# CFA 2009 Level I Certification

## With Preliminary Reading Assignments

## The Candidates Question And Answer Workbook For Chartered Financial Analyst

**Author**

**Jane Vessey, CFA**

**TotalRecall Publications, Inc.**

**TotalRecall Publications, Inc.**

This Book Sponsored by The Center For Financial Certification, Inc.



Printed in United States of America, Canada, and England

| | | |
|---|---|---|
| **Paper Back:** | **ISBN:** | **978-1-59095-937-4** |
| | **UPC:** | **6-43977-93703-2** |
| **eBook:** | **ISBN:** | **978-1-59095-938-1** |
| | **UPC:** | **6-43977-93763-6** |

The sponsoring editor for this book is Bruce Moran and the production supervisor is Corby R. Tate.

This book is dedicated to our fantastic children Adam and Julia who we love very much.

*Jane Vessey*

# ExamWise®

# Volume 1

# CFA 2009 Level I Certification

# With

# Preliminary Reading Assignments

# The Candidates Question And Answer Workbook For Chartered Financial Analyst

## About the Author:

**Jane Vessey, CFA** manages a training company in the United Kingdom specializing in financial analysis and investment. She is a visiting lecturer at Cass Business School teaching classes in asset management and valuation. She also teaches a CFA® revision course at ISMA (the business school at Reading University) and is an associate at a leading London financial training company where she teaches courses covering investment management and related topics. She has developed online training programs for students taking the CFA examinations and teaches CFA courses for UKSIP (the UK Society of Investment Professionals).

Jane graduated in Mathematics from Oxford University, United Kingdom, and is a CFA charter holder. She has some eighteen years experience working in the investment industry, starting out as an equity analyst before becoming an investment manager. She was based in London and Tokyo and took responsibility for managing equity portfolios invested in the Japanese and other Asian markets. In 1990, Jane moved to Indonesia and established and ran an investment management operation on behalf of Mees Pierson. She took responsibility for all areas of the business, including investment, operations, marketing and administration. While in Asia, Jane was involved in providing training to capital market participants and state officials and teaching in courses provided by local universities.

## About the Book:

ExamWise For CFA Level I Concept Check Q&A Workbook With Preliminary Reading Assignments is designed to give you plenty of practice questions to test your readiness for the CFA exam. It offers 360+ concept check questions based 18 exam study sessions that cover the Learning Outcome Statements and their associated CFA Assigned Readings. For additional practice, there is an accompanying free download test engine that generates multiple mock exams similar in design and difficulty to the real CFA exam. The questions and explanations have references to the page number in the related Reading and to the related LOS.

Use this workbook to test your understanding of the basic concepts covered in the CFA Readings and identify your strengths and weaknesses. Then you can move on to more advanced study materials to sharpen your weakest knowledge areas.

This book is divided into Study Sessions (1 – 18) that cover the 76 Learning Outcome Statements and the associated Assigned Readings. Appendix A (Exhibits 1 – 4), is a collection of exhibits and flow charts for condensed reference and review, including examples of accounting statements, puts and calls, PE breakdown, and financial ratios.

### The 18 2006 CFA Level I Study Sessions breakout is as follows:

#### *Ethical and Professional Standards*

1. Study Session 1: Ethical and Professional Standards

#### *Investment Tools*

2. Study Session 2. Quantitative Methods: Basic Concepts
3. Study Session 3. Quantitative Methods: Application
4. Study Session 4. Economics: Microeconomic Analysis
5. Study Session 5. Economics: Market Structure and Macroeconomic Analysis
6. Study Session 6. Economics: Monetary and Fiscal Economics
7. Study Session 7. Financial Reporting & Analysis: Introduction
8. Study Session 8. FR&A: Income Statement, Balance Sheet, and Cash Flow Statements
9. Study Session 9. FR&A: Inventories, Long-Term Assets, Deferred Taxes, and On- and Off-Balance Sheet Debt
10. Study Session 10. FR&A: Techniques, Apps, & International Standards Convergence
11. Study Session 11. Corporate Finance

#### *Portfolio Management*

12. Study Session 12. Portfolio Management

#### *Asset Valuation*

13. Study Session 13. Analysis of Equity Investments: Securities Markets
14. Study Session 14. Analysis of Equity Investments: Industry and Company Analysis
15. Study Session 15. Analysis of Fixed Income Investments: Basic Concepts
16. Study Session 16. Analysis of Fixed Income Investments: Analysis and Valuation
17. Study Session 17. Derivatives
18. Study Session 18. Alternative Investments

## Online Information:

1. What is CFA Institute

http://www.cfainstitute.org/aboutus/index.html

2. CFA Program: http://www.cfainstitute.org/cfaprogram

3. The Code of Ethics (Full Text) http://www.cfainstitute.org/centre/ethics/code/

The Standards of Professional Conduct

Standard I: Fundamental Responsibilities

Standard II: Relationships with and Responsibilities to the Profession

Standard III: Relationships with and Responsibilities to the Employer

Standard IV: Relationships with and Responsibilities to Clients and Prospects

Standard V: Relationships with and Responsibilities to the Public

4. **Why The CFA Designation Matters to You: Individual Investor FAQ**

http://www.cfainstitute.org/aboutus/investors/articles/cfamatters.html

5. Soft Dollar Standards http://www.cfainstitute.org/centre/ethics/softdollar/

6. CFA Institute-PPSTM AIMR Performance Presentation Standards

http://www.cfapubs.org/doi/ref/10.2469/faj.v57.n2.2433

7. Global Investment Performance Standards http://www.cfainstitute.org/centre/ips/

**Click the picture and link to a free CFA Candidates online glossary.**

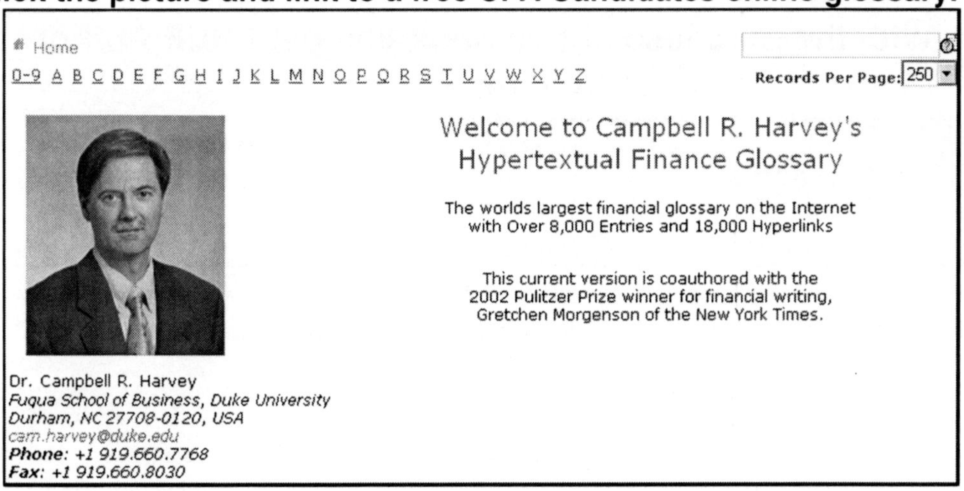

# List of Chapters

# Table of Contents

# Study Session 01:
# Ethical and Professional Standards:

The readings in this study session present a framework for ethical conduct in the investment profession by focusing on the CFA Institute Code of Ethics and Standards of Professional Conduct as well as the Global Investment Performance Standards (GIPS®).

The principles and guidance presented in the CFA Institute Standards of Practice Handbook (SOPH) form the basis for the CFA Institute self-regulatory program to maintain the highest professional standards among investment practitioners. "Guidance" in the SOPH addresses the practical application of the Code of Ethics and Standards of Professional Conduct. The guidance reviews the purpose and scope of each standard, presents recommended procedures for compliance, and provides examples of the standard in practice.

The Global Investment Performance Standards (GIPS) facilitate efficient comparison of investment performance across investment managers and country borders by prescribing methodology and standards that are consistent with a clear and honest presentation of returns. Having a global standard for reporting investment performance minimizes the potential for ambiguous or misleading presentations.

**Reading 1: Code of Ethics and Standards of Professional Conduct**

***Standards of Practice Handbook*, Ninth Edition**

**Reading 2: "Guidance" for Standards I–VII**

***Standards of Practice Handbook*, Ninth Edition**

**Reading 3: Introduction to the Global Investment Performance Standards (GIPS)**

**Reading 4: Global Investment Performance Standards (GIPS)**

1. (QID 1) Which of the following is classified as a firm under the Global Investment Performance Standards (GIPS)?

A. All the assets that are managed in one or more base currencies fall under the definition of a firm.

B. An investment firm, subsidiary, or division held out to clients or potential clients as a distinct business unit.

C. An entity registered with the appropriate national regulatory authority overseeing its investment management activities.

---

2. (QID 2) Adrian Johns has just been awarded a CFA charter following his successful completion of the CFA program. Which of the following statements made by Johns is an inappropriate reference to the CFA program and designation?

A. As a CFA charterholder I am committed to maintaining high ethical standards of conduct.

B. As I passed the CFA examinations in three consecutive years I am highly qualified to manage client funds.

C. I believe the CFA program provides the highest qualification in the international investment management industry.

1. (QID 1) Which of the following is classified as a firm under the Global Investment Performance Standards (GIPS)?

A. All the assets that are managed in one or more base currencies fall under the definition of a firm.

***B. An investment firm, subsidiary, or division held out to clients or potential clients as a distinct business unit.**

C. An entity registered with the appropriate national regulatory authority overseeing its investment management activities.

Explanation: LOS: Reading 4-b

Firms must be an investment firm, subsidiary, or division held out to clients or potential clients as a distinct business unit. Firms are encouraged to adopt the broadest interpretation of 'firm', and so include all offices operating under the same brand name.

**Reference:** CFA® Program Curriculum, Volume 1, p. 132.

---

2. (QID 2) Adrian Johns has just been awarded a CFA charter following his successful completion of the CFA program. Which of the following statements made by Johns is an inappropriate reference to the CFA program and designation?

A. As a CFA charterholder I am committed to maintaining high ethical standards of conduct.

***B. As I passed the CFA examinations in three consecutive years I am highly qualified to manage client funds.**

C. I believe the CFA program provides the highest qualification in the international investment management industry.

Explanation: LOS: Reading 2-b

Statements which are factual with respect to passing the exams are acceptable, but to claim superiority in doing so is unacceptable. Statements that emphasise the rigour of the CFA program or its commitment to ethical standards are permitted.

**Reference:** CFA® Program Curriculum, Volume 1, pp. 103-107.

3. (QID 3) Which of the following is least likely to be an example of market manipulation according to the Code and Standards?

A. Taking advantage of market inefficiencies to make profits on arbitrage strategies.

B. Agreeing to issue stock in an IPO to market participants if they agree to generate turnover in the stock subsequent to listing.

C. Purchasing leading stocks in an index just prior to the expiry date of futures contracts on the index in order to make a profit on a long position in the futures contract.

---

4. (QID 4) Which of the following parties do the Global Investment Performance Standards (GIPS) mainly benefit?

A. CFA Institute members and investment management firms only.

B. Investment management firms, and prospective and current clients of investment management firms only.

C. CFA Institute members, investment management firms, and prospective and current clients of investment management firms.

3. (QID 3) Which of the following is least likely to be an example of market manipulation according to the Code and Standards?

***A. Taking advantage of market inefficiencies to make profits on arbitrage strategies.**

B. Agreeing to issue stock in an IPO to market participants if they agree to generate turnover in the stock subsequent to listing.

C. Purchasing leading stocks in an index just prior to the expiry date of futures contracts on the index in order to make a profit on a long position in the futures contract.

Explanation: LOS: Reading 2-a

Market manipulation is artificially creating stock market prices or volumes. Arbitrage strategies are not a form of manipulation since they are taking advantage of pricing inefficiencies existing in the market, and are a legitimate practice.

**Reference:** CFA® Program Curriculum, Volume 1, pp. 45-48.

---

4. (QID 4) Which of the following parties do the Global Investment Performance Standards (GIPS) mainly benefit?

A. CFA Institute members and investment management firms only.

***B. Investment management firms, and prospective and current clients of investment management firms only.**

C. CFA Institute members, investment management firms, and prospective and current clients of investment management firms.

Explanation: LOS: Reading 3-a

The main parties benefiting from Global Investment Performance Standards (GIPS) are prospective and current clients of investment management firms and the firm itself since they ensure past and current performance figures are accurately and fairly presented.

**Reference:** CFA® Program Curriculum, Volume 1, pp. 120-121.

5. (QID 5) Which of the following statements is the least accurate statement regarding verification of compliance with the Global Investment Performance Standards (GIPS)?

A. Verification has been a requirement since 1 January 2000.

B. Verification must be performed by an independent third party.

C. Verification checks whether the calculation procedures meet Global Investment Performance Standards (GIPS) requirements.

---

6. (QID 6) Elizabeth Salami and Albert Toffee have both passed Level II of the CFA Exam Program. Salami advertises a resumé stating that she is a candidate for the CFA designation and has passed Level II of the CFA Program. Toffee circulates a resume stating that he is a CFA candidate who has passed Level II and expects to obtain his CFA charter in 2009, the following year. Both have enrolled to take Level III in 2009. Which of the following statements is most accurate?

A. Only Toffee has violated the Code and Standards.

B. Only Salami has violated the Code and Standards.

C. Both Salami and Toffee have violated the Code and Standards.

5. (QID 5) Which of the following statements is the least accurate statement regarding verification of compliance with the Global Investment Performance Standards (GIPS)?

***A. Verification has been a requirement since 1 January 2000.**

B. Verification must be performed by an independent third party.

C. Verification checks whether the calculation procedures meet Global Investment Performance Standards (GIPS) requirements.

Explanation: LOS: Reading 3-c

Verification is recommended but not required. Verification must be done by an independent third party who will check if a firm's processes and procedures to calculate performance numbers are in compliance with GIPS, and whether composite construction has complied with Global Investment Performance Standards (GIPS).

**Reference:** CFA® Program Curriculum, Volume 1, p. 121.

---

6. (QID 6) Elizabeth Salami and Albert Toffee have both passed Level II of the CFA Exam Program. Salami advertises a resumé stating that she is a candidate for the CFA designation and has passed Level II of the CFA Program. Toffee circulates a resume stating that he is a CFA candidate who has passed Level II and expects to obtain his CFA charter in 2009, the following year. Both have enrolled to take Level III in 2009. Which of the following statements is most accurate?

***A. Only Toffee has violated the Code and Standards.**

B. Only Salami has violated the Code and Standards.

C. Both Salami and Toffee have violated the Code and Standards.

Explanation: LOS: Reading 2-b

Standard VII(B) indicates that candidates should not cite the expected date of the exam completion and award of the charter. If Salami had not enrolled for the Level III examination, she would have also violated the Code and Standards by claiming to be a (current) candidate.

**Reference:** CFA® Program Curriculum, Volume 1, pp. 103-107.

7. (QID 7) According to the Standards of Professional Conduct, when writing material for circulation to the public:

A. members may copy or use charts or graphs without stating the sources and members may orally, for example in a group meeting, without acknowledgment, use excerpts from articles or reports prepared by others.

B. members may not copy or use charts or graphs without stating the sources but members may orally, for example in a group meeting, without acknowledgment, use excerpts from articles or reports prepared by others.

C. members may not copy or use charts or graphs without stating the sources and members may not orally, for example in a group meeting, without acknowledgment, use excerpts from articles or reports prepared by others.

---

8. (QID 8) Jason Vasco, CFA, is the director for a major Talia-owned investment management firm branch in Rasen. Talia is known as the world's centre of investment management with securities laws stricter than the CFA Institute Code and Standards, and Vasco is governed by Talia's laws. In Rasen, an emerging market, the local securities laws and regulations are lenient. They are very vague in the definition of insider trading and have no provision regulating soft-dollars. Which of the following is most accurate?

A. Vasco must comply with Talia's law.

B. Vasco only has to comply with Rasen's law and therefore can take the fullest advantage of soft-dollar arrangements.

C. Vasco should not worry about Rasen's law, it is an early stage emerging market and the law enforcement will be lax, if any at all.

7. (QID 7) According to the Standards of Professional Conduct, when writing material for circulation to the public:

A. members may copy or use charts or graphs without stating the sources and members may orally, for example in a group meeting, without acknowledgment, use excerpts from articles or reports prepared by others.

B. members may not copy or use charts or graphs without stating the sources but members may orally, for example in a group meeting, without acknowledgment, use excerpts from articles or reports prepared by others.

***C. members may not copy or use charts or graphs without stating the sources and members may not orally, for example in a group meeting, without acknowledgment, use excerpts from articles or reports prepared by others.**

Explanation: LOS: Reading 2-b

Standard I(C) prohibits plagiarism, whether it is a written or oral form of communication of another's work. Other parties' research (charts, graphs, articles, reports etc.) may be quoted but the research must be attributed to the original author.

**Reference:** CFA® Program Curriculum, Volume 1, pp. 29-34.

---

8. (QID 8) Jason Vasco, CFA, is the director for a major Talia-owned investment management firm branch in Rasen. Talia is known as the world's centre of investment management with securities laws stricter than the CFA Institute Code and Standards, and Vasco is governed by Talia's laws. In Rasen, an emerging market, the local securities laws and regulations are lenient. They are very vague in the definition of insider trading and have no provision regulating soft-dollars. Which of the following is most accurate?

***A. Vasco must comply with Talia's law.**

B. Vasco only has to comply with Rasen's law and therefore can take the fullest advantage of soft-dollar arrangements.

C. Vasco should not worry about Rasen's law, it is an early stage emerging market and the law enforcement will be lax, if any at all.

Explanation: LOS: Reading 2-b

Standard I (A) stipulates that in foreign jurisdictions members must comply with the stricter of the applicable laws and the Code of Standards, in this case Talia's law is the strictest.

**Reference:** CFA® Program Curriculum, Volume 1, pp. 15-17.

9. (QID 9) Mary Chew, CFA, is a junior research analyst with XYZ Securities and she has been asked by her Head of Research to prepare a research report on First Beverages InC. Chew is aware than XYZ Securities has acted as underwriter to First Beverages on a number of occasions in the past. She thoroughly analyses First Beverages and decides that First Beverages' shares are undervalued. Chew's best course of action is to:

A. write the research report but not make the recommendation that the shares are undervalued.

B. write the report including the recommendation as long as she discloses the relationship between XYZ Securities and First Beverages.

C. keep the analysis on file but not write any report to be circulated to clients given the relationship between XYZ Securities and First Beverages.

---

10. (QID 11) Catherine Cleves, CFA, heads the Asian research department in Hong Kong of a New York-based brokerage firm. The firm employs many analysts spread about in different countries in Asia, some of whom are members of CFA Institute. If Cleves delegates some supervisory duties in the different offices in Asia, which of the following statements best describes her responsibilities under the Code and Standards?

A. Cleves retains supervisory responsibility for all subordinates despite her delegation of some duties.

B. Cleves' supervisory responsibilities only apply to those subordinates who are subject to the Code and Standards.

C. The Code and Standards prevent Cleves from delegating supervisory duties to subordinates in a developing or emerging market.

9. (QID 9) Mary Chew, CFA, is a junior research analyst with XYZ Securities and she has been asked by her Head of Research to prepare a research report on First Beverages InC. Chew is aware than XYZ Securities has acted as underwriter to First Beverages on a number of occasions in the past. She thoroughly analyses First Beverages and decides that First Beverages' shares are undervalued. Chew's best course of action is to:

A. write the research report but not make the recommendation that the shares are undervalued.

***B. write the report including the recommendation as long as she discloses the relationship between XYZ Securities and First Beverages.**

C. keep the analysis on file but not write any report to be circulated to clients given the relationship between XYZ Securities and First Beverages.

Explanation: LOS: Reading 2-a

Under Standard V1(A) Disclosure of Conflicts, disclosure of the relationship is required regardless of whether a recommendation is made, although management should not put pressure on Chew to make a favourable recommendation.

**Reference:** CFA® Program Curriculum, Volume 1, pp. 89-94.

---

10. (QID 11) Catherine Cleves, CFA, heads the Asian research department in Hong Kong of a New York-based brokerage firm. The firm employs many analysts spread about in different countries in Asia, some of whom are members of CFA Institute. If Cleves delegates some supervisory duties in the different offices in Asia, which of the following statements best describes her responsibilities under the Code and Standards?

***A. Cleves retains supervisory responsibility for all subordinates despite her delegation of some duties.**

B. Cleves' supervisory responsibilities only apply to those subordinates who are subject to the Code and Standards.

C. The Code and Standards prevent Cleves from delegating supervisory duties to subordinates in a developing or emerging market.

Explanation: LOS: Reading 2-a

Standard IV(C) Responsibilities of Supervisors states that supervisory responsibility remains with the supervisor although the actual supervision can be delegated. Members who are supervisors can rely on reasonable procedures to detect and prevent violations to applicable statutes, regulations and provisions of the Code and Standards.

**Reference:** CFA® Program Curriculum, Volume 1, pp. 76-80.

11. (QID 13) Toby Green, CFA, works in an equity brokerage department at Mulberry Securities. Green has reviewed a report from the firm's research department that suggests Crown Appliances is rated a "buy" because the sales figures for the firm's new products have been better than those of the closest competition. Green lives on the same street as the CFO of Crown Appliances. While waiting for the train to work, Green accidentally overheard the Chief Financial Officer of Crown Appliances report to his colleague on a mobile phone about an announcement in the morning newspaper that a competitor has just launched a website for appliance distribution over the internet. Upon returning to his office, Green tipped his father to sell his holding based on this new information, but he still recommends a buy to all Mulberry's clients. Green:

A. was in full compliance with the Code and Standards.

B. violated the Code and Standards because he failed to maintain priority of transactions for his firm's clients.

C. violated the Code and Standards because he gave a recommendation based on material nonpublic information.

11. (QID 13) Toby Green, CFA, works in an equity brokerage department at Mulberry Securities. Green has reviewed a report from the firm's research department that suggests Crown Appliances is rated a "buy" because the sales figures for the firm's new products have been better than those of the closest competition. Green lives on the same street as the CFO of Crown Appliances. While waiting for the train to work, Green accidentally overheard the Chief Financial Officer of Crown Appliances report to his colleague on a mobile phone about an announcement in the morning newspaper that a competitor has just launched a website for appliance distribution over the internet. Upon returning to his office, Green tipped his father to sell his holding based on this new information, but he still recommends a buy to all Mulberry's clients. Green:

***A. was in full compliance with the Code and Standards.**

B. violated the Code and Standards because he failed to maintain priority of transactions for his firm's clients.

C. violated the Code and Standards because he gave a recommendation based on material nonpublic information.

Explanation: LOS: Reading 2-b

Green did not violate Standard II(A) Material Nonpublic Information because the announcement appears in the morning newspaper. His buy recommendation is consistent with that of his firm's research department and no violation of Priority of Transactions occurs here.

**Reference:** CFA® Program Curriculum, Volume 1, pp. 36-39.

12. (QID 15) Bud Clayton, CFA, manages the discretionary account of the Lewin Jones Corporation employees' profit-sharing plan. Diane Lewin, the company president, recently asked Clayton to vote on behalf of the shares in the firm's profit-sharing plan in favor of the company-nominated slate of directors and against the slate of directors sponsored by a corporate-raider stockholder group. Clayton does not want to lose Lewin Jones as a client, because the account generates more than 20 percent of his firm's revenues. Clayton investigates the proxy-fight issue and realizes that the corporate raider's slate of directors would probably be better for the long-run performance of the firm than that recommended by the management. However Clayton fears that the new board, which he hardly knows, will shift the business to a competing investment firm as often happens in corporate takeovers. According to the Code and Standards, Clayton should:

A. vote in the manner requested by Lewin due to her importance as a major client.

B. vote against the corporate raider's recommendation as corporate raiding is unethical.

C. vote in favor of the corporate raider's recommendation since it is in the best interest of the participants and beneficiaries of the employees' profit sharing plan.

---

13. (QID 17) Which one of the following requirements is least likely to help to ensure the establishment of an information barrier (fire wall)?

A. Place securities on a restricted list when the firm has access to material nonpublic information.

B. Limit the number of people in the firm who have access to material nonpublic information

C. Limit the number of major institutional clients who regularly receive 'special investment tips' prior to information being made public.

12. (QID 15) Bud Clayton, CFA, manages the discretionary account of the Lewin Jones Corporation employees' profit-sharing plan. Diane Lewin, the company president, recently asked Clayton to vote on behalf of the shares in the firm's profit-sharing plan in favor of the company-nominated slate of directors and against the slate of directors sponsored by a corporate-raider stockholder group. Clayton does not want to lose Lewin Jones as a client, because the account generates more than 20 percent of his firm's revenues. Clayton investigates the proxy-fight issue and realizes that the corporate raider's slate of directors would probably be better for the long-run performance of the firm than that recommended by the management. However Clayton fears that the new board, which he hardly knows, will shift the business to a competing investment firm as often happens in corporate takeovers. According to the Code and Standards, Clayton should:

A. vote in the manner requested by Lewin due to her importance as a major client.

B. vote against the corporate raider's recommendation as corporate raiding is unethical.

***C. vote in favor of the corporate raider's recommendation since it is in the best interest of the participants and beneficiaries of the employees' profit sharing plan.**

Explanation: LOS: Reading 2-b

This is a test case on the execution of a fiduciary duty by investment managers as stated in Standard III (A) Loyalty, Prudence, and Care. Clayton's main obligation is to maintain the interest of his client namely the Lewin Jones employees' profit-sharing plan.

**Reference:** CFA® Program Curriculum, Volume 1, pp. 48-53.

---

13. (QID 17) Which one of the following requirements is least likely to help to ensure the establishment of an information barrier (fire wall)?

A. Place securities on a restricted list when the firm has access to material nonpublic information.

B. Limit the number of people in the firm who have access to material nonpublic information

***C. Limit the number of major institutional clients who regularly receive 'special investment tips' prior to information being made public.**

Explanation: LOS: Reading 2-a

Firewalls are intended to block the dissemination of material nonpublic information. The conscious effort of dissemination, albeit to a limited number of clients, therefore is in violation of Standard II(A) Material Nonpublic Information.

**Reference:** CFA® Program Curriculum, Volume 1, pp. 36-45.

14. (QID 16) Victoria Anderson, CFA, works for Pluto Capital, a newly established investment counseling firm. The founding partners of Pluto Capital came from Vulcan Investments which was recently taken over by a large financial services group. Jonathan Beecham, a prospective client of the firm, is meeting with Anderson for the first time. Beecham has been a client of Vulcan Investments for years, but is now considering switching his account to Pluto Capital because he has been disappointed by Vulcan's underperformance following the takeover. At the beginning of their meeting, Anderson sympathized with his situation, then immediately explains to Beecham that she has discovered a highly undervalued stock that offers large potential gains. Anderson then promises Beecham that she can buy the stock for his account at the current price if he switches the account within 48 hours. Anderson's actions violated the Code and Standards. Which of the following statements best describes the action Anderson should have taken? Anderson should have:

A. elaborated on the technical features of Pluto's standard valuation method used to identify the undervaluation.

B. avoided the meeting with Beecham in the first place because the founding partners of Pluto came from Vulcan.

C. determined Beecham's investment needs, objectives, and tolerance for risk before making any investment recommendation.

---

15. (QID 18) Which one of the following is least likely to be a required part of the verification process for a firm claiming compliance with Global Investment Performance Standards (GIPS)?

A. Checking that fees charged to client accounts are in line with market practice.

B. Checking that required disclosures have been made in the performance presentation.

C. Checking that composites have been set up in line with client objectives or the strategy followed.

14. (QID 16) Victoria Anderson, CFA, works for Pluto Capital, a newly established investment counseling firm. The founding partners of Pluto Capital came from Vulcan Investments which was recently taken over by a large financial services group. Jonathan Beecham, a prospective client of the firm, is meeting with Anderson for the first time. Beecham has been a client of Vulcan Investments for years, but is now considering switching his account to Pluto Capital because he has been disappointed by Vulcan's underperformance following the takeover. At the beginning of their meeting, Anderson sympathized with his situation, then immediately explains to Beecham that she has discovered a highly undervalued stock that offers large potential gains. Anderson then promises Beecham that she can buy the stock for his account at the current price if he switches the account within 48 hours. Anderson's actions violated the Code and Standards. Which of the following statements best describes the action Anderson should have taken? Anderson should have:

A. elaborated on the technical features of Pluto's standard valuation method used to identify the undervaluation.

B. avoided the meeting with Beecham in the first place because the founding partners of Pluto came from Vulcan.

***C. determined Beecham's investment needs, objectives, and tolerance for risk before making any investment recommendation.**

Explanation: LOS: Reading 2-b

Prior to recommending any investments, Anderson should determine Beecham's investment needs, objectives, and tolerance for risk as stated in Standard III(C) Suitability.

**Reference:** CFA® Program Curriculum, Volume 1, pp. 60-64.

---

15. (QID 18) Which one of the following is least likely to be a required part of the verification process for a firm claiming compliance with Global Investment Performance Standards (GIPS)?

***A. Checking that fees charged to client accounts are in line with market practice.**

B. Checking that required disclosures have been made in the performance presentation.

C. Checking that composites have been set up in line with client objectives or the strategy followed.

Explanation: LOS: Reading 4-a

There is no requirement to check the fairness of fees being charged to clients in terms of whether they are in line with market standards.

**Reference:** CFA® Program Curriculum, Volume 1, pp. 126-128.

16. (QID 19) Cliff Bardots, CFA, is a research analyst who has accumulated and analyzed several pieces of nonpublic information through his industry contacts. Although each piece of information is not material, Bardots correctly deduced that the earnings of one of the firms under his coverage would unexpectedly decline significantly in the coming year. According to the Code and Standards, Bardots:

A. is allowed to use the information to make investment recommendations and decisions

B. should urge his industry contacts to publicly disseminate the information immediately.

C. is not allowed to make investment recommendations or actions based on this information.

---

17. (QID 20) Which of the following is not a concept covered by the CFA Institute Code of Ethics?

A. Competence.

B. Integrity and diligence.

C. Remuneration levels of investment professionals.

16. (QID 19) Cliff Bardots, CFA, is a research analyst who has accumulated and analyzed several pieces of nonpublic information through his industry contacts. Although each piece of information is not material, Bardots correctly deduced that the earnings of one of the firms under his coverage would unexpectedly decline significantly in the coming year. According to the Code and Standards, Bardots:

***A. is allowed to use the information to make investment recommendations and decisions**

B. should urge his industry contacts to publicly disseminate the information immediately.

C. is not allowed to make investment recommendations or actions based on this information.

Explanation: LOS: Reading 2-b

This is an example of an application of mosaic theory. It is legitimate to employ an educated deduction over pieces of 'nonmaterial' nonpublic information and to arrive at an investment recommendation, Standard V(A) Diligence and Reasonable Basis.

**Reference:** CFA® Program Curriculum, Volume 1, pp. 38-39.

---

17. (QID 20) Which of the following is not a concept covered by the CFA Institute Code of Ethics?

A. Competence.

B. Integrity and diligence.

***C. Remuneration levels of investment professionals.**

Explanation: LOS: Reading 1-c

Remuneration of investment professionals is not explicitly covered in the Code of Ethics. Disclosure of compensation is stipulated in Standard IV(B) Additional Compensation Arrangements and in Standard VI(C) Referral Fees.

**Reference:** CFA® Program Curriculum, Volume 1, pp. 12-14.

18. (QID 21) Martha Birch, CFA, is a financial analyst at Granders Securities Corporation. Granders has information firewalls between different departments in compliance with recommendations made in the Code and Standards. Birch is preparing a purchase recommendation on B&D Corporation. Which of the following situations would be least likely to present a conflict of interest for Birch and, therefore, needs not be disclosed?

A. Birch has been a member of the board of directors of B&D until three months ago.

B. Granders, through its investment advisory arm, holds for its clients' accounts a substantial holding of common stock in B&D Corporation.

C. Birch was formerly married to the Chief Financial Officer of B&D and has recently received a significant stock holding as part of her divorce settlement.

---

19. (QID 10) Kevin Dudman, CFA, has just been offered an exciting new position with Walton Asset Management and decides that he will resign from his current position with Trust Asset Management. Before he resigns he decides to ensure that he uses some of the skills and materials he has developed at Trust Asset Management. He is least likely to violate the Code and Standards, if he takes:

A. stock market analysis prepared by Dudman when he was working at Trust Asset Management.

B. internal contact information on Trust Asset Management's major clients which is available from other eternal sources.

C. experience in pricing unlisted securities which he gained while attending training courses which were paid for by Trust Asset Management.

18. (QID 21) Martha Birch, CFA, is a financial analyst at Granders Securities Corporation. Granders has information firewalls between different departments in compliance with recommendations made in the Code and Standards. Birch is preparing a purchase recommendation on B&D Corporation. Which of the following situations would be least likely to present a conflict of interest for Birch and, therefore, needs not be disclosed?

A. Birch has been a member of the board of directors of B&D until three months ago.

***B. Granders, through its investment advisory arm, holds for its clients' accounts a substantial holding of common stock in B&D Corporation.**

C. Birch was formerly married to the Chief Financial Officer of B&D and has recently received a significant stock holding as part of her divorce settlement.

Explanation: LOS: Reading 2-a

Granders, does not present a potential conflict of interest as stated in Standard VI(A), Disclosure of Conflicts, as the appropriate firewall between an investment advisory arm and the brokerage operation would be established pursuant to the Code and Standards.

**Reference:** CFA® Program Curriculum, Volume 1, pp. 89-94.

---

19. (QID 10) Kevin Dudman, CFA, has just been offered an exciting new position with Walton Asset Management and decides that he will resign from his current position with Trust Asset Management. Before he resigns he decides to ensure that he uses some of the skills and materials he has developed at Trust Asset Management. He is least likely to violate the Code and Standards, if he takes:

A. stock market analysis prepared by Dudman when he was working at Trust Asset Management.

B. internal contact information on Trust Asset Management's major clients which is available from other eternal sources.

***C. experience in pricing unlisted securities which he gained while attending training courses which were paid for by Trust Asset Management.**

Explanation: LOS: Reading 2-b

Models and research which he worked on when employed by Trust Asset Management belong to Trust Asset Management. Client contact details should not be taken from his employer, although he is not prohibited from collecting client information from outside sources. However skills and experience gained at Trust Asset Management can be used in his new job, so "experience in pricing" is the correct choice.

**Reference:** CFA® Program Curriculum, Volume 1, pp. 69-74.

20. (QID 23) Rachael Jocund, CFA, is an equity analyst following cigarette companies and a rising star in her firm. Her supervisor has been recommending D. Morass as a 'buy' and asks Jocund to take over the coverage of the company. He tells Jocund that she can only change the recommendation with his approval. The Code and Standards say that:

A. Jocund must be independent and objective in her analysis.

B. Jocund should follow her supervisor's direction but notify the legal officer of her firm of the situation.

C. Jocund should follow her supervisor's direction as she reports to him, although she should keep records of any information that would lead her to feel uncomfortable with the buy recommendation.

---

21. (QID 22) Ken Janzen, CFA, is an economist at a large bank and he has never made direct investment decisions. Jenzen is the latest winner of a well-publicized portfolio management competition in a national newspaper. Followint this success he is launching an investment fund. In the prospectus he tells the prospective clients, "The fund has no long-term track record as yet, but the investment manager has shown considerable skills in managing hypothetical portfolios. In a competition the manager has demonstrated a portfolio total return above 26 percent per year annualized, and that is more than 12 percent above the benchmark for the same period." He managed to raise a significant amount of money from retail investors who are interested in investing in the fund. Has Janzen violated the Code and Standards?

A. Yes, because the statement misrepresents Janzen's track record.

B. Yes, because he cannot quote performance for a hypothetical portfolio.

C. No, because the statement is a true and accurate description of Janzen's track record.

20. (QID 23) Rachael Jocund, CFA, is an equity analyst following cigarette companies and a rising star in her firm. Her supervisor has been recommending D. Morass as a 'buy' and asks Jocund to take over the coverage of the company. He tells Jocund that she can only change the recommendation with his approval. The Code and Standards say that:

***A. Jocund must be independent and objective in her analysis.**

B. Jocund should follow her supervisor's direction but notify the legal officer of her firm of the situation.

C. Jocund should follow her supervisor's direction as she reports to him, although she should keep records of any information that would lead her to feel uncomfortable with the buy recommendation.

Explanation: LOS: Reading 2-a

As part of responsibilities to clients and prospects, members must personally maintain independence and objectivity so their clients will have the benefit of their work and opinions unaffected by any potential conflict of interest or other circumstance adversely affecting their judgment

**Reference:** CFA® Program Curriculum, Volume 1, pp. 21-25.

---

21. (QID 22) Ken Janzen, CFA, is an economist at a large bank and he has never made direct investment decisions. Jenzen is the latest winner of a well-publicized portfolio management competition in a national newspaper. Followint this success he is launching an investment fund. In the prospectus he tells the prospective clients, "The fund has no long-term track record as yet, but the investment manager has shown considerable skills in managing hypothetical portfolios. In a competition the manager has demonstrated a portfolio total return above 26 percent per year annualized, and that is more than 12 percent above the benchmark for the same period." He managed to raise a significant amount of money from retail investors who are interested in investing in the fund. Has Janzen violated the Code and Standards?

A. Yes, because the statement misrepresents Janzen's track record.

B. Yes, because he cannot quote performance for a hypothetical portfolio.

***C. No, because the statement is a true and accurate description of Janzen's track record.**

Explanation: LOS: Reading 2-b

Although Janzen's experience in managing investments is only based on his winning a hypothetical portfolio management competition, he does not misrepresent his capabilities and experience as described in Standard III(D) Performance Presentation. Whether it is appropriate for an investor to subscribe to his investment fund is a different matter. The role of the Code and Standards is to guide self-regulation of CFA Institute members, not to certify the merit of an investment.

**Reference:** CFA® Program Curriculum, Volume 1, pp. 64-67.

22. (QID 12) Wimpy Greenback, CFA, is the research analyst responsible for following Brown Appliances Company. This analysis suggests the stock should be rated a "sell" because the market outlook for the firm's new products is bleak compared with that of the closest competition. Greenback lives on the same street as the CFO of Brown Appliances. During a recent neighborhood gathering, Greenback's wife overheard the wife of the Chief Financial Officer of Brown Appliances complaining that her husband had been working late due to a hostile takeover threat from a foreign appliances group. This fact has not yet been made public by Brown Appliances. Upon returning to his office, Greenback released a strong "buy" recommendation to the public based on this new information. Greenback:

A. did not violate the Code and Standards because he used mosaic theory to arrive at his recommendation.

B. violated the Code and Standards by failing to distinguish between facts and opinions in his recommendation.

C. violated the Code and Standards because he did not have a reasonable and adequate basis for his recommendation.

---

23. (QID 14) The fixed-income corporate finance department of Golden Brothers, an investment banking firm, has decided to compete for the advisory and underwriting bond offering of Kia Telcom, a 'hot' telecommunications company. The firm's equity brokerage unit is about to publish a "sell" recommendation on Kia Telcom due to an unexpected announcement of cost overruns. The head of fixed-income investment banking has asked the head of the equity brokerage unit to change the recommendation from "sell" to "buy" before distributing the research report to clients. According to the Code and Standards, the best course of action for the equity brokerage unit is to:

A. place Kia Telcom on a restricted list and publish only factual information about the company.

B. increase the rating by no more than one increment (in this case, to a "hold" recommendation) since little harm is done by being a bit more positive, while the firm's overall interest is served.

C. assign a more senior analyst to decide if the stock deserves a higher rating for the sake of objectivity since less senior analysts may err in judgment.

22. (QID 12) Wimpy Greenback, CFA, is the research analyst responsible for following Brown Appliances Company. This analysis suggests the stock should be rated a "sell" because the market outlook for the firm's new products is bleak compared with that of the closest competition. Greenback lives on the same street as the CFO of Brown Appliances. During a recent neighborhood gathering, Greenback's wife overheard the wife of the Chief Financial Officer of Brown Appliances complaining that her husband had been working late due to a hostile takeover threat from a foreign appliances group. This fact has not yet been made public by Brown Appliances. Upon returning to his office, Greenback released a strong "buy" recommendation to the public based on this new information. Greenback:

A. did not violate the Code and Standards because he used mosaic theory to arrive at his recommendation.

B. violated the Code and Standards by failing to distinguish between facts and opinions in his recommendation.

***C. violated the Code and Standards because he did not have a reasonable and adequate basis for his recommendation.**

Explanation: LOS: Reading 2-b

Standard V(A) Diligence and Reasonable Basis, states that members must have a reasonable and adequate basis for a recommendation. Greenback should have reinvestigated the company's situation and not only relied on unofficial information. This may well be a misappropriation of material nonpublic information as stated in Standard V(A) Prohibition against Use of Material Nonpublic Information, if a tender offer to Brown Appliances follows.

**Reference:** CFA® Program Curriculum, Volume 1, pp. 80-84.

23. (QID 14) The fixed-income corporate finance department of Golden Brothers, an investment banking firm, has decided to compete for the advisory and underwriting bond offering of Kia Telcom, a 'hot' telecommunications company. The firm's equity brokerage unit is about to publish a "sell" recommendation on Kia Telcom due to an unexpected announcement of cost overruns. The head of fixed-income investment banking has asked the head of the equity brokerage unit to change the recommendation from "sell" to "buy" before distributing the research report to clients. According to the Code and Standards, the best course of action for the equity brokerage unit is to:

***A. place Kia Telcom on a restricted list and publish only factual information about the company.**

B. increase the rating by no more than one increment (in this case, to a "hold" recommendation) since little harm is done by being a bit more positive, while the firm's overall interest is served.

C. assign a more senior analyst to decide if the stock deserves a higher rating for the sake of objectivity since less senior analysts may err in judgment.

Explanation: LOS: Reading 2-a

In this case, any action to accommodate the interest of the investment banking department that may compromise the independence and objectivity of the brokerage research efforts can violate Standard I(B) and the Code of Ethics.

**Reference:** CFA® Program Curriculum, Volume 1, pp. 21-25.

# Study Session 02: Quantitative Methods: Basic Concepts

This introductory study session presents the fundamentals of those quantitative techniques that are essential in almost any type of financial analysis, and which will be used throughout the remainder of the CFA curriculum. This session introduces two main building blocks of the quantitative analytical tool kit:

(1) the time value of money and

(2) statistics and probability theory.

The time value of money concept is one of the main principles of financial valuation. The calculations based on this principle (e.g., present value, future value, and internal rate of return) are the basic tools used to support corporate finance decisions and estimate the fair value of fixed income, equity, or any other type of security or investment.

Similarly, the basic concepts of statistics and probability theory constitute the essential tools used in describing the main statistical properties of a population and understanding and applying various probability concepts in practice.

**Reading 5: The Time Value of Money**

**Reading 6: Discounted Cash Flow Applications**

**Reading 7: Statistical Concepts and Market Returns**

**Reading 8: Probability Concepts**

1. (QID 24) The number of cars sold per month over the last three years by ABC Car Distributor is as follows:

| | J | F | M | A | M | J | J | A | S | O | N | D |
|---|---|---|---|---|---|---|---|---|---|---|---|---|
| Year 1 | 30 | 35 | 45 | 46 | 52 | 48 | 40 | 35 | 35 | 28 | 20 | 16 |
| Year 2 | 19 | 25 | 34 | 41 | 43 | 37 | 34 | 27 | 26 | 20 | 15 | 14 |
| Year 3 | 32 | 34 | 30 | 44 | 51 | 55 | 60 | 45 | 44 | 38 | 34 | 26 |

You have been asked to build a frequency distribution using 6 classes and you select the first class to be '10 up to 20':

What is the class frequency and relative class frequency of the second class?

| Class frequency | Relative class frequency |
|---|---|
| A. 7 | 0.194 |
| B. 7 | 0.278 |
| C. 10 | 0.194 |

1. (QID 24) The number of cars sold per month over the last three years by ABC Car Distributor is as follows:

| | J | F | M | A | M | J | J | A | S | O | N | D |
|---|---|---|---|---|---|---|---|---|---|---|---|---|
| Year 1 | 30 | 35 | 45 | 46 | 52 | 48 | 40 | 35 | 35 | 28 | 20 | 16 |
| Year 2 | 19 | 25 | 34 | 41 | 43 | 37 | 34 | 27 | 26 | 20 | 15 | 14 |
| Year 3 | 32 | 34 | 30 | 44 | 51 | 55 | 60 | 45 | 44 | 38 | 34 | 26 |

You have been asked to build a frequency distribution using 6 classes and you select the first class to be '10 up to 20':

What is the class frequency and relative class frequency of the second class?

| Class frequency | Relative class frequency |
|---|---|
| *A. 7 | 0.194 |
| B. 7 | 0.278 |
| C. 10 | 0.194 |

Explanation: LOS: Reading 7-b

The second class is for sales from 20 up to 30 cars per month, there are 7 observations in this range which is the class frequency. The relative frequency is the percentage of observations in each class, for the second class this is 7 36 = 19.4%

**Reference:** CFA® Program Curriculum, Volume 1, pp. 243-251.

2. (QID 27) The forecast rate of return from an investment has the following probability distribution:

| Rate of Return | Probability |
|---|---|
| 15% | 0.250 |
| 20% | 0.500 |
| 24% | 0.125 |
| 26% | 0.125 |

The standard deviation of the rate of return is closest to:

A. 0.0013.

B. 0.0250.

C. 0.0357.

---

3. (QID 30) A series of data is normally distributed, has a mean of 50 and standard deviation of 4. Approximately 95% of the readings will fall between:

A. 46 to 54.

B. 42 to 58.

C. 38 to 62.

2. (QID 27) The forecast rate of return from an investment has the following probability distribution:

| Rate of Return | Probability |
|---|---|
| 15% | 0.250 |
| 20% | 0.500 |
| 24% | 0.125 |
| 26% | 0.125 |

The standard deviation of the rate of return is closest to:

A. 0.0013.

B. 0.0250.

***C. 0.0357.**

Explanation: LOS: Reading 8-k

**The mean is:**

$$E(X) = \sum_{i=1}^{n} P(X_i) \times X_i$$

$$= (0.25 \times 15\%) + (0.5 \times 20\%) + (0.125 \times 24\%) + (0.125 \times 26\%) = 20\%$$

**The standard deviation is:**

$$\sigma^2(X) = \sum_{i=1}^{n} P(X_i)[X_i - E(X)]^2$$

$$\{[0.25 \times (0.05)^2] + [0.125 \times (0.04)^2] + [0.125 \times (0.06)^2]\}^{1/2} = 0.0357$$

**Reference:** CFA® Program Curriculum, Volume 1, pp. 332-337.

---

3. (QID 30) A series of data is normally distributed, has a mean of 50 and standard deviation of 4. Approximately 95% of the readings will fall between:

A. 46 to 54.

***B. 42 to 58.**

C. 38 to 62.

Explanation: LOS: Reading 7-i

For a normal distribution 95% of the observations will fall between the mean plus or minus 2 standard deviations, i.e. between 50 ± 8.

**Reference:** CFA® Program Curriculum, Volume 1, pp. 297-298.

4. (QID 28) Two investment managers have their performance analyzed. The first, A, achieves an average (arithmetic mean) performance of 20% with a standard deviation of 2%. The second, B, achieves an average performance of 12%, with a standard deviation of 1.5%. Which of the following statements is the most accurate?

A. The coefficient of variation of A's returns is equal to that of B's.

B. The coefficient of variation of A's returns is lower than that of B's.

C. The coefficient of variation of A's returns is higher than that of B's.

---

5. (QID 26) A team of four people is to be selected from a group of nine students. How many ways can they be selected?

A. 24.

B. 126.

C. 3,024.

4. (QID 28) Two investment managers have their performance analyzed. The first, A, achieves an average (arithmetic mean) performance of 20% with a standard deviation of 2%. The second, B, achieves an average performance of 12%, with a standard deviation of 1.5%. Which of the following statements is the most accurate?

A. The coefficient of variation of A's returns is equal to that of B's.

***B. The coefficient of variation of A's returns is lower than that of B's.**

C. The coefficient of variation of A's returns is higher than that of B's.

Explanation: LOS: Reading 7-h

The coefficient of variation is (in percentage terms) $\frac{\sigma}{\mu} \times 100$

For A this is $\frac{2\% \times 100}{20\%} = 10.0\%$ and

for B = $\frac{1.5\% \times 100}{12\%} = 12.5\%$

**Reference:** CFA® Program Curriculum, Volume 1, pp. 291-293.

---

5. (QID 26) A team of four people is to be selected from a group of nine students. How many ways can they be selected?

A. 24.

***B. 126.**

C. 3,024.

Explanation: LOS: Reading 8-n

Since the order of the four students to be selected does not matter we can use the combination (binomial) formulA. The number of ways is:

Apply the combination formula

$$\frac{n!}{(n-r)! \times r!} = \frac{9!}{4!5!} = \frac{9 \times 8 \times 7 \times 6}{4 \times 3 \times 2 \times 1} = 126$$

**Reference:** CFA® Program Curriculum, Volume 1, pp. 355-358.

6. (QID 29) The following income streams will be paid from an investment:

| | |
|---|---|
| End year 1 | $15,000 |
| End year 2 | $25,000 |
| End year 3 | $10,000 |

At the end of year 3 the investment will have no remaining value. If the discount rate is 8% the present value of the investment is closest to:

A. $46,721.

B. $39,692.

C. $43,260.

---

7. (QID 31) If an investment costs $15 and will make a single payment of $25 in four years' time the annual interest rate that will be earned on the investment is closest to:

A. 8.8%.

B. 13.6%.

C. 16.7%.

6. (QID 29) The following income streams will be paid from an investment:

| | |
|---|---|
| End year 1 | $15,000 |
| End year 2 | $25,000 |
| End year 3 | $10,000 |

At the end of year 3 the investment will have no remaining value. If the discount rate is 8% the present value of the investment is closest to:

A. $46,721.

B. $39,692.

***C. $43,260.**

Explanation: LOS: Reading 5-d

$$PV = \frac{\$15{,}000}{1.08} + \frac{\$25{,}000}{(1.08)^2} + \frac{\$10{,}000}{(1.08)^3}$$
$$= \$13{,}889 + \$21{,}433 + \$7{,}938 = \$43{,}260$$

**Reference:** CFA® Program Curriculum, Volume 1, pp. 197-198.

---

7. (QID 31) If an investment costs $15 and will make a single payment of $25 in four years' time the annual interest rate that will be earned on the investment is closest to:

A. 8.8%.

***B. 13.6%.**

C. 16.7%.

Explanation: LOS: Reading 5-d

$$FV_N = PV(1+r)^N$$
$$\$25 = \$15(1+r)^4$$
$$r = 13.62\%$$

Or use a financial calculator.

**Reference:** CFA® Program Curriculum, Volume 1, pp. 174-179.

8. (QID 32) Equal numbers of red, white, green and blue folders are manufactured but one in ten of the folders is faulty. The probability that a folder is faulty is equal for each of the colors. What is the probability that if you select one folder that it will be green or faulty?

A. 31.5%.

B. 32.5%.

C. 37.5%.

9. (QID 37) Which of the following statements about variance is least accurate? Variance is:

A. the arithmetic mean of the squared deviations from the mean.

B. the square of the standard deviation.

C. in the same units as the original data.

8. (QID 32) Equal numbers of red, white, green and blue folders are manufactured but one in ten of the folders is faulty. The probability that a folder is faulty is equal for each of the colors. What is the probability that if you select one folder that it will be green or faulty?

A. 31.5%.

***B. 32.5%.**

C. 37.5%.

Explanation: LOS: Reading 8-e

The Rule of Addition for events, A and B, that are not mutually exclusive, is:

P(A or B) = P(A) + P(B) - P(A and B)

So the probability that a folder will be green or faulty is:

P(green) + P(faulty) - P(green and faulty)

= 0. 25 + 0.10 - 0.025

= 0.325 or 32.5%

**Reference:** CFA® Program Curriculum, Volume 1, pp. 327-328.

---

9. (QID 37) Which of the following statements about variance is least accurate? Variance is:

A. the arithmetic mean of the squared deviations from the mean.

B. the square of the standard deviation.

***C. in the same units as the original data.**

Explanation: LOS: Reading 7-f

The standard deviation, not the variance, is in the same units as the original data, since the deviations are squared, summed and then square rooted.

**Reference:** CFA® Program Curriculum, Volume 1, pp. 282-287.

10 (QID 33) A portfolio increases in value from $10 million to $12 million over the first year. New cash of $2 million is then invested in the fund and the fund increases in value to $15 million at the end of the second year. The money-weighted and time-weighted rates of return are closest to (respectively):

A. 12.8%, 13.4%.

B. 12.8%, 27.1%.

C. 13.4%, 22.5%.

---

11. (QID 46) An analyst states

" .... the odds against the company increasing its dividend are twelve to one."

This means that the analyst believes that the probability of it increasing the dividend is closest to:

A. 0.0769.

B. 0.0833.

C. 0.9166.

10. (QID 33) A portfolio increases in value from $10 million to $12 million over the first year. New cash of $2 million is then invested in the fund and the fund increases in value to $15 million at the end of the second year. The money-weighted and time-weighted rates of return are closest to (respectively):

***A. 12.8%, 13.4%.**

B. 12.8%, 27.1%.

C. 13.4%, 22.5%.

Explanation: LOS: Reading 6-c

**The money-weighted return is calculated by solving** $10+\frac{2}{(1+R)}=\frac{15}{(1+R)^2}$

**So, R = 12.8%.**

**The time-weighted return is the geometric average of the returns in each period,**

$(1.20)(1.0714)=(1+r)^2$ **so r = 13.39%**

**Reference:** CFA® Program Curriculum, Volume 1, pp. 222-223.

---

11. (QID 46) An analyst states

" .... the odds against the company increasing its dividend are twelve to one."

This means that the analyst believes that the probability of it increasing the dividend is closest to:

***A. 0.0769.**

B. 0.0833.

C. 0.9166.

Explanation: LOS: Reading 8-c

Odds against of twelve to one, means the probability is

1/(12 + 1) = 0.0769,

there is a one in thirteen chance it will happen.

**Reference:** CFA® Program Curriculum, Volume 1, pp. 320-321.

12. (QID 35) It is estimated that a stock has the following probabilities of return:

| Return | Probability |
|---|---|
| 15% | 0.2 |
| 20% | 0.4 |
| 30% | 0.4 |

The stock's expected return is closest to:

A. 25.0%.

B. 21.7%.

C. 23.0%.

---

13. (QID 36) If a distribution has positive excess kurtosis it means:

A. the mean of the distribution is greater than zero.

B. the distribution is positively skewed.

C. the distribution has fatter tails than a normal distribution.

12. (QID 35) It is estimated that a stock has the following probabilities of return:

| Return | Probability |
|---|---|
| 15% | 0.2 |
| 20% | 0.4 |
| 30% | 0.4 |

The stock's expected return is closest to:

A. 25.0%.

B. 21.7%.

***C. 23.0%.**

Explanation: LOS: Reading 8-k

Use the formula for expected value,

$$E(X) = \sum_{1}^{n} P(X_i)X_i = (0.2 \times 15\%) + (0.4 \times 20\%) + (0.4 \times 30\%) = 23\%$$

Reference:, CFA® Program Curriculum, Volume 1, pp. 334-337.

---

13. (QID 36) If a distribution has positive excess kurtosis it means:

A. the mean of the distribution is greater than zero.

B. the distribution is positively skewed.

***C. the distribution has fatter tails than a normal distribution.**

Explanation: LOS: Reading 7-j

Positive excess kurtosis means the distribution will be more peaked and have fatter tails than a normal distribution.

**Reference:** CFA® Program Curriculum, Volume 1, pp. 302-305.

14. (QID 38) The Sharpe ratio calculates:

A. the excess risk taken in a portfolio.

B. the excess return earned per unit of risk taken.

C. the standard deviation relative to the return earned.

15. (QID 39) A portfolio's performance over 5 years is +14%, −2%, + 10%, +14%, +8%. The portfolio's arithmetic mean return and median were:

| | Arithmetic mean | Median |
|---|---|---|
| A. | 8.8% | 10.0% |
| B. | 8.6% | 10.0% |
| C. | 8.6% | 14.0% |

14. (QID 38) The Sharpe ratio calculates:

A. the excess risk taken in a portfolio.

***B. the excess return earned per unit of risk taken.**

C. the standard deviation relative to the return earned.

Explanation: LOS: Reading 7-h

The Sharpe ratio measures the excess return over the risk-free rate in units of risk (standard deviation) taken. It is a common measure used to evaluate the performance of fund managers.

**Reference:** CFA® Program Curriculum, Volume 1, pp. 293-296.

---

15. (QID 39) A portfolio's performance over 5 years is +14%, –2%, + 10%, +14%, +8%. The portfolio's arithmetic mean return and median were:

| Arithmetic mean | Median |
|---|---|
| ***A. 8.8%** | **10.0%** |
| B. 8.6% | 10.0% |
| C. 8.6% | 14.0% |

Explanation: LOS: Reading 7-d

The arithmetic mean is $\frac{14\% - 2\% + 10\% + 14\% + 8\%}{5} = 8.8\%$

The median is the middle value of the ordered display

-2%, +8%, + 10%, +14%, +14%, which is 10%.

**Reference:** CFA® Program Curriculum, Volume 1, pp. 255-263.

16. (QID 40) Which of the following statements is most accurate about a frequency distribution histogram?

A. I. The individual observations cannot be identified.

B. II. Neighboring points on the graph are connected by a straight line.

C. III. The frequency of a class is shown by the width of the corresponding bar.

---

17. (QID 41) In a positively skewed distribution which of the following is most likely to occur?

A. Median mean mode.

B. Mode median mean.

C. Median mode mean.

16. (QID 40) Which of the following statements is most accurate about a frequency distribution histogram?

***A. I. The individual observations cannot be identified.**

B. II. Neighboring points on the graph are connected by a straight line.

C. III. The frequency of a class is shown by the width of the corresponding bar.

Explanation: LOS: Reading 7-c

II. refers to a frequency polygon.

III. is not correct; the frequency of a class is shown by the height.

**Reference:** CFA® Program Curriculum, Volume 1, pp. 251-255.

---

17. (QID 41) In a positively skewed distribution which of the following is most likely to occur?

A. Median mean mode.

***B. Mode median mean.**

C. Median mode mean.

Explanation: LOS: Reading 7-i

A positively skewed distribution will have one or more observations that are very large. This will lead to the average (mean) being 'pulled' to the right. The median (the middle reading) will be higher than the mode (the most frequently occurring observation).

**Reference:** CFA® Program Curriculum, Volume 1, pp. 297-302.

18. (QID 42) The money market yield of a 90-day Treasury bill offering a bank discount yield of 4% is closest to:

A. 16.99%.

B. 4.00%.

C. 4.04%.

---

19. (QID 43) The value of $1,000 invested today, at an interest rate of 12% per year compounded quarterly, in 2 years' time is closest to:

A. $1,259.48.

B. $1,254.40.

C. $1,266.77.

18. (QID 42) The money market yield of a 90-day Treasury bill offering a bank discount yield of 4% is closest to:

A. 16.99%.

B. 4.00%.

***C. 4.04%.**

Explanation: LOS: Reading 6-d

$$r_{MM} = \frac{360 \times r_{BD}}{360 - t \times r_{BD}} = \frac{360 \times 0.04}{360 - (90 \times 0.04)} = 4.04\%$$

**Reference:** CFA® Program Curriculum, Volume 1, pp. 229-233.

---

19. (QID 43) The value of $1,000 invested today, at an interest rate of 12% per year compounded quarterly, in 2 years' time is closest to:

A. $1,259.48.

B. $1,254.40.

***C. $1,266.77.**

Explanation: LOS: Reading 5-c

$$FV_N = PV\left(1 + \frac{r_S}{m}\right)^{m \times N} = \$1{,}000\left(1 + \frac{0.12}{4}\right)^{4 \times 2} = \$1{,}266.77$$

Or use a financial calculator.

**Reference:** CFA® Program Curriculum, Volume 1, pp. 179-180.

20. (QID 45) A manager is offered two investments projects X and Y with net cash flows, in $ million, from each investment as shown below. The cost of X is $2 million and the cost of Y is $10 million. The cost of capital for X is 10% and for Y is 8%. Which should be accepted for investment?

| End of Year | X | Y |
|---|---|---|
| 1 | 1.1 | 3.0 |
| 2 | 1.8 | 9.0 |

A. Both projects should be accepted.

B. X should be accepted and Y rejected.

C. Y should be accepted and X rejected.

---

21. (QID 44) The mean absolute deviation of the data 1, 5, 7, 8, 14 is:

A. 18.0.

B. 3.2.

C. 4.2.

20. (QID 45) A manager is offered two investments projects X and Y with net cash flows, in $ million, from each investment as shown below. The cost of X is $2 million and the cost of Y is $10 million. The cost of capital for X is 10% and for Y is 8%. Which should be accepted for investment?

| End of Year | X | Y |
|---|---|---|
| 1 | 1.1 | 3.0 |
| 2 | 1.8 | 9.0 |

***A. Both projects should be accepted.**

B. X should be accepted and Y rejected.

C. Y should be accepted and X rejected.

Explanation: LOS: Reading 6-a

$$NPV(X) = \sum_{t=0}^{N} \frac{CF_t}{(1+r)^t} = -2 + \frac{1.1}{1.10} + \frac{1.8}{1.10^2} = 0.49$$

$$NPV(Y) = \sum_{t=0}^{N} \frac{CF_t}{(1+r)^t} = -10 + \frac{3.0}{1.08} + \frac{9.0}{1.08^2} = 0.49$$

Both investments have positive NPVs so they should both be accepted.

**Reference:** CFA® Program Curriculum, Volume 1, pp. 214-216.

---

21. (QID 44) The mean absolute deviation of the data 1, 5, 7, 8, 14 is:

A. 18.0.

***B. 3.2.**

C. 4.2.

Explanation: LOS: Reading 7-f

The mean is: $(1 + 5 + 7 + 8 + 14)/5 = 7$

The absolute mean deviation is:

$$\frac{\sum_{1}^{n} |X_i - \overline{X}|}{n} = \frac{|1-7| + |5-7| + |7-7| + |7-8| + |7-14|}{5} = 3.2$$

**Reference:** CFA® Program Curriculum, Volume 1, pp. 279-281.

22. (QID 25) A person invests $10,000 at the end of each year for the next ten years, if the investment earns 6% interest annually, the value of the investment at the end of ten years will be closest to:

A. $131,808.

B. $134,350.

C. $139,708.

---

23. (QID 34) An investor wants to buy an annuity that will pay out $10,000 a year at the end of each of the next 15 years. He can earn an interest rate of 8% on the annuity. The purchase price of the annuity is closest to:

A. $85,595.

B. $102,037.

C. $138,889.

22. (QID 25) A person invests $10,000 at the end of each year for the next ten years, if the investment earns 6% interest annually, the value of the investment at the end of ten years will be closest to:

***A. $131,808.**

B. $134,350.

C. $139,708.

Explanation: LOS: Reading 5-d

This is a question asking for the future value of an annuity, use the annuity formula or a financial calculator:

This is an annuity type question.

**Future value =**

$$FV = A\left[\frac{(1+r)^N - 1}{r}\right] = \$10{,}000 \times \frac{\left[(1.06)^{10} - 1\right]}{0.06} = \$131{,}800$$

Or use a financial calculator.

| Explicit use of annuity formula: | Calculator keystrokes for: | |
|---|---|---|
| | **HP-12C** | **BA II Plus** |
| $A = \$10{,}000$ | [f] CLEAR [FIN] | [2nd] [QUIT] [2nd] [CLR TVM] |
| $r = 6\% = 0.06$ | 10000 [CHS] [PMT] -10,000.00 | 10000 [+/-] [PMT] PMT = -10,000.00 |
| $N = 10$ | 6 [i] 6.00 | 6 [I/Y] I/Y = 6.00 |
| $FV_N = A\dfrac{(1+r)^N - 1}{r}$ | 10 [n] 10.00 | 10 [N] N = 10.00 |
| $= \$10{,}000\dfrac{(1+0.06)^{10} - 1}{0.06}$ | [FV] FV = 131,807.95 | [CPT] [FV] FV = 131,807.95 |
| $= \$10{,}000 \times 13.1808$ | | |
| $= \$131808$ | | |

**Reference:** CFA® Program Curriculum, Volume 1, pp. 183-185.

23. (QID 34) An investor wants to buy an annuity that will pay out $10,000 a year at the end of each of the next 15 years. He can earn an interest rate of 8% on the annuity. The purchase price of the annuity is closest to:

***A. $85,595.**

B. $102,037.

C. $138,889.

Explanation: LOS: Reading 5-d

This is a question asking for the present value of an annuity, use the annuity formula or a financial calculator:

$$PV = A\frac{\left[1-\frac{1}{(1+r)^N}\right]}{r} = \$10{,}000\frac{\left[1-\frac{1}{(1.08)^{15}}\right]}{008} = \$85{,}595$$

Or use a financial calculator.

| **Explicit use of annuity formula:** | **Calculator keystrokes for:** | | | |
|---|---|---|---|---|
| | **HP-12C** | | **BA II Plus** | |
| $A = \$10{,}000$ | | | | |
| $r = 8\% = 0.08$ | [f] CLEAR [FIN] | | [2nd] [QUIT] [2nd] [CLR TVM] | |
| $N = 15$ | [g] END | | 10000 [+/-] [PMT] | |
| $PV = A\frac{1 \quad \frac{1}{(1+r)^N}}{r}$ | 10000 [CHS] [PMT] | | | **PMT = -102,000.00** |
| | | **-10,000.00** | 8 [I/Y] | **I/Y = 8.00** |
| $= \$10{,}000\frac{1 \quad \frac{1}{(1+0.08)^{15}}}{0.08}$ | 8 [i] | **8.00** | 15 [N] | **N = 15.00** |
| | 15 [n] | **15.00** | [CPT] [PV] | **PV =85,594.79** |
| $= \$10{,}000 \times 8.5595$ | [PV] | 85,594.79 | | |
| $= \$85{,}595$ | | | | |

**Reference:** CFA® Program Curriculum, Volume 1, pp. 190-194.

# Study Session 03: Quantitative Methods: Applications

This study session introduces the discrete and continuous probability distributions that are most commonly used to describe the behavior of random variables. Probability theory and calculations are widely applied in finance, for example, in the field of investment and project valuation and in financial risk management.

Furthermore, this session teaches how to estimate different parameters (e.g., mean and standard deviation) of a population if only a sample, rather than the whole population, can be observed. Hypothesis testing is a closely related topic. This session presents the techniques that can be applied to accept or reject an assumed hypothesis (null hypothesis) about various parameters of a population. Finally, you will also learn about the fundamentals of technical analysis. It is important that analysts properly understand the assumptions and limitations when applying these tools as mis-specified models or improperly used tools can result in misleading conclusions.

**Reading 9: Common Probability Distributions**

**Reading 10: Sampling and Estimation**

**Reading 11: Hypothesis Testing**

**Reading 12: Technical Analysis**

1. (QID 47) An analyst is collecting data on mutual fund performance. He estimates that the standard deviation of funds' returns is 4% and returns are independent across funds. To achieve a standard error of sample mean of 0.5% how many funds does he need to include in his sample?

A. 8.

B. 128.

C. 64.

---

2. (QID 48) Which of the following statements is least accurate?

A. The null hypothesis should always contain the equal sign.

B. Type I error is accepting the null hypothesis when it is false.

C. The level of significance is the probability of rejecting the null hypothesis when it is true.

1. (QID 47) An analyst is collecting data on mutual fund performance. He estimates that the standard deviation of funds' returns is 4% and returns are independent across funds. To achieve a standard error of sample mean of 0.5% how many funds does he need to include in his sample?

A. 8.

B. 128.

***C. 64.**

Explanation: LOS: Reading 10-e

**Standard error of sample mean is**

$\frac{\sigma}{\sqrt{n}}$. **So** $\sqrt{n} = 4\% / 0.5\%$

**and n = 64**

**Reference:** CFA® Program Curriculum, Volume 1, pp. 429-431.

---

2. (QID 48) Which of the following statements is least accurate?

A. The null hypothesis should always contain the equal sign.

***B. Type I error is accepting the null hypothesis when it is false.**

C. The level of significance is the probability of rejecting the null hypothesis when it is true.

Explanation: LOS: Reading 11-b

A Type I error is rejecting the null hypothesis when it is true.

**Reference:** CFA® Program Curriculum, Volume 1, pp. 456-461.

3. (QID 49) A binomial distribution model is created to analyze the performance of a fund relative to an index over 36 trial periods. In each period there is a 60% probability of success which is defined as the fund matching or outperforming the index, in each period the performance is assumed to be independent. The mean of the binomial random variable is closest to:

A. 14.4.

B. 8.64.

C. 21.6.

---

4. (QID 50) An analyst does a test of a sample of 100 observations to determine whether the mean of a normally distributed population is less than or equal to zero. The z-value is calculated to be 1.95. At the 1% significance level which of the following should the analyst conclude:

A. reject the null hypothesis and accept the alternative hypothesis that the mean is significantly lower than zero.

B. reject the null hypothesis and accept the alternative hypothesis that the mean is significantly higher than zero.

C. do not reject the null hypothesis that the sample mean is less than or equal to zero and reject the alternative hypothesis.

3. (QID 49) A binomial distribution model is created to analyze the performance of a fund relative to an index over 36 trial periods. In each period there is a 60% probability of success which is defined as the fund matching or outperforming the index, in each period the performance is assumed to be independent. The mean of the binomial random variable is closest to:

A. 14.4.

B. 8.64.

***C. 21.6.**

Explanation: LOS: Reading 9-d

The mean is np where n is the number of trials, 36, and p is the probability of success, 0.60, so the mean is 36 x 0.60 = 21.6

**Reference:** CFA® Program Curriculum, Volume 1, pp. 384-387.

---

4. (QID 50) An analyst does a test of a sample of 100 observations to determine whether the mean of a normally distributed population is less than or equal to zero. The z-value is calculated to be 1.95. At the 1% significance level which of the following should the analyst conclude:

A. reject the null hypothesis and accept the alternative hypothesis that the mean is significantly lower than zero.

B. reject the null hypothesis and accept the alternative hypothesis that the mean is significantly higher than zero.

***C. do not reject the null hypothesis that the sample mean is less than or equal to zero and reject the alternative hypothesis.**

Explanation: LOS: Reading 11-e

The critical z-value for a one tailed test is 2.33, the z-value is below this so do not reject the null hypothesis.

**Reference:** CFA® Program Curriculum, Volume 1, pp. 466-474.

5. (QID 51) Which of the following would be seen as a buy signal by a contrary opinion technical analyst?

A. The bearish sentiment index for investment advisory opinions is high

B. OTC volume is high relative to volume on the NYSE.

C. A low put/call ratio on the Chicago Board Options Exchange.

---

6. (QID 52) When a technical analyst notes that a stock has risen to a price range where she expects to see major sellers of the stock enter the market, then the stock is most likely to have:

A. broken its trend line.

B. broken through its moving average line from below.

C. reached a resistance level.

5. (QID 51) Which of the following would be seen as a buy signal by a contrary opinion technical analyst?

***A. The bearish sentiment index for investment advisory opinions is high**

B. OTC volume is high relative to volume on the NYSE.

C. A low put/call ratio on the Chicago Board Options Exchange.

Explanation: LOS: Reading 12-c

Contrarians believe that investment advisors are trend followers so the number of bears is greatest near the bottom of the market.

**Reference:** CFA® Program Curriculum, Volume 1, pp. 509-511.

---

6. (QID 52) When a technical analyst notes that a stock has risen to a price range where she expects to see major sellers of the stock enter the market, then the stock is most likely to have:

A. broken its trend line.

B. broken through its moving average line from below.

***C. reached a resistance level.**

Explanation: LOS: Reading 12-c

A resistance level is when technical analysts would expect to see an increase in supply of stock (which has been overhanging the market) lead to selling pressure and price reversal.

**Reference:** CFA® Program Curriculum, Volume 1, pp. 515-516.

7. (QID 53) A sample of 100 observations is taken from a normal population, the sample mean is 50 and the population standard deviation is 6. The 99% confidence interval for the population mean is closest to:

A. 48.46 up to 51.55.

B. 48.82 up to 51.18.

C. 49.34 up to 50.63.

---

8. (QID 54) When we are using a hypothesis test to test the variance of a single normally distributed population we should use the:

A. F-test.

B. z-test.

C. chi-square test.

7. (QID 53) A sample of 100 observations is taken from a normal population, the sample mean is 50 and the population standard deviation is 6. The 99% confidence interval for the population mean is closest to:

***A. 48.46 up to 51.55.**

B. 48.82 up to 51.18.

C. 49.34 up to 50.63.

Explanation: LOS: Reading 10-j

The result of (2.575 * 6) / Square root of 100 is 1.545

So 50 + 1.545 = 51.545 and 50 – 1.545 = 48.455

Specific 48.455 to 51.545

**99% confidence interval for the mean is** $\bar{x} \pm \frac{2.575\sigma}{\sqrt{n}}$

$$= 50 \pm \frac{2.575 \times 6}{\sqrt{100}} = 50 \pm 1.548 = 48.452 \text{ to } 51.458$$

**Reference:** CFA® Program Curriculum, Volume 1, pp. 433-441.

---

8. (QID 54) When we are using a hypothesis test to test the variance of a single normally distributed population we should use the:

A. F-test.

B. z-test.

***C. chi-square test.**

Explanation: LOS: Reading 11-f

The chi-square test is used to test the variance of a single normally distributed population.

**Reference:** CFA® Program Curriculum, Volume 1, pp. 482-484.

9. (QID 55) When a contrary opinion technical analyst sees a build-up of credit balances in brokerage accounts they would see this as:

A. a bearish signal for the market, since it indicates a lack of funds available to buy stocks in the market.

B. a bearish signal for the market, since investors are negative on the market prospects.

C. a bullish signal for the market, since there are funds available to buy stocks in the market.

---

10. (QID 56) Which of the following is least likely to be an assumption of technical analysis?

A. The prices of securities move in long-term trends.

B. Market values are determined by supply and demand.

C. The prices of securities reflect all past market trading data.

9. (QID 55) When a contrary opinion technical analyst sees a build-up of credit balances in brokerage accounts they would see this as:

A. a bearish signal for the market, since it indicates a lack of funds available to buy stocks in the market.

B. a bearish signal for the market, since investors are negative on the market prospects.

***C. a bullish signal for the market, since there are funds available to buy stocks in the market.**

Explanation: LOS: Reading 12-c

High credit balances imply that investors are planning to invest the money in the short term so it is a bullish signal for the market.

**Reference:** CFA® Program Curriculum, Volume 1, pp. 509-511.

---

10. (QID 56) Which of the following is least likely to be an assumption of technical analysis?

A. The prices of securities move in long-term trends.

B. Market values are determined by supply and demand.

***C. The prices of securities reflect all past market trading data.**

Explanation: LOS: Reading 12-a

"The prices of securities reflect all" is the weak form of the Efficient Market Hypothesis which says that all past price and trading information is reflected in current stock prices. The implication is that technical analysis does not improve returns.

**Reference:** CFA® Program Curriculum, Volume 1, pp. 504-506.

11. (QID 57) A coin has a 50% chance of landing head up and a 50% chance of landing tail up. What is the probability, if a coin is thrown four times, of it landing head up once or not at all?

A. 25.00%.

B. 31.25%.

C. 37.50%.

---

12. (QID 58) The population is defined as the 1,500 employees of a company and the wages of the employees range from $10.00 per hour to $25.00 per hour with a mean of $14.00 per hour. A sample of 100 employees is taken and the mean wage of the sample is $12.50. The sampling error is closest to:

A. - $1.50.

B. + $1.50.

C. + 15.00.

11. (QID 57) A coin has a 50% chance of landing head up and a 50% chance of landing tail up. What is the probability, if a coin is thrown four times, of it landing head up once or not at all?

A. 25.00%.

***B. 31.25%.**

C. 37.50%.

Explanation: LOS: Reading 9-d

Apply the binomial probability distribution formula where we are solving for p(0) and p(1).

$$p(0) = \frac{4!}{4! \times 0!} 0.5^0 (1-0.5)^4 = 0.0625$$

$$p(1) = \frac{4!}{(4-1)! \times 1!} 0.5^1 (1-0.5)^3 = 0.2500$$

**p(0) + p(1) = 0.3125 or 31.25%**

**Reference:** CFA® Program Curriculum, Volume 1, pp. 376-384.

---

12. (QID 58) The population is defined as the 1,500 employees of a company and the wages of the employees range from $10.00 per hour to $25.00 per hour with a mean of $14.00 per hour. A sample of 100 employees is taken and the mean wage of the sample is $12.50. The sampling error is closest to:

***A. - $1.50.**

B. + $1.50.

C. + 15.00.

Explanation: LOS: Reading 10-a

**The sampling error is**

$$\overline{X} - \mu = \$12.50 - \$14.00 = -\$1.50$$

**Reference:** CFA® Program Curriculum, Volume 1, p 423.

13. (QID 59) Which of the following statements concerning a multivariate distribution is least accurate?

A. The distribution describes the probability of different outcomes for a group of random variables.

B. If the random variables are normally distributed it is usually assumed the multivariate distribution is normally distributed.

C. A multivariate distribution describes the outcomes for a single random variable under different scenarios.

---

14. (QID 60) Which group of people believes that the adjustment of stock prices to new information takes the longest period of time?

A. Technical analysts.

B. Fundamental analysts.

C. Supporters of the efficient market hypothesis.

13. (QID 59) Which of the following statements concerning a multivariate distribution is least accurate?

A. The distribution describes the probability of different outcomes for a group of random variables.

B. If the random variables are normally distributed it is usually assumed the multivariate distribution is normally distributed.

***C. A multivariate distribution describes the outcomes for a single random variable under different scenarios.**

Explanation: LOS: Reading 9-f

If it is a single random variable it is a univariate distribution.

**Reference:** CFA® Program Curriculum, Volume 1, p. 392.

---

14. (QID 60) Which group of people believes that the adjustment of stock prices to new information takes the longest period of time?

***A. Technical analysts.**

B. Fundamental analysts.

C. Supporters of the efficient market hypothesis.

Explanation: LOS: Reading 12-a

Technical analysts believe that it takes a period of time for a new trend to establish itself.

**Reference:** CFA® Program Curriculum, Volume 1, pp. 504-506.

15. (QID 61) In hypothesis testing a test statistic is:

A. the level of significance of the test.

B. the probability of correctly rejecting the null hypothesis.

C. a value which will decide whether to accept or reject the null hypothesis.

---

16. (QID 69) When selecting a sample a population is first divided into subpopulations and then random samples are taken from each subpopulation, the number taken proportional to the size of the subpopulation. This is an example of:

A. structured sampling.

B. stratified random sampling.

C. systematic sampling.

15. (QID 61) In hypothesis testing a test statistic is:

A. the level of significance of the test.

B. the probability of correctly rejecting the null hypothesis.

***C. a value which will decide whether to accept or reject the null hypothesis.**

Explanation: LOS: Reading 11-b

A test statistic is calculated based on a sample and will be used to decide whether to accept or reject the null hypothesis, t and z-statistics are commonly used test statistics.

**Reference:** CFA® Program Curriculum, Volume 1, pp. 459-466.

---

16. (QID 69) When selecting a sample a population is first divided into subpopulations and then random samples are taken from each subpopulation, the number taken proportional to the size of the subpopulation. This is an example of:

A. structured sampling.

***B. stratified random sampling.**

C. systematic sampling.

Explanation: LOS: Reading 10-b

Stratified random sampling ensures that different subdivisions within a population are represented in the sample.

**Reference:** CFA® Program Curriculum, Volume 1, pp. 422-425.

17. (QID 63) In technical analysis the breadth of the stock market might be measured by:

A. the confidence index.

B. the moving-averages.

C. the advance-decline ratio.

---

18. (QID 64) Technical analysts are least likely to believe that they have the following advantages over fundamental analysts:

A. they do not need to use financial statements.

B. they can select the right timing for buying and selling securities.

C. their decisions will not be affected by changes in investor sentiment.

17. (QID 63) In technical analysis the breadth of the stock market might be measured by:

A. the confidence index.

B. the moving-averages.

***C. the advance-decline ratio.**

Explanation: LOS: Reading 12-c

The breadth of the market looks at the number of issues that have increased versus the number that have declined; this information can be seen in the advance-decline ratio. It provides additional information to the market index which is often dominated by a small number of large stocks which can move the market in one direction even when the majority of issues are moving in the opposite direction.

**Reference:** CFA® Program Curriculum, Volume 1, pp. 513-514.

---

18. (QID 64) Technical analysts are least likely to believe that they have the following advantages over fundamental analysts:

A. they do not need to use financial statements.

B. they can select the right timing for buying and selling securities.

***C. their decisions will not be affected by changes in investor sentiment.**

Explanation: LOS: Reading 12-b

Changes in sentiment will affect supply and demand for stocks that, in technical analysis, are the determinants of stock price moves. A fundamental analyst, if depending on the financial statements, may not take into account sentiment changes.

Reference CFA® Program Curriculum, Volume 1, pp. 506-507.

19. (QID 65) An analyst has extensively tested past stock data to identify a stock valuation model. He has looked at numerous variables and has arrived at a model, using six different variables, which he believes successfully identifies undervalued stocks. His analysis is likely to exhibit:

A. look-ahead bias.

B. data-mining bias.

C. data-snooping bias.

---

20. (QID 66) The level of significance in hypothesis testing is the probability of:

A. rejecting the null hypothesis when it is true.

B. accepting the null hypothesis when it is false.

C. rejecting the alternate hypothesis when it is true.

19. (QID 65) An analyst has extensively tested past stock data to identify a stock valuation model. He has looked at numerous variables and has arrived at a model, using six different variables, which he believes successfully identifies undervalued stocks. His analysis is likely to exhibit:

A. look-ahead bias.

***B. data-mining bias.**

C. data-snooping bias.

Explanation: LOS: Reading 10-k

Data-mining biases occur when an analyst searches through data to identify patterns or significant variables. It can be detected by doing out-of-sample tests which will often show the variable is not significant.

**Reference:** CFA® Program Curriculum, Volume 1, pp. 442-444.

---

20. (QID 66) The level of significance in hypothesis testing is the probability of:

***A. rejecting the null hypothesis when it is true.**

B. accepting the null hypothesis when it is false.

C. rejecting the alternate hypothesis when it is true.

Explanation: LOS: Reading 11-b

The level of significance is alpha or the probability of making a Type I error. This refers to the probability of rejecting the null hypothesis when it is true.

**Reference:** CFA® Program Curriculum, Volume 1, pp. 456-462.

21. (QID 67) A normal distribution has a mean of 25 and a standard deviation of 5. What is the standardized normal random variable representing an observation of 15?

A. -2.00.

B. 1.67.

C. 3.00.

---

22. (QID 68) If mutual fund cash positions rise to 13% of the net asset value of the funds, then a contrary-opinion technical analyst would see this as a:

A. sell signal since it means that they are raising cash to meet redemptions from the fund.

B. buy signal since it indicates that the majority of investors are bearish.

C. sell signal since it means that they are receiving large cash flows into the funds.

21. (QID 67) A normal distribution has a mean of 25 and a standard deviation of 5. What is the standardized normal random variable representing an observation of 15?

***A. -2.00.**

B. 1.67.

C. 3.00.

Explanation: LOS: Reading 9-h

$$Z = \frac{X - \mu}{\sigma} = \frac{15 - 25}{5} = -2.0$$

**which is the number of standard deviations below the mean.**

Which is the number of standard deviations of the observation below the mean.

**Reference:** CFA® Program Curriculum, Volume 1, pp. 391-397.

---

22. (QID 68) If mutual fund cash positions rise to 13% of the net asset value of the funds, then a contrary-opinion technical analyst would see this as a:

A. sell signal since it means that they are raising cash to meet redemptions from the fund.

***B. buy signal since it indicates that the majority of investors are bearish.**

C. sell signal since it means that they are receiving large cash flows into the funds.

Explanation: LOS: Reading 12-c

A contrarian would take the opposite view to the majority of investors and high cash balances indicate that mutual fund managers, who are an indicator of institutional investors, are bearish. Also high cash balances indicate future buying power of the funds.

**Reference:** CFA® Program Curriculum, Volume 1, pp. 509-511.

23. (QID 62) If the mean of a normal distribution is 0 and the standard deviation is 20, the probability of an observation lying between -40 and 20 is closest to:

A. 95.4%.

B. 40.9%.

C. 81.8%.

---

24. (QID 66) A client wishes to protect the value of his capital. Which of the following portfolios will be optimal from a safety-first analysis?

| Asset | Expected Return | Standard Deviation |
|---|---|---|
| A | 25 | 12 |
| B | 15 | 8 |
| C | 10 | 6 |

A. Portfolio A.

B. Portfolio B.

C. Portfolio C.

23. (QID 62) If the mean of a normal distribution is 0 and the standard deviation is 20, the probability of an observation lying between -40 and 20 is closest to:

A. 95.4%.

B. 40.9%.

***C. 81.8%.**

Explanation: LOS: Reading 9-h

First, calculate the z-value of

–40: $z = (X - u)/\sigma = -40/20 = -2.0$

Therefore the area between 0 and –4 is 47.7, since 95.4% of observations lie within two standard deviations of the mean.

The z value of 20 is 1.

Therefore the area between 0 and 20 is 34.1, since 68.26% of observations lie within one standard deviation of the mean.

So the probability that a reading lies between

–44 and 20 is 47.7% +34.1% = 81.8%.

This looks like an area under the lopsided curve question

If the area under a standard (normal) curve is 68.26 (1 sigma) then ½ would be on each side (34.13 on each side),

And, the area under the curve for 2 sigma is 95.4 (1/2 each side would be 47.7 on each side), then the negative side would be 47.7 (1/2 of 2 standard deviation sigmas to the left) and the positive side would be 34.13 (1/2 of the sigma to the right).

34.13 | 34.13

Add the area under the curve to the right (using ½ of 1 sigma)

47.70 | 47.70

To the area under the curve on the left (using ½ of 2 sigma)

**Reference:** CFA® Program Curriculum, Volume 1, pp. 391-397.

24. (QID 66) A client wishes to protect the value of his capital. Which of the following portfolios will be optimal from a safety-first analysis?

| Asset | Expected Return | Standard Deviation |
|---|---|---|
| A | 25 | 12 |
| B | 15 | 8 |
| C | 10 | 6 |

***A. Portfolio A.**

B. Portfolio B.

C. Portfolio C.

Explanation: LOS: Reading 9-i

$$S\,F\,Ratio = \left[E(R_P) - R_L\right] / \sigma_P$$

**where**

$R_P$ = **portfolio return**

$R_L$ = **threshold level**

$\sigma_P$ = **portfolio standard deviation**

Calculate the S F Ratio for each portfolio:

S F Ratio(A) = 25/12 = 2.08

S F Ratio(B) = 15/8 = 1.875

S F Ratio(C) = 10/6 = 1.667

Portfolio A has the highest S F Ratio and is the correct choice.

**Reference:** CFA® Program Curriculum, Volume 1, pp. 397-400.

# Study Session 4: Economics Introduction:

## Introductory Readings

Economics: Private and Public Choice, 10th edition, James D. Gwartney, Richard L. Stroup, Russell S. Sobel, and David A. Macpherson (South-Western, 2003)
"Supply, Demand, and the Market Process," Ch. 3
"Supply and Demand: Applications and Extensions" Ch. 4
"Taking the Nation's Economic Pulse," Ch. 7
"Working with Our Basic Aggregate Demand/Aggregate Supply Model," Ch. 10
"Keynesian Foundations of Modern Macroeconomics," Ch. 11

## Supply, Demand, and the Market Process CH 5

### Introduction

This chapter is centered on the laws of supply and demand. The law of supply says that a higher price means producers produce more of the product, and the law of demand says that consumers buy less of a good if the price rises, and vice versa. Candidates should know what type of factors cause shifts in the supply and demand curves and movements along the curves and understand the concept of market equilibrium.

## Consumer choice and the Law of Demand

Consumers are forced to make choices regarding how they spend their income in order to get the most value for their money. **The Law of Demand** states that there is an inverse relationship between the price of a product and the amount or quantity of it that consumers are willing to purchase.

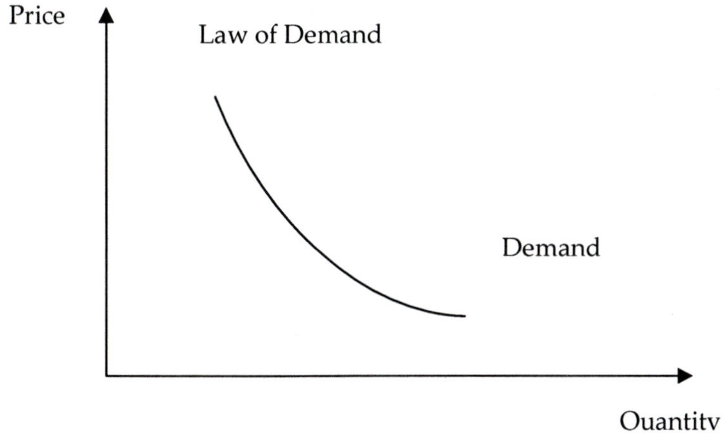


A **consumer surplus** is the difference between the maximum price that consumers are willing to pay and the price that they actually pay; this is a net gain to the buyers of the good.

## Producer choice and the Law of Supply

All economic participants in an economy are aiming to generate profit, which is the excess of sales revenue over the production costs. The Law of Supply states that there is a direct relationship between the price of a product and the amount of it that is offered for sale.

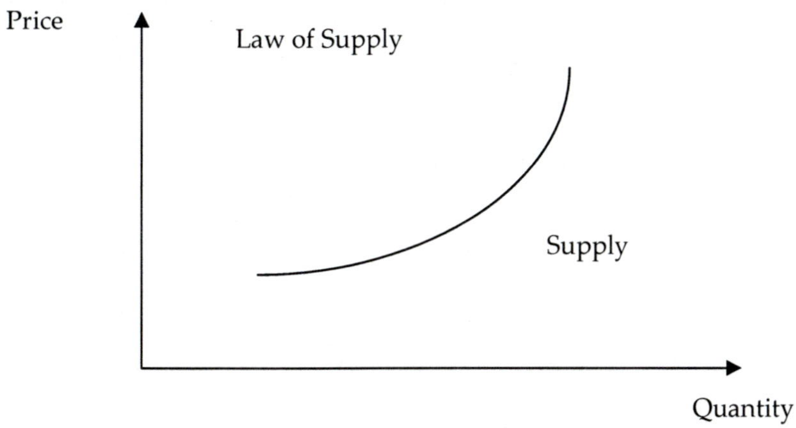

## Price changes and demand and supply

Consumers buy less of a product as the price increases because of the availability of substitutes. The availability of substitutes is a major factor in deciding the sensitivity to the quantity demanded to a change in price. If the demand for a product is elastic it means a small price change will lead to a large change in demand. In the diagram below when the price moves from P1 to P2, the quantity demanded falls sharply from Q1 to Q2. If demand is inelastic it means that a change in price only has a small impact on the quantity demanded, so prices move from Q1 to Q2. Unitary elastic means that a percent change in quantity demanded leads to a percent change in price.

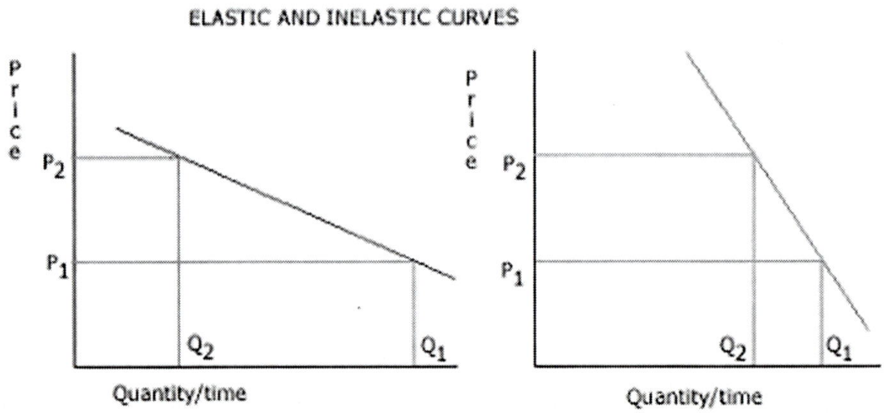


Similarly a supply curve is elastic when the quantity supplied is very responsive to a change in price (a flat curve) and inelastic when quantity supplied is not very responsive to a change in price (a steep curve).

## Shifts in demand

A **shift** in the demand curve will be a result of a change in demand due to factors other than price. Factors that lead to a shift include increases in consumer income, changes in taxes on the product, changes in price or availability of competing products, and changes in expectations of future prices. It is important to differentiate between **changes in demand** (a shift of the demand curve) and **changes in quantity demanded** (a movement along the same demand curve).

Demand curve shifts

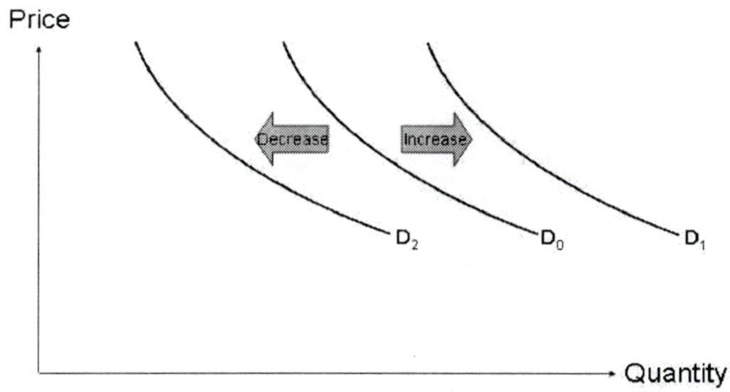


Movement along demand curve (from A to B)

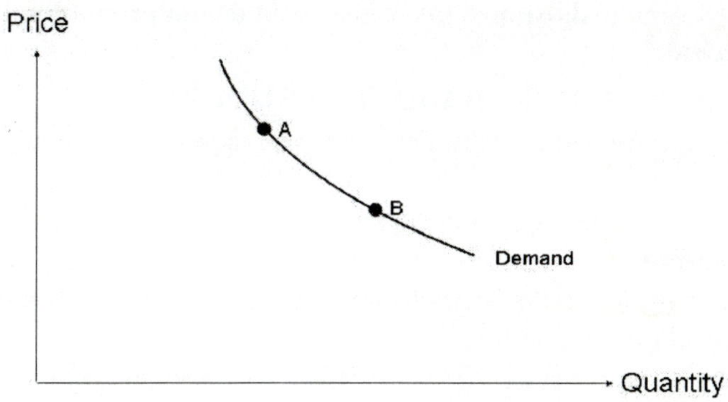

## Shifts in supply

A change in supply indicates a shift in the supply curve. The following are examples of factors that could lead to a change in supply – changes in resource costs, technology improvements, natural disasters which limit supply of a product, changes in taxes on the producers of the product.

**Equilibrium** is defined as a state of balance between forces such as supply and demand. It is important to differentiate between **short run** (an insufficient time period for decision makers to fully adjust to changes in market conditions) and **long run** (a sufficient time for decision makers to make adjustments).

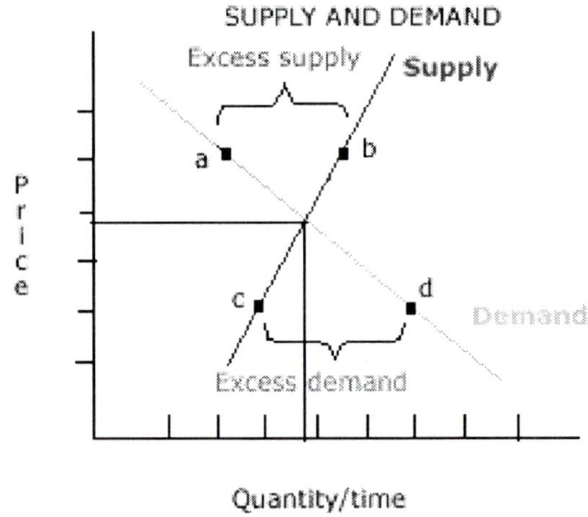


High prices will tend to lead to an excess supply illustrated by the points a and b, producers will tend to lower prices until supply and demand are in balance. On the other hand if prices are too low, demand will exceed supply, illustrated by points c and d, and producers will increase prices until equilibrium is reached.

## Impact of changes in demand and supply

**Increase in demand** – the demand curve shifts to the right, which will increase both the equilibrium price and quantity.

**Decrease in demand** – the demand curve shifts to the left, which will decrease both the equilibrium price and quantity.

**Increase in supply** – the supply curve shifts to the right, which will decrease the equilibrium price and increase the equilibrium quantity.

**Decrease in supply** – the supply curve shifts to the left, which will increase the equilibrium price and decrease the equilibrium quantity.

An unanticipated cut in supply will, in the short run, lead to a sharp increase in price, but in the long run demand will respond to the price change. Similarly an unanticipated surge in demand for a product will initially push up prices but longer-term supply will be increased.

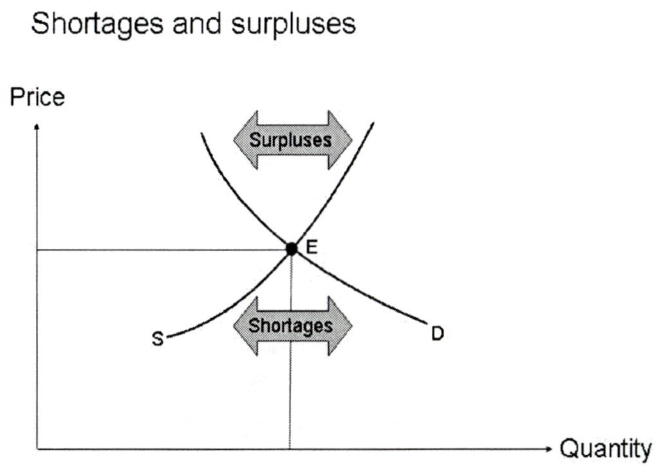


The **invisible hand principle** says that market prices act as an inducement to individuals to pursue productive activities that also promote the economic well being of society.

# Supply and Demand: Applications and Extensions CH 4

## Introduction

This chapter examines some of the applications of supply and demand analysis covered in the previous Reading. First we look at the impact of wage rates, interest rates and foreign exchange on supply and demand. Then we look at the impact of government action, including price controls on markets, and of black markets which are operating outside the legal system. Finally we consider taxation and how it relates to elasticity of supply and demand.

## Resources

The first step in a firm's production process is the purchase of **resources**. Resources include raw materials, labor etc. Resource markets generally have downward-sloping demand curves and upward-sloping supply curves. There is a close link between the markets for the end-product and the resources used to make the product. For example, when the price of a resource increases, costs increase leading to a reduction in supply and higher prices for the end-product.

The **loanable funds** market refers to the market that coordinates the borrowing and lending decisions of firms and households. Participants in the market include commercial banks, and stock and bond markets. The interest rate is the price of loanable funds.

The demand curve will slope downwards to the right since firms and households will borrow more at low interest rates. On the other hand, low interest rates will make it less attractive to save so the supply curve will be upward sloping to the right. Market forces will drive interest rates to a level, E, where the quantity of funds demanded will equal the quantity of funds supplied.

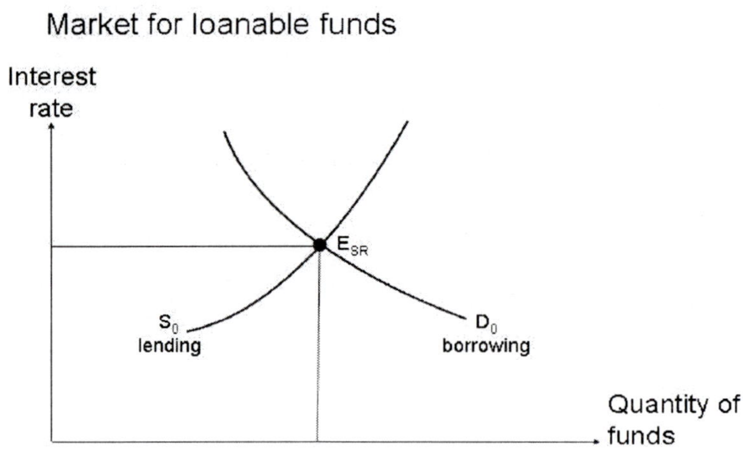


The interest rate is important because it is the link between the price of something today with its price in the future.

The **foreign exchange market** is the market in which different currencies are bought and sold. Exchange rates between currencies are very important since they determine the price of all goods and services that are traded in international markets. They will also influence decision makers who are looking at producing goods in different countries, although other issues such as transport costs, legal issues will be factors to consider before a decision is made to move production overseas.

A **price ceiling** is a legal restriction that establishes a maximum price that a good can be sold at. If the price ceiling is set below the equilibrium price it will increase demand and reduce the quantity supplied creating a **shortage** of the good. Non-price factors (e.g. waiting lists) will determine who is able to buy the product. Suppliers will be tempted to reduce the quality of the good supplied if they cannot increase prices.

**Price floors** establish a minimum price that can be charged for a good. If the price is fixed above the equilibrium price then a **surplus** of the good will appear.

The minimum wage is an example of a price floor, and has led to the substitution of machines or more highly-skilled workers for low-paid workers. Also employers will have little incentive to offer non-wage benefits to workers on the minimum wage.

A **black market** is a market that operates outside the legal system, either the sale of illegal goods or goods at illegal prices or terms. Black markets are characterized by higher profit margins for suppliers who do not get caught (to compensate the supplier for the higher risk), defective products and violence (to settle disputes). The point is made that a legal system that allows for settlement of disputes is essential for the smooth operation of markets.

**Tax incidence** refers to how the burden of a tax is distributed between buyers and sellers and related parties (the actual incidence). This will often be quite different to the **statutory incidence** which is the legal assignment of the responsibility to pay the tax. It can be shown that the actual incidence is independent of its statutory incidence, i.e. whether it is imposed on the buyer or the seller.

Looking at the example of when a tax is imposed on the seller of a product, this will shift the supply curve up by the amount of the tax. The intersection of the demand curve and supply curve will move, splitting the tax burden between the buyer and seller. The reduction in overall trade (and loss of benefit of this trade to both parties) results in a deadweight loss; this is the loss over and above the actual payment of tax to the government.

## Elasticity and the incidence of tax

In the case that demand is inelastic and supply elastic the burden of tax will largely fall on the buyer (e.g. when oil prices rise). Conversely when demand is relatively elastic compared to supply, the sellers will bear the largest burden.

If either demand or supply is relatively inelastic fewer trades will be eliminated so a rise in tax will result in a relatively small deadweight loss.

# Taking the Nation's Economic Pulse CH 7

## Introduction

The focus of this chapter is on the measurement of GDP as the most commonly quoted measure of economic performance. Candidates need to know how to calculate GDP using both the expenditure and the resources cost-income approaches. They also need to be familiar with the differences between GDP and GNP, and how to switch between nominal and real GDP given the rate of inflation. At the end of the chapter we look at alternative measures for the performance of the economy.

## Gross domestic product

Gross domestic product (GDP) is defined as the total market value of all final goods and services produced within a country's borders during a specific time period. GDP is a broad measure of current production of goods and services, and GDP calculations exclude second-hand goods, intermediate goods, and financial transactions.

There are two main approaches to measuring GDP:

19. 1. Expenditure approach, where GDP is the sum of:

Consumption (C)
Gross private investment (Ig)
Government expenditure (G)
Net Exports (NX)

The expenditure approach is commonly stated as:

$$GDP = C + I_g + G + NX$$

Gross private investment includes depreciation expense; gross investment is the sum of net investment ($I_n$) plus depreciation. Net exports (NX) is equal to exports minus imports (X – IM), and NX can be either positive or negative. If exports are higher than imports, NX will be positive and added to GDP; if imports are higher than exports, NX will be negative and subtracted from GDP.

20. 2. Cost resource-income approach, where GDP is the sum of:

Wages, salaries, self-employed income
Rents, profits, and interest
Indirect business taxes
Depreciation
Net income of foreigners

Net income of foreigners can be positive or negative. If foreigners bring in more investment income into a country than the residents of the same country pay abroad, then net income will be positive.

GDP calculated by the expenditure approach and GDP calculated by the cost-income approach must be equal.

e.g.

### Example Int-1 Calculating GDP

The fictitious country of Euphoria has the following expenditure and income categories and amounts (in millions):

- Imports $95
- Net investment $100
- Wages and salaries $295
- Government expenditure $70
- Depreciation $25
- Indirect business taxes $60
- Issuance of corporate bonds $35
- Self-employed income $95
- Exports $150
- Rents, profits, and interest $140
- Net income of foreigners -$40
- Consumption expenditure $325

The trick to calculating GDP is to identify expenditure versus cost-income components.

To use the GDP expenditure approach, we must first compute two preliminary items:

$$I_g = \text{net investment} + \text{depreciation} = \$100 + \$25 = \$125$$

$$NX = \text{exports} - \text{imports} = \$150 - \$95 = \$55$$

$$GDP = C + I_g + G + NX$$

$$GDP = \$325 + \$125 + \$70 + \$55$$

$$GDP = \$575$$

To use the GDP cost-income approach, sum up all cost-income components:

GDP = wages and salaries + self-employed income + rents, profits, and interest + depreciation + indirect business taxes + net income of foreigners

$$GDP = \$295 + \$95 + \$140 + \$25 + \$60 + (-\$40)$$

$$GDP = \$575$$

Notice that GDP is equal using either approach. The issuance of bonds is a financial flow, which is excluded from GDP calculations. (Assume that the asset financed by the bond flotation has already been counted under gross business investment).

GDP counts the value of goods and services produced inside a nation by residents of that nation and by foreigners living there, too. Whereas, GNP counts the value of goods and services produced by the citizens of a country, whether they are living in the country itself or living abroad. GDP and GNP will be equal only when net income of foreigners is zero.

GDP is measured in the U.S. in dollars. In simple terms, GDP is the sum of price multiplied by quantity (P × Q) of all final goods and services produced. Quantity represents real production within an economy; if quantity (or output) changes, then economic activity reported by GDP will change. However, GDP can change, even if there is no change in output, if prices by themselves change.

Nominal GDP measures economic activity by multiplying current prices with current output; nominal GDP can increase because of either increasing prices and/or increasing output. Whereas, real GDP measures economic activity by multiplying historical prices referenced to a particular year by current output; because prices are held constant, real GDP can only change because of output changes.

When newspapers or television report GDP forecasts, they almost always mean real GDP.

Inflation is the increase in prices over time, and there are two main ways in which inflation can be measured. The Consumer Price Index (CPI) measures narrow price changes in a typical "basket" of goods bought by consumers, captured in the consumption component of GDP calculations. The GDP deflator measures broad price changes across all categories of economic activity, captured by consumption, investment, government, and net exports.

Both CPI and the GDP deflator are referenced to a base year, which is assigned a value of 100.0. As inflation rises, so does the index value of the CPI or the GDP deflator.

The Equation below is used to calculate real GDP when we are given nominal GDP and the GDP deflator for any given year:

**Equation Int-1**

$$\text{real GDP}_{\text{period t}} = \text{nominal GDP}_{\text{period t}} \times \frac{\text{GDP deflator}_{\text{base year}}}{\text{GDP deflator}_{\text{period t}}}$$

Recall that the GDP deflator in the base year is equal to 100.0. Therefore, real GDP will always equal nominal GDP in the base year.

**Example Int-2 Calculating real GDP**

Given the following information:

- Nominal GDP in 2005 = $11,381.2 billion
- GDP deflator in 2005 = 121.4
- GDP base year is 1986

Calculate real GDP in 2005:

$$\text{real GDP}_{\text{period t}} = \text{nominal GDP}_{\text{period t}} \times \frac{\text{GDP deflator}_{\text{base year}}}{\text{GDP deflator}_{\text{period t}}}$$

$$= \$11{,}381.2 \text{ billion} \times \frac{100.0}{121.4}$$

$$= \$9{,}375.0 \text{ billion}$$

Although GDP attempts to capture a nation's economic activity, some activities will elude statisticians and will be excluded from any measure. Such excluded activities include:

- Leisure and human costs;
- Unreported and illegal activities, such as the underground economy;
- Value of unpaid household production, including chores;
- Harmful side effects of production, including pollution of air, water, soil; and
- Quality and variety of product improvements which occur through innovation.

GDP and GNP are the broadest measures of output. However, there are several alternative measures of economic performance:

- National income (NI) is the earnings of all resource owners, which is the sum of employment compensation (salaries), rents, corporate profits, interest, and self-employment income. However, not all of this income is available for personal use.
- Personal income (PI) adjusts NI by subtracting corporate profits and social insurance taxes and adding transfer payments and dividends. PI can be spent on consumption, saving, or paying of personal taxes.
- Disposable income (DI) strips away personal taxes from PI. Out of the five output measures, DI is the narrowest. DI can either be consumed or saved.

# Working with Our Basic Aggregate Demand/ Aggregate Supply Model CH 10

## Introduction

We now look at the effects of changes in aggregate demand and supply on other economic indicators, such as growth, prices and employment. First of all we examine the factors that change supply and demand and then differentiate between the short-run and long-run impact of anticipated versus unanticipated changes on the economy. We also consider the self-correcting mechanisms that will help stabilise the economy.

## Aggregate demand

There are, in fact, three separate curves: aggregate demand, short-run aggregate supply, and long-run aggregate supply

The aggregate demand (AD) curve is a downward-sloping curve, with the price level (P) plotted on the vertical axis and real GDP (Y) plotted on the horizontal axis. There are six factors that will shift AD to the right ($AD_1$), also known as an increase in aggregate demand:

- Increase in real wealth
- Decrease in real interest rates
- Increased optimism in the economy
- Higher expected inflation in the future
- Higher incomes abroad, thereby boosting exports
- Domestic currency depreciation, thereby boosting exports and restricting imports

The opposite of these factors will cause the AD curve to shift to the left, also known as a decrease in aggregate demand ($AD_2$). The diagram below depicts the shape of the original aggregate demand curve ($AD_0$) and the shifted curves.

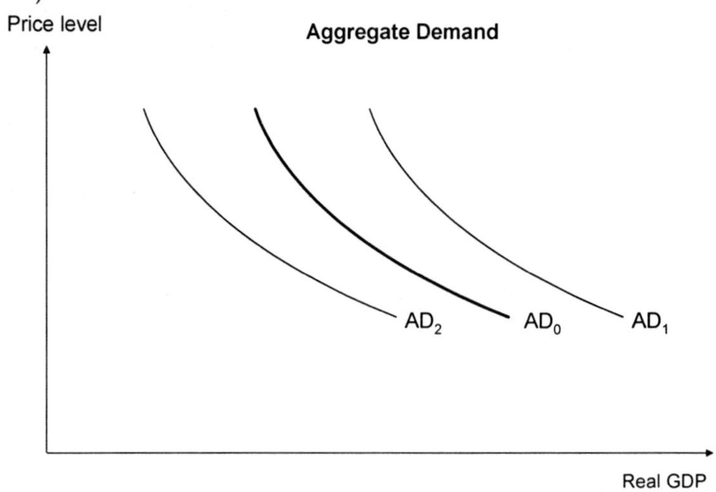


The short-run aggregate supply (SRAS) curve is an upward-sloping curve, with the price level (P) plotted on the vertical axis and real GDP (Y) plotted on the horizontal axis. There are five factors that will shift SRAS to the right ($SRAS_1$), also known as an increase in short-run aggregate supply:

- Increase in the stock of capital
- Technological improvements
- Reduction in input prices
- Lower expected inflation in the future
- Favourable shocks, such as good weather

The opposite of these factors will cause the SRAS curve to shift to the left, also known as a decrease in short-run aggregate supply ($SRAS_2$). The diagram below depicts the shape of the original short-run aggregate supply curve ($SRAS_0$) and the shifted curves.

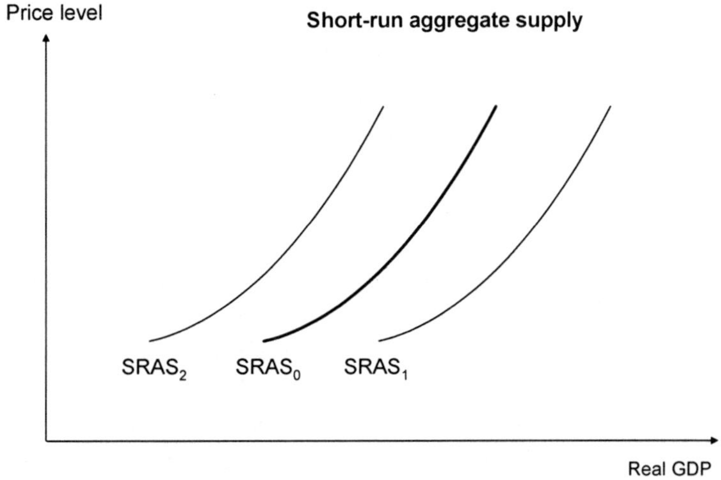


The long-run aggregate supply (LRAS) curve is a vertical curve, with the price level (P) plotted on the vertical axis and real GDP (Y) plotted on the horizontal axis. There are two factors that will shift LRAS to the right ($SRAS_1$), also known as an increase in long-run aggregate supply:

- Increase in the stock of capital
- Technological improvements

Observe that these factors are common to SRAS, which means that whenever the LRAS curve shifts, the SRAS curve will move with it in the same direction. The opposite of these factors will cause the LRAS curve to shift to the left, also known as a decrease in long-run aggregate supply ($LRAS_2$). The diagram below depicts the shape of the original long-run aggregate supply curve ($LRAS_0$) and the shifted curves.

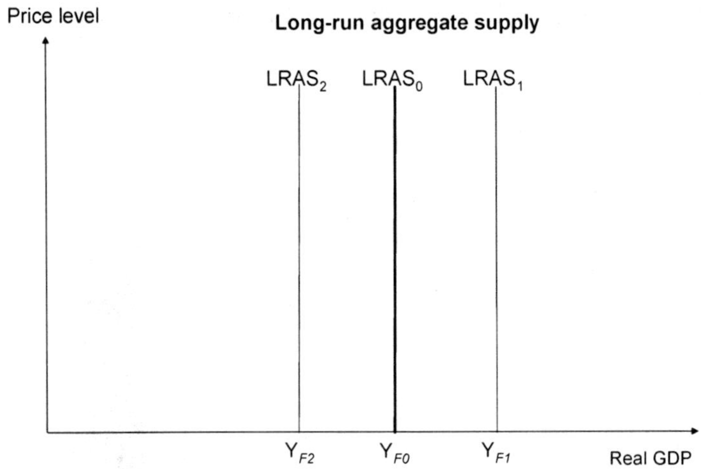


The LRAS curve plays a significant role in regulating the macro economy: the position of LRAS determines the level of economic activity corresponding to full employment ($Y_{F0}$). Full employment can only be achieved when an economy is operating somewhere along the LRAS curve.

An unanticipated change in macroeconomics suggests that people are caught off guard by the change, but over time, the market will react to it. When people initially react to unanticipated changes in either AD or SRAS, then output can change, but only in the short run. (Remember that LRAS represents the limit of production in the economy in the long run.)

Consider an unanticipated increase in government expenditure, a component of AD. If the AD curve shifts upwards, then the new short-run equilibrium will occur at the intersection of the new AD curve and the original SRAS curve. Thus, output (Y) and price level (P) will be higher in the short run. However, the economy is now operating beyond its capacity, which exerts pressure on resource prices. As resource prices increase, SRAS will shift to the left until equilibrium is restored along LRAS. Thus, output (Y) is restored to full employment and the price level is higher. In the long run, unanticipated changes in AD result in changes to the price level only.

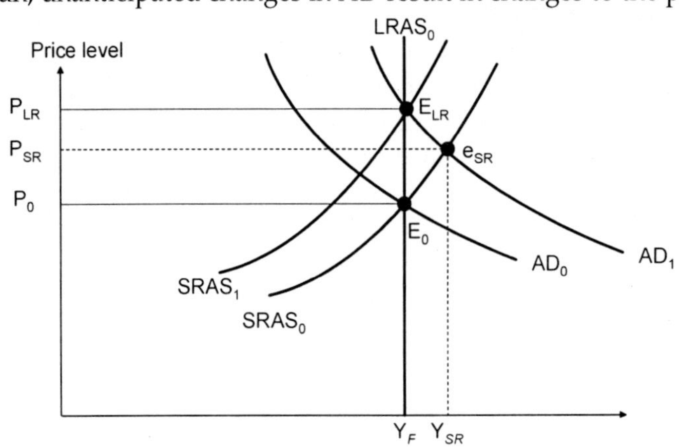

Unanticipated changes in SRAS will only affect the short-run position of the SRAS curve itself; there will be no affect on aggregate demand. Consider an economy dependent on agriculture, and an unexpected warm summer boosts the economy's main crop. In the short run, the favorable boost in production will shift the SRAS curve to the right, leading to a lower price level but a higher level of output. However, the economy is operating beyond its long-run capacity, and there is upward pressure on resource prices. As resource prices increase, SRAS will shift to the left until long-run equilibrium is restored along the LRAS curve. In the long run, unanticipated changes in SRAS result in neither a change to the price level nor change in output.

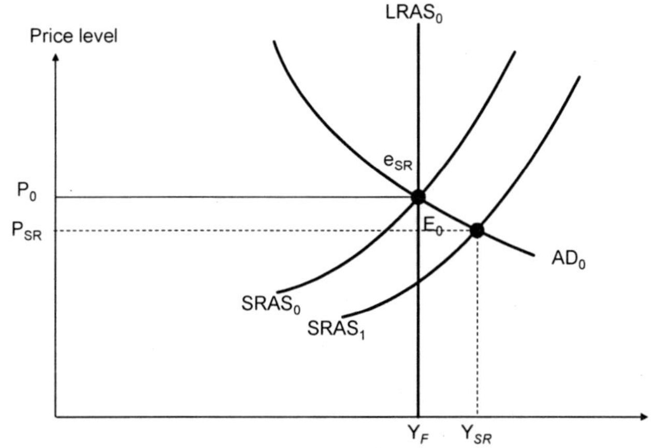


Market economies respond when they operate at an output level above or below full employment (along the LRAS curve). There are two self-correcting mechanisms that tend to restore long-run equilibrium:

- Changes in resource prices affect the SRAS curve. We have discussed this in the previous LOS. For example, when output is higher than full employment, increasing resource prices tends to decrease SRAS, causing higher price levels and eventually restoring the economy to full employment.
- Changes in real interest rates affect the AD curve. For example, when output is higher than full employment, real (inflation-adjusted) interest rates will increase as the demand for money increases. Higher real interest rates depress business investment, which is a component of AD. Thus, there is a tendency for AD to automatically decrease, which can help restore the economy to its full employment level of output.

The third self-correcting mechanism relates to consumption expenditure, which is a large component of AD. (Consumption represents approximately 65 percent of GDP in most developed economies.) Compared with other components of AD, consumption is the most stable component of GDP. The inherent stability of consumption expenditure helps to mitigate changes to other less stable components of GDP, such as net exports (tied to the exchange rate) and business investment (tied to interest rates and fickle business sentiment).

# Keynesian Foundations of Modern Macroeconomics CH 11

## Introduction

In this section we explore the main principles of Keynesian theory which was developed by a British economist to explain the prolonged unemployment in the 1930s; it has had a major influence on subsequent economic thinking. Keynes focused on demand rather than supply and the role of the government's fiscal policy in taking an economy out of recession. He believed that the government should run a budget deficit in order to stimulate demand and bring the economy back to full employment. This chapter examines the rationale behind his thinking including the importance of the expenditure multiplier.

## Keynesian economics

The distinction between classical and Keynesian economics stems from the assumptions made on the length of recessions. The classical school assumed that the economy operated mostly at or near its long-run level of output; recessions tended to be short lived as the economy automatically reverted to long-run output and employment through the SRAS mechanism discussed in the previous Reading.

Keynesians are followers of John Maynard Keynes, a British economist of the early 20th century. Writing during the Great Depression, Keynes (hence Keynesians) believed that the economy could get stuck in prolonged recession, with reduced output and widespread unemployment. Keynesians do not believe that adjustments to SRAS will restore equilibrium. Rather, they believe that recessions stem from a deficiency of AD, and the government can only restore long-run output and employment levels by boosting AD. According to the Keynesians, SRAS adjustments are too slow, if indeed they operate at all.

The Keynesian model explains the output level at which an economy can operate, in the absence of either an explicit SRAS or LRAS curve.

The model distinguishes between autonomous verses induced expenditure. (Recall the major components of expenditure: C, I, G, and NX.) Autonomous expenditure has no relationship with levels of income; whereas induced expenditure is a function of income. For example, consumption expenditure increases as disposable income increases (induced). However, even when disposable income is equal to zero, the economy will maintain a level of consumption by drawing down assets (autonomous).

In a simplified economy consisting of consumers, total expenditure is equal to consumption expenditure. Total expenditure is an upward sloping function of GDP (output), and even when GDP is zero, there will be autonomous expenditure. The aggregate expenditure curve is shown as the AE curve in the graph below.

Businesses plan for a certain level of expenditure, and they build inventories to meet consumption expenditure. In the graph below, businesses wish to operate along a 45-degree line, where planned aggregate expenditure is equal to actual output. If people consume more than is planned, then businesses inventories will be depleted faster than expected. Businesses increase production to meet the unanticipated expenditure, which boosts output. Alternatively, if people consume less than is planned, then businesses inventories will be unexpectedly increased. In response, businesses decrease their production, resulting in lower output.

Keynesian equilibrium

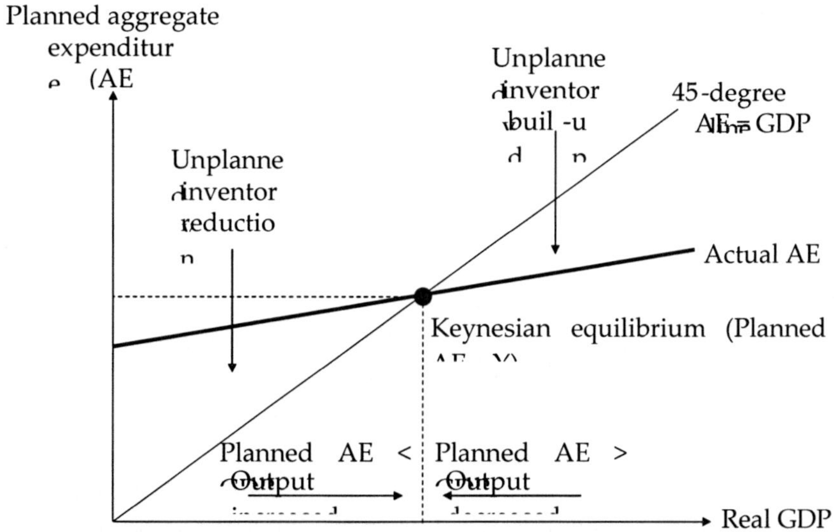


Keynesian macro-equilibrium occurs along the 45-degree line, when real GDP is equal to planned aggregate expenditure.

The marginal propensity to consume (MPC) is additional consumption related to an additional unit of disposable income, is shown in the Equation Int-2 below:

**Equation Int-2**

$$\text{marginal propensity to consume} = \frac{\Delta \text{ consumption expenditure}}{\Delta \text{ disposable income}}$$

where Δ is uppercase Greek letter delta meaning change.

The MPC is a number greater than zero but less than one (0 < MPC <1). Recall that disposable income can be either consumed or saved; therefore, we can define the marginal propensity to save (MPS) as 1 – MPC. Note that MPC + MPS = 1.

The expenditure multiplier is related to the MPC and MPS, as shown below:

**Equation Int-3**

$$\text{expenditure multiplier} = \frac{1}{1 - \text{MPC}} = \frac{1}{\text{MPS}}$$

**Example Int-3 Marginal propensity to consume and expenditure multiplier**

When disposable income is $150, consumption expenditure is $120; and when disposable income is $200, consumption expenditure is $157.50. Calculate the marginal propensity to consume and the expenditure multiplier.

Use Equations Int-2 and Int-3, respectively:

marginal propensity to consume

$$= \frac{\Delta \text{ consump. exp.}}{\Delta \text{ disposable income}} = \frac{\$157.50 - \$120}{\$200 - \$150} = \frac{\$37.5}{\$50} = 0.75$$

Note that the MPS = 1 – MPC = 1 – 0.75 = 0.25

$$\text{expenditure multiplier} = \frac{1}{1 - \text{MPC}} = \frac{1}{1 - 0.75} = \frac{1}{0.25} = 4$$

The expenditure multiplier explains the total increase in output caused by an initial change in autonomous expenditure. The expenditure multiplier is positively related to the MPC and negatively related to MPS. Intuitively, if some of the increase in autonomous expenditure is saved rather than spent, the effect of the autonomous stimulus on the economy will be reduced.

Assume that the MPC = 0.75, which yields an expenditure multiplier of 4. If the government increased autonomous expenditure by $10, then the total effect of the government's increased expenditure would be a $10 × 4 = $40 increase in total output (Y).

If, however, people had a tendency to consume more of the autonomous increase (MPC = 0.80), then the new expenditure multiplier would be:

$$\text{expenditure multiplier} = \frac{1}{1 - \text{MPC}} = \frac{1}{1 - 0.80} = \frac{1}{0.20} = 5$$

If the government increased autonomous expenditure by $10, then the total effect of the government's increased expenditure would be a $10 × 5 = $50 increase in total output (Y).

In terms of the Keynesian model, an increase in autonomous expenditure would shift the actual AE curve upwards, resulting in a multiplied increase in output (Y) until planned aggregate expenditure equals output.

Keynesians believe that private investment is the most volatile component of aggregate expenditure. An unexplained decline in business confidence results in an autonomous decrease in private investment, which reverberates throughout the entire economy by the multiplier effect. The decrease in aggregate demand causes a decline in output and employment levels. The economy's built-in stabilizers might not be enough to offset the decline in AD, so Keynesian believe that the government ought to increase expenditure to restore full employment.

Alternatively, an increase in business confidence would result in an autonomous increase in investment expenditure, which would reverberate throughout the economy via the expenditure multiplier. If output expands beyond full employment, inflation pressures would emerge.

## Introductory Readings Concept Check Questions

1. It is noticed that a small change in price has a big impact on demand for a product. This means the demand is:

   A. elastic, with a flat demand curve.

   B. elastic, with a steep demand curve.

   C. inelastic, with a flat demand curve.

   D. inelastic, with a steep demand curve.

---

2. A natural disaster will often cause:

   A. a shift in the supply curve to the left.

   B. a shift in the supply curve to the right.

   C. a move to the left along the supply curve.

   D. a move to the right along the supply curve.

---

3. If the GDP deflator in a country has risen from 100 in 1985, to 130 in 2005 and nominal GDP has risen from $85 billion to $125 billion then the change in real GDP over the period is *closest* to:

   A. a fall of 3.9%.

   B. an increase of 13.1%.

   C. an increase of 17.1%.

   D. an increase of 62.5%.

4. Which of the following statements is **CORRECT** regarding gross national product (GNP) and gross domestic product (GDP)?

A. GNP and GDP are both the same, but different terms are used in different countries.

B. GNP is GDP less the income of foreigners in the country plus the income earned by the country's citizens overseas.

C. GNP is GDP less depreciation costs.

D. GNP is calculated using the expenditure approach and GDP using the income approach.

---

5. Which of the following would cause a shift in aggregate demand?

I. An increase in real interest rates.

II. New technology increasing productivity.

III. A change in inflationary expectations.

IV. A significant change in the exchange rate.

A. II only.

B. I and III only.

C. I, III and IV only.

D. All of the above.

---

6. When economic output is less than the economy's potential, which of the following will act as a self-correcting mechanism?

A. Fiscal stimulus.

B. Real interest rates will decline.

C. Real resource prices will rise.

D. Rising inflation.

7. The Keynesian model implies that:

A. market forces are sufficient to ensure that the economy operates at the full employment level in the long term.

B. adjusting money supply is the primary tool that should be used to stimulate aggregate demand.

C. adjusting interest rates is the primary tool that should be used to stimulate aggregate demand.

D. macroeconomic policy should focus on maintaining aggregate expenditures at the level that leads to full employment .

---

8. If the marginal propensity to consume (MPC) is 0.7 and investment spending is increased by $3 billion then the additional income generated is closest to:

A. $3.33 billion.

B. $4.28 billion.

C. $7.00 billion.

D. $10.00 billion

# Introductory Readings Concept Check Answers

1. It is noticed that a small change in price has a big impact on demand for a product. This means the demand is:

   A. elastic, with a flat demand curve.

   B. elastic, with a steep demand curve.

   C. inelastic, with a flat demand curve.

   D. inelastic, with a steep demand curve.

**Correct Answer: 1. A**

Demand is elastic since it is highly responsive to a change in price, this will lead to a flat demand curve.

---

2. A natural disaster will often cause:

   A. a shift in the supply curve to the left.

   B. a shift in the supply curve to the right.

   C. a move to the left along the supply curve.

   D. a move to the right along the supply curve.

**Correct Answer: 2. A**

The supply curve shifts to the left as supply is decreased. This will in turn increase the equilibrium price.

3. If the GDP deflator in a country has risen from 100 in 1985, to 130 in 2005 and nominal GDP has risen from $85 billion to $125 billion then the change in real GDP over the period is *closest* to:

A. a fall of 3.9%.

B. an increase of 13.1%.

C. an increase of 17.1%.

D. an increase of 62.5%.

**Correct Answer: 3. B**

Real GDP (2004) = $125 billion x (100/130) = $96.15 billion

This is an increase of 13.1%

---

4. Which of the following statements is **CORRECT** regarding gross national product (GNP) and gross domestic product (GDP)?

A. GNP and GDP are both the same, but different terms are used in different countries.

B. GNP is GDP less the income of foreigners in the country plus the income earned by the country's citizens overseas.

C. GNP is GDP less depreciation costs.

D. GNP is calculated using the expenditure approach and GDP using the income approach.

**Correct Answer: 4. B**

5. Which of the following would cause a shift in aggregate demand?

I. An increase in real interest rates.

II. New technology increasing productivity.

III. A change in inflationary expectations.

IV. A significant change in the exchange rate.

A. II only.

B. I and III only.

C. I, III and IV only.

D. All of the above.

**Correct Answer: 5. C**

Item II would lead to a shift in the supply curve.

---

6. When economic output is less than the economy's potential, which of the following will act as a self-correcting mechanism?

A. Fiscal stimulus.

B. Real interest rates will decline.

C. Real resource prices will rise.

D. Rising inflation.

**Correct Answer: 6. B**

The main self-correcting mechanisms will be the fall in real interest rates and resource prices (including labor costs).

7. The Keynesian model implies that:

A. market forces are sufficient to ensure that the economy operates at the full employment level in the long term.

B. adjusting money supply is the primary tool that should be used to stimulate aggregate demand.

C. adjusting interest rates is the primary tool that should be used to stimulate aggregate demand.

D. macroeconomic policy should focus on maintaining aggregate expenditures at the level that leads to full employment .

**Correct Answer: 7. D**

---

8. If the marginal propensity to consume (MPC) is 0.7 and investment spending is increased by $3 billion then the additional income generated is closest to:

A. $3.33 billion.

B. $4.28 billion.

C. $7.00 billion.

D. $10.00 billion

**Correct Answer: 8. D**

The expenditure multiplier is 1/(1 – 0.7) or 3.33. Therefore the additional income is $3 billion x 3.33 or $10 billion.

# Study Session 04: Economics:

## Microeconomic Analysis

This study session focuses on microeconomic concepts and how firms are affected by these concepts. One of the main concepts related to the equilibrium between demand and supply is elasticity, which measures the dependency between demand and supply and the impact of changes in either on the equilibrium price level. A second key concept is efficiency, which is a measure of the firm's "optimal" output given its cost and revenue functions. Understanding these concepts enables analysts to differentiate among various companies on an individual level, and to determine their attractiveness for an investor.

**Reading 13: Elasticity**

**Reading 14: Efficiency and Equity**

**Reading 15: Markets in Action**

**Reading 16: Organizing Production**

**Reading 17: Output and Costs**

1. (QID 70) One of the arguments against utilitarianism is:

A. high tax rates make people work less.

B. fairness can only be achieved with state ownership of key assets.

C. the marginal benefit of receiving an extra dollar is higher for poor people.

---

2. (QID 71) Which of the following concentration ratios for a firm is most likely to indicate that the firm is operating in an oligopoly?

| Four-firm ratio | Herfindahl-Hirschman Index |
|---|---|
| A. 40% | 3,000 |
| B. 70% | 2,200 |
| C. 90% | 1,200 |

1. (QID 70) One of the arguments against utilitarianism is:

***A. high tax rates make people work less.**

B. fairness can only be achieved with state ownership of key assets.

C. the marginal benefit of receiving an extra dollar is higher for poor people.

Explanation: LOS: Reading 14-f

Utilitarianism proposes that money should be transferred from the rich to the poor. One of the arguments against this is that it reduces the size of the economic pie since the rich will work or save less. The other argument is that the cost of administration or tax collection causes inefficiency.

**Reference:** CFA® Program Curriculum, Volume 2, pp. 49-52.

---

2. (QID 71) Which of the following concentration ratios for a firm is most likely to indicate that the firm is operating in an oligopoly?

| Four-firm ratio | Herfindahl-Hirschman Index |
|---|---|
| A. 40% | 3,000 |
| ***B. 70%** | **2,200** |
| C. 90% | 1,200 |

Explanation: LOS: Reading 16-g

A four-firm measure of over 60%, and a HHI index of over 1,800 indicate an oligopoly, so "70% 2,200" is the best choice.

**Reference:** CFA® Program Curriculum, Volume 2, pp. 108-112.

3. (QID 72) There are two companies in an industry that produce the same product. Their annual inputs are shown below:

| | Labor | Capital |
|---|---|---|
| Company A | 5 | 100 |
| Company B | 10 | 70 |

Labor costs $40,000 per annum and capital costs $10,000 per annum.

Which statement is the most accurate?

A. Only company B is both technologically and economically efficient.

B. Only company A is both technologically and economically efficient.

C. Companies A and B are both technologically efficient but only B is economically efficient.

---

4. (QID 73) The supply of a product which is made from a resource with low resource mobility is generally:

A. elastic in both the short and long run.

B. elastic in the short run and inelastic in the long run.

C. inelastic in the short run but more elastic in the long run.

3. (QID 72) There are two companies in an industry that produce the same product. Their annual inputs are shown below:

| | Labor | Capital |
|---|---|---|
| Company A | 5 | 100 |
| Company B | 10 | 70 |

Labor costs $40,000 per annum and capital costs $10,000 per annum.

Which statement is the most accurate?

A. Only company B is both technologically and economically efficient.

B. Only company A is both technologically and economically efficient.

***C. Companies A and B are both technologically efficient but only B is economically efficient.**

Explanation: LOS: Reading 16-c

Both firms are technologically efficient since they use the least amount of inputs, although the mix of inputs is different.

The cost of inputs for company A is $200,000 + $1,000,000 = $1,200,000,

for company B $400,000 + $700,000 = $1,100,000.

Therefore B is economically efficient.

**Reference:** CFA® Program Curriculum, Volume 2, pp. 100-103.

---

4. (QID 73) The supply of a product which is made from a resource with low resource mobility is generally:

A. elastic in both the short and long run.

B. elastic in the short run and inelastic in the long run.

***C. inelastic in the short run but more elastic in the long run.**

Explanation: LOS: Reading 13-a

Low resource mobility will make the supply relatively inelastic in the short run since the resource cannot be easily transferred to another use. Generally long-run elasticity is more elastic than short-run elasticity, as suppliers have time to adjust to the change in prices.

**Reference:** CFA® Program Curriculum, Volume 2, pp. 22-27.

5. (QID 74) Which of the following is least likely to lead to a shift in the demand curve for a product? A change in:

A. consumer preferences.

B. the price of the product.

C. the price of a substitute product.

---

6. (QID 75) If the price of televisions produced by manufacturer is increased by 10% from $500 to $550 then demand is forecast to fall by 20%, from 100,000 units to 80,000 units. The elasticity of demand is closest to:

A. 2.22.

B. 2.33.

C. 2.50.

5. (QID 74) Which of the following is least likely to lead to a shift in the demand curve for a product? A change in:

A. consumer preferences.

***B. the price of the product.**

C. the price of a substitute product.

Explanation: LOS: Reading 13-a

Price will lead to a change in the quantity demanded along the same demand curve. The other factors will lead to a shift in the entire demand curve.

**Reference:** CFA® Program Curriculum, Volume 2, pp. 8-22.

---

6. (QID 75) If the price of televisions produced by manufacturer is increased by 10% from $500 to $550 then demand is forecast to fall by 20%, from 100,000 units to 80,000 units. The elasticity of demand is closest to:

A. 2.22.

***B. 2.33.**

C. 2.50.

Explanation: LOS: Reading 13-b

**Price elasticity of demand** $= \dfrac{\%\Delta Q_{Dem}}{\%\Delta P}$

**where**

$Q_{Dem}$ = **quantity demanded**

P = **price**

$\%\Delta Q_{Dem}$ = **percentage change in quantity demanded, this is** $\Delta Q / Q_{ave}$

$$\frac{\%\Delta Q_{Dem}}{\%\Delta P} = \frac{20/90}{50/525} = 2.33.$$

Note: percentages are calculated on the average price and average quantity. We also ignore minus signs; we are measuring the magnitude of elasticity.

**Reference:** CFA® Program Curriculum, Volume 2, pp. 8-10.

7. (QID 76) If the price elasticity of demand for a product is elastic, it means that:

A. total expenditure on the product will remain constant as the price changes.

B. price and total expenditure on the product will move in the same direction.

C. a percent increase in prices leads to a larger percent reduction in the amount purchased.

8. (QID 77) Following contamination of drinking water and a surge in demand for bottled water the government decides to buy all available bottled water at the higher market price, sell this water at pre-contamination prices, and ration the water sold to each individual. Which statement best describes the position?

A. The consumer surplus is eliminated if the water is rationed.

B. The consumer and producer surpluses are reallocated due to the government action.

C. The producer surplus is eliminated if the water is sold at the pre-contamination price to consumers.

7. (QID 76) If the price elasticity of demand for a product is elastic, it means that:

A. total expenditure on the product will remain constant as the price changes.

B. price and total expenditure on the product will move in the same direction.

***C. a percent increase in prices leads to a larger percent reduction in the amount purchased.**

Explanation: LOS: Reading 13-b

The amount purchased will be highly sensitive to price changes; this will mean that the price and total expenditure on the product will move in opposite directions.

**Reference:** CFA® Program Curriculum, Volume 2, pp. 14-16.

---

8. (QID 77) Following contamination of drinking water and a surge in demand for bottled water the government decides to buy all available bottled water at the higher market price, sell this water at pre-contamination prices, and ration the water sold to each individual. Which statement best describes the position?

A. The consumer surplus is eliminated if the water is rationed.

***B. The consumer and producer surpluses are reallocated due to the government action.**

C. The producer surplus is eliminated if the water is sold at the pre-contamination price to consumers.

Explanation: LOS: Reading 14-f

There will still be a consumer surplus (they are buying water at a price below the new market price), there will still be a producer surplus since they will sell to the government at a higher price. Not all participants benefit since taxpayers will be paying part of the cost. The best choice is the consumer and producer surpluses are reallocated by the government action.

**Reference:** CFA® Program Curriculum, Volume 2, pp. 46-48.

9. (QID 78) Which one of the following statements is most accurate?

A. Demand for products is usually more elastic in the long run than short run.

B. Demand for products is usually more elastic in the short run than long run.

C. Demand elasticity for products will usually increase more rapidly in the long run.

---

10. (QID 79) Luxury goods usually have a:

A. low income elasticity of demand.

B. high income elasticity of demand.

C. negative income elasticity of demand.

9. (QID 78) Which one of the following statements is most accurate?

***A. Demand for products is usually more elastic in the long run than short run.**

B. Demand for products is usually more elastic in the short run than long run.

C. Demand elasticity for products will usually increase more rapidly in the long run.

Explanation: LOS: Reading 13-a

Demand will be more elastic in the long run since consumers will have had more time to adjust to a price change.

**Reference:** CFA® Program Curriculum, Volume 2, pp. 16-18.

---

10. (QID 79) Luxury goods usually have a:

A. low income elasticity of demand.

***B. high income elasticity of demand.**

C. negative income elasticity of demand.

Explanation: LOS: Reading 13-a

Luxury goods usually have a high (greater than one) income elasticity which means that as incomes rise, the demand for these goods rises at an even faster rate.

**Reference:** CFA® Program Curriculum, Volume 2, pp. 21-22.

11. (QID 80) When a government imposes a minimum wage above the equilibrium wage, which of the following best describes the impact of its action?

A. There is a reallocation of a portion of the producer surplus to the worker surplus.

B. The worker surplus is eliminated as workers spend time and money in job searches.

C. The producer surplus is reduced as they are required to pay marginal workers a minimum wage rather than the equilibrium wage.

---

12. (QID 81) A government decides to subsidize the production of cars in a country. Which of the following is least likely to happen as a result of the subsidy?

A. The price of cars will drop.

B. There is a deadweight loss due to overproduction of cars.

C. The marginal cost of car production drops below marginal benefit.

11. (QID 80) When a government imposes a minimum wage above the equilibrium wage, which of the following best describes the impact of its action?

A. There is a reallocation of a portion of the producer surplus to the worker surplus.

B. The worker surplus is eliminated as workers spend time and money in job searches.

***C. The producer surplus is reduced as they are required to pay marginal workers a minimum wage rather than the equilibrium wage.**

Explanation: LOS: Reading 15-b

The producer and worker surplus will both be reduced as a deadweight loss is created. Unemployment will rise as marginal workers fail to find jobs.

**Reference:** CFA® Program Curriculum, Volume 2, pp. 68-73.

---

12. (QID 81) A government decides to subsidize the production of cars in a country. Which of the following is least likely to happen as a result of the subsidy?

A. The price of cars will drop.

B. There is a deadweight loss due to overproduction of cars.

***C. The marginal cost of car production drops below marginal benefit.**

Explanation: LOS: Reading 15-d

The quantity of cars produced and the price of cars sold drops leading to overproduction, and marginal cost is higher than marginal benefit leading to a deadweight loss.

**Reference:** CFA® Program Curriculum, Volume 2, pp. 83-85.

13. (QID 82) Which of the following is an accurate description of an owner's liability and tax position in the U.S. for different business structures?

| Has unlimited liability | Pays taxes at two levels |
|---|---|
| A. Corporation | Corporation |
| B. Corporation | Partnership |
| C. Partnership | Corporation |

14. (QID 83) Which of the following is least likely to be included in opportunity costs of a firm owned by Julia Painter?

A. Bank interest costs.

B. Painter's interest forgone.

C. Accounting depreciation costs.

13. (QID 82) Which of the following is an accurate description of an owner's liability and tax position in the U.S. for different business structures?

| | Has unlimited liability | Pays taxes at two levels |
|---|---|---|
| A. | Corporation | Corporation |
| B. | Corporation | Partnership |
| ***C.** | **Partnership** | **Corporation** |

Explanation: LOS: Reading 16-e

A partner has unlimited liability but only pays tax as owner's income. An owner of a corporation has limited liability but is taxed at both the corporate and individual level.

**Reference:** CFA® Program Curriculum, Volume 2, pp. 105-108.

---

14. (QID 83) Which of the following is least likely to be included in opportunity costs of a firm owned by Julia Painter?

A. Bank interest costs.

B. Painter's interest forgone.

***C. Accounting depreciation costs.**

Explanation: LOS: Reading 16-a

Opportunity costs include all explicit and implicit costs. Economic rather than accounting depreciation would be included.

**Reference:** CFA® Program Curriculum, Volume 2, pp. 97-98.

15. (QID 84) In the short run, as a company increases production levels towards operating at full capacity marginal costs will generally:

A. fall but average total costs will rise.

B. generally fall and average total costs will also fall.

C. generally rise and average total costs will also rise.

---

16. (QID 85) If a company is unable to expand the size of its production facilities it means that as more and more units of a variable resource are used output will eventually:

A. decrease and marginal costs will increase towards average total costs.

B. increase at a decreasing rate and marginal costs will exceed average total costs.

C. increase at a decreasing rate and average fixed costs will increase as a percentage of total costs.

15. (QID 84) In the short run, as a company increases production levels towards operating at full capacity marginal costs will generally:

A. fall but average total costs will rise.

B. generally fall and average total costs will also fall.

***C. generally rise and average total costs will also rise.**

Explanation: LOS: Reading 17-c

Marginal costs are the change in total costs to produce an additional unit of output. As a firm approaches operating at full capacity, marginal costs will rise and average total costs will therefore also rise.

**Reference:** CFA® Program Curriculum, Volume 2, pp. 133-136

---

16. (QID 85) If a company is unable to expand the size of its production facilities it means that as more and more units of a variable resource are used output will eventually:

A. decrease and marginal costs will increase towards average total costs.

***B. increase at a decreasing rate and marginal costs will exceed average total costs.**

C. increase at a decreasing rate and average fixed costs will increase as a percentage of total costs.

Explanation: LOS: Reading 17-b

The law of diminishing returns states that as more and more units of a variable resource are allocated to production they will eventually increase output at a decreasing rate. Mathematically, as the marginal costs increase, they will become higher than the average total cost, thereby increasing the average total cost.

**Reference:** CFA® Program Curriculum, Volume 2, pp. 133-136.

17. (QID 86) Which of the following statements regarding the relationship between costs of larger firms relative to costs of smaller firms is least accurate?

A. Constant returns to scale can exist in an industry for different sizes of firm.

B. Firms that are smaller than the minimum efficient size have higher average total unit costs.

C. Long-run average total unit costs will always be lower for large firms due to economies of scale.

---

18. (QID 87) It costs $20 a manufacturer to produce the first kettle and $50 to produce the 10,000th kettle, assume the cost increases linearly from $20 to $50. The manufacturer sells 10,000 kettles at a unit price of $50. Its producer surplus is closest to:

A. $150,000.

B. $250,000.

C. $300,000.

17. (QID 86) Which of the following statements regarding the relationship between costs of larger firms relative to costs of smaller firms is least accurate?

A. Constant returns to scale can exist in an industry for different sizes of firm.

B. Firms that are smaller than the minimum efficient size have higher average total unit costs.

***C. Long-run average total unit costs will always be lower for large firms due to economies of scale.**

Explanation: LOS: Reading 17-d

Large firms are not always more efficient. For example, it is often harder to motivate the work force in a large firm and communication between employer and employees becomes harder.

**Reference:** CFA® Program Curriculum, Volume 2, pp. 142-144.

---

18. (QID 87) It costs $20 a manufacturer to produce the first kettle and $50 to produce the 10,000th kettle, assume the cost increases linearly from $20 to $50. The manufacturer sells 10,000 kettles at a unit price of $50. Its producer surplus is closest to:

***A. $150,000.**

B. $250,000.

C. $300,000.

Explanation: LOS: Reading 14-d

The producer surplus is $30 on the first kettle decreasing steadily to $0 on the 10,000th kettle, so the area of the producer surplus triangle is 10,000 x ($30 + 0)/2 = $150,000.

**Reference:** CFA® Program Curriculum, Volume 2, pp. 42-43.

19. (QID 88) When the government imposes a tax on a product, the buyers of the product will generally pay most of the tax if:

| Demand | Supply |
|---|---|
| A. Elastic | Inelastic |
| B. Inelastic | Elastic |
| C. Inelastic | Inelastic |

---

20. (QID 89) A company purchased a piece of machinery five years ago which had an estimated useful life of ten years. The machine cost $1,000,000 and is being depreciated in the accounts at $100,000 per year. The other costs associated with using the machine are $300,000 per year, and the annual revenue generated from using the machine is $325,000 per year. The machine has no alternative use or scrap value. The company should

A. continue to operate the machine.

B. stop using the machine since it is generating an economic loss.

C. stop using the machine since it is generating an accounting loss.

19. (QID 88) When the government imposes a tax on a product, the buyers of the product will generally pay most of the tax if:

| | Demand | Supply |
|---|---|---|
| A. | Elastic | Inelastic |
| ***B.** | **Inelastic** | **Elastic** |
| C. | Inelastic | Inelastic |

Explanation: LOS: Reading 15-c

Inelastic demand means that buyers will continue to buy the product even at a higher price including tax. If supply is elastic producers are willing to increase the quantity to reflect the higher price which includes tax, so again buyers pay most of the tax.

**Reference:** CFA® Program Curriculum, Volume 2, pp. 73-81.

---

20. (QID 89) A company purchased a piece of machinery five years ago which had an estimated useful life of ten years. The machine cost $1,000,000 and is being depreciated in the accounts at $100,000 per year. The other costs associated with using the machine are $300,000 per year, and the annual revenue generated from using the machine is $325,000 per year. The machine has no alternative use or scrap value. The company should

***A. continue to operate the machine.**

B. stop using the machine since it is generating an economic loss.

C. stop using the machine since it is generating an accounting loss.

Explanation: LOS: Reading 16-a

Although the machine is generating an accounting loss it generates an economic profit of $25,000. This is because there is no economic depreciation charge - the opportunity cost of using the machine is zero, the cost of the machine is a sunk cost and it has no alternative use. Therefore the company should continue to operate the machine.

**Reference:** CFA® Program Curriculum, Volume 2, pp. 96-98.

21. (QID 90) It is noticed that a small change in price has a big impact on demand for a product. This means the demand is:

A. elastic, with a flat demand curve.

B. elastic, with a steep demand curve.

C. inelastic, with a flat demand curve.

---

22. (QID 91) Which of the following would lead to a shift in the demand curve for wine?

A. I. Beer prices increase.

B. II. An increase in bottling costs.

C. III. An increase in the price of wine.

21. (QID 90) It is noticed that a small change in price has a big impact on demand for a product. This means the demand is:

***A. elastic, with a flat demand curve.**

B. elastic, with a steep demand curve.

C. inelastic, with a flat demand curve.

Explanation: LOS: Reading 13-a

Demand is elastic since it is highly responsive to a change in price, this will lead to a flat demand curve.

**Reference:** CFA® Program Curriculum, Volume 2, pp. 11-12.

---

22. (QID 91) Which of the following would lead to a shift in the demand curve for wine?

***A. I. Beer prices increase.**

B. II. An increase in bottling costs.

C. III. An increase in the price of wine.

Explanation: LOS: Reading 13-a

II. mainly impacts on the supply of wine.

III. affects the change in quantity demanded (downwards) and therefore leads to a movement along the same demand curve.

**Reference:** CFA® Program Curriculum, Volume 2, pp. 16-18.

23. (QID 92) The law of diminishing returns implies that

A. total profits diminish as output increases.

B. marginal product is initially upward sloping then downward sloping as quantities increase.

C. as more units of a variable resource are added marginal product eventually decreases.

---

24. (QID 111) An industry has five participants with market shares of 30%, 25%, 25% 10% and 10%. The four firm concentration ratio and Herfindahl-Hirschman Index are:

| Four firm concentration ratio | Herfindahl-Hirschman Index |
|---|---|
| A. 90% | 470 |
| B. 10% | 2,350 |
| C. 90% | 2,350 |

---

25. (QID 112) The law of diminishing returns implies that

A. total profits diminish as output increases.

B. marginal product is initially upward sloping then downward sloping as quantities increase.

C. as more units of a variable resource are added marginal product eventually decreases.

23. (QID 92) The law of diminishing returns implies that

A. total profits diminish as output increases.

B. marginal product is initially upward sloping then downward sloping as quantities increase.

***C. as more units of a variable resource are added marginal product eventually decreases.**

Explanation: LOS: Reading 17-c

The law of diminishing returns sates that marginal product starts to decline as quantities increase due to technological constraints.

---

24. (QID 111) An industry has five participants with market shares of 30%, 25%, 25% 10% and 10%. The four firm concentration ratio and Herfindahl-Hirschman Index are:

| Four firm concentration ratio | Herfindahl-Hirschman Index |
|---|---|
| A. 90% | 470 |
| B. 10% | 2,350 |
| ***C. 90%** | **2,350** |

Explanation: LOS: Reading 16-g

Four-firm concentration ratio is (30% + 25% + 25% + 10%) = 90%

Herfindahl-Hirschman Index is 302 + 252 + 252 + 102 = 2350

**Reference:** CFA® Program Curriculum, Volume 2, pp. 108-112.

25. (QID 112) The law of diminishing returns implies that

A. total profits diminish as output increases.

B. marginal product is initially upward sloping then downward sloping as quantities increase.

***C. as more units of a variable resource are added marginal product eventually decreases.**

Explanation: LOS: Reading 17-c

The law of diminishing returns sates that marginal product starts to decline as quantities increase due to technological constraints.

**Reference:** CFA® Program Curriculum, Volume 2, pp. 131-132.

# Study Session 05: Economics:

## Market Structure and Macroeconomic Analysis

This study session first compares and contrasts the different market structures in which firms operate. The market environment influences the price a firm can demand for its goods or services. Among the most important of these market forms are monopoly and perfect competition, although monopolistic competition and oligopoly are also covered.

The study session then introduces the macroeconomic concepts that have an impact on all firms in the same environment, be it a country, a group of related countries, or a particular industry. The readings explain the business cycle, and how to forecast changes in the business cycle and the impact on, among other things, price levels and profitability. The study session concludes by describing how an economy's aggregate supply and aggregate demand are determined.

1. (QID 93) A railway company provides low fares to travelers prepared to start their journey after 10 am. This is an example of:

A. collusion.

B. profiteering.

C. price discrimination.

---

2. (QID 94) A sustained rise in interest rates will tend to lead to a change in demand for:

| | Physical Capital | Financial Capital |
|---|---|---|
| A. | Static | Decrease |
| B. | Decrease | Increase |
| C. | Decrease | Decrease |

1. (QID 93) A railway company provides low fares to travelers prepared to start their journey after 10 am. This is an example of:

A. collusion.

B. profiteering.

***C. price discrimination.**

Explanation: LOS: Reading 19-c

Price discrimination is when a seller charges different customers different prices for the same product or service.

**Reference:** CFA® Program Curriculum, Volume 2, pp. 193-195.

---

2. (QID 94) A sustained rise in interest rates will tend to lead to a change in demand for:

| | Physical Capital | Financial Capital |
|---|---|---|
| A. | Static | Decrease |
| B. | Decrease | Increase |
| ***C.** | **Decrease** | **Decrease** |

Explanation: LOS: Reading 21-e

The present value of the physical capital required falls; this also reduces the financial capital required.

Static = Remain the same or no change.

**Reference:** CFA® Program Curriculum, Volume 2, pp. 271-280.

3. (QID 95) It can be argued that monopolistic competition is efficient because:

A. price exceeds marginal cost.

B. excess capacity is minimized.

C. product variety offsets the difference between marginal revenue and marginal cost.

---

4. (QID 96) In a perfectly competitive market if prices fall below a firm's average total cost, the firm:

A. should increase prices to marginal cost to reach breakeven.

B. could temporarily shutdown their operations to reduce losses.

C. should increase prices to average total cost to reach breakeven.

3. (QID 95) It can be argued that monopolistic competition is efficient because:

A. price exceeds marginal cost.

B. excess capacity is minimized.

***C. product variety offsets the difference between marginal revenue and marginal cost.**

Explanation: LOS: Reading 20-b

Although in monopolistic competition price exceeds marginal cost, marginal benefit is not equal to marginal cost, and there is excess capacity produced. It can be argued that the variety of goods on offer compensates customers for these inefficiencies.

**Reference:** CFA® Program Curriculum, Volume 2, p. 213-218.

---

4. (QID 96) In a perfectly competitive market if prices fall below a firm's average total cost, the firm:

A. should increase prices to marginal cost to reach breakeven.

***B. could temporarily shutdown their operations to reduce losses.**

C. should increase prices to average total cost to reach breakeven.

Explanation: LOS: Reading 18-b

Shutting down the operations temporarily will eliminate variable costs and losses will be limited to fixed costs. If the owners expect a rise in prices in the future this would be probably preferable to going out of business. Increasing prices is not an option since the firm is a price taker, if they increase prices sales would fall to zero.

**Reference:** CFA® Program Curriculum, Volume 2, pp. 155-159.

5. (QID 97) Which of the following statements is most accurate regarding the behavior of monopolists?

A. Monopolists do not need to advertise since they are not facing competition.

B. Monopolists will expand output until marginal revenue equals marginal cost.

C. Monopolists can always make an economic profit since other firms cannot easily enter their markets.

---

6. (QID 98) Monopolies use price discrimination in order to:

A. reduce long-run average cost to the minimum level.

B. transfer the potential consumer surplus to economic profit.

C. reduce output to the level where marginal revenue equal marginal cost.

5. (QID 97) Which of the following statements is most accurate regarding the behavior of monopolists?

A. Monopolists do not need to advertise since they are not facing competition.

***B. Monopolists will expand output until marginal revenue equals marginal cost.**

C. Monopolists can always make an economic profit since other firms cannot easily enter their markets.

Explanation: LOS: Reading 19-b

As is the case with other price searchers, monopolists will expand output until marginal revenue equals marginal cost. Monopolists still have a downward sloping demand curve and will need to attract demand (through advertising etc.) in order to make sales at a certain price level. Monopolists can lose money, as can any firm, if costs exceed revenue.

**Reference:** CFA® Program Curriculum, Volume 2, pp. 183-188.

---

6. (QID 98) Monopolies use price discrimination in order to:

A. reduce long-run average cost to the minimum level.

B. transfer the potential consumer surplus to economic profit.

***C. reduce output to the level where marginal revenue equal marginal cost.**

Explanation: LOS: Reading 19-c

Price discrimination among buyers means aiming to charge different groups of customers the maximum price they are willing to pay. This will transfer the consumer surplus to the monopoly and increase its economic profit.

**Reference:** CFA® Program Curriculum, Volume 2, pp. 193-198.

7. (QID 99) Classical macroeconomists believe that:

A. the economy is self regulating.

B. tax rates do not have a major impact on supply of labor.

C. money wage rates are very slow to adjust if there is a recession.

---

8. (QID 100) In monopolistic competition advertising to promote a certain brand name:

A. does not affect product pricing since consumers are under no obligation to buy goods that are heavily advertised.

B. is never of benefit to consumers since the cost of advertising will mean that consumers are overpaying for the product.

C. can be beneficial to consumers since once a brand name has value the owners of the brand name will be careful to protect the reputation of their product.

7. (QID 99) Classical macroeconomists believe that:

***A. the economy is self regulating.**

B. tax rates do not have a major impact on supply of labor.

C. money wage rates are very slow to adjust if there is a recession.

Explanation: LOS: Reading 23-d

Classical economists believe that the economy is self regulating and taxes are a disincentive to work.

**Reference:** CFA® Program Curriculum, Volume 2, p. 335-336.

---

8. (QID 100) In monopolistic competition advertising to promote a certain brand name:

A. does not affect product pricing since consumers are under no obligation to buy goods that are heavily advertised.

B. is never of benefit to consumers since the cost of advertising will mean that consumers are overpaying for the product.

***C. can be beneficial to consumers since once a brand name has value the owners of the brand name will be careful to protect the reputation of their product.**

Explanation: LOS: Reading 20-c

Advertising can provide consumers with information about the product so it does have some benefit to consumers, but the cost of advertising will often be passed on to consumers through higher prices. It is true, however, that consumers are under no obligation to pay higher prices since they have the option to buy a cheaper product that is not heavily advertised. Consumers will benefit in that a firm that has spent heavily to establish a brand name will be anxious to maintain the value of the brand name, and therefore provide an attractive product to the consumer.

**Reference:** CFA® Program Curriculum, Volume 2, pp. 219-223.

9. (QID 101) A firm which is operating in monopolistic competition will make:

A. economic profits in the short and long run.

B. either economic profits or losses in the short run and economic profits in the long run.

C. either economic profits or losses in the short run and zero economic profit in the long run.

---

10. (QID 102) Which of the following statements concerning the Consumer Price Index (CPI) is least accurate?

A. Quality change bias will lead to the CPI overstating the true inflation rate.

B. Outlet substitution bias will lead to the CPI overstating the true inflation rate.

C. Social security payments which are linked to the CPI have risen more slowly than the true inflation rate.

9. (QID 101) A firm which is operating in monopolistic competition will make:

A. economic profits in the short and long run.

B. either economic profits or losses in the short run and economic profits in the long run.

***C. either economic profits or losses in the short run and zero economic profit in the long run.**

Explanation: LOS: Reading 20-a

Since monopolistic competition has low barriers to entry, if a firm is making economic profits new competitors will enter the market which will drive prices down. Similarly if firms are making economic losses it will lead to firms dropping out of the market and prices increasing until economic losses are eliminated. In both cases firms will make zero economic profit in the long run.

**Reference:** CFA® Program Curriculum, Volume 2, pp. 213-216.

---

10. (QID 102) Which of the following statements concerning the Consumer Price Index (CPI) is least accurate?

A. Quality change bias will lead to the CPI overstating the true inflation rate.

B. Outlet substitution bias will lead to the CPI overstating the true inflation rate.

***C. Social security payments which are linked to the CPI have risen more slowly than the true inflation rate.**

Explanation: LOS: Reading 22-d

Upward biases will be created by the quality change bias (goods more expensive but better quality, so the price rise is not all inflation effect) and outlet substitution bias (people use discount stores more if prices are rising). The CPI-based inflation number overstates true inflation so workers or social security recipients, with CPI-related contracts, benefit.

**Reference:** CFA® Program Curriculum, Volume 2, pp. 304-309.

11. (QID 103) Which of the following statements is the least accurate? The labor force participation rate:

A. rises when the number of discouraged workers is low.

B. reflects the number of people in the labor force that cannot find jobs.

C. reflects the likelihood that more people start to look for jobs during an expansion phase of a business cycle.

---

12. (QID 104) In an increasing-cost industry which is perfectly competitive the long-run market supply curve:

A. is horizontal.

B. slopes upwards to the right.

C. slopes downwards to the right.

11. (QID 103) Which of the following statements is the least accurate? The labor force participation rate:

A. rises when the number of discouraged workers is low.

***B. reflects the number of people in the labor force that cannot find jobs.**

C. reflects the likelihood that more people start to look for jobs during an expansion phase of a business cycle.

Explanation: LOS: Reading 22-a

The number of people in the labor force that cannot find jobs refers to the unemployment rate. The labor force participation rate is the labor force divided by the working age population.

**Reference:** CFA® Program Curriculum, Volume 2, pp. 291-294.

---

12. (QID 104) In an increasing-cost industry which is perfectly competitive the long-run market supply curve:

A. is horizontal.

***B. slopes upwards to the right.**

C. slopes downwards to the right.

Explanation: LOS: Reading 18-c

In an increasing-cost industry the cost of production increases as output expands, usually since resource prices increase. Therefore market output will only increase as higher prices push the supply curve upwards to the right.

**Reference:** CFA® Program Curriculum, Volume 2, pp. 169-171.

13. (QID 105) A government decides to regulate a natural monopoly using marginal cost pricing where the price the monopoly can charge equals marginal cost. This will have the effect of:

A. maximizing the producer surplus.

B. consumers overpaying for the product.

C. ensuring the monopoly makes an economic loss.

14. (QID 106) A firm will maximize profits when:

A. marginal product returns start to diminish.

B. marginal revenue product equals the wage rate.

C. the marginal revenue product curve crosses the demand curve.

13. (QID 105) A government decides to regulate a natural monopoly using marginal cost pricing where the price the monopoly can charge equals marginal cost. This will have the effect of:

A. maximizing the producer surplus.

B. consumers overpaying for the product.

***C. ensuring the monopoly makes an economic loss.**

Explanation: LOS: Reading 19-e

A marginal cost pricing rule will mean, since the average total cost is above the marginal cost, that the monopoly makes an economic loss.

**Reference:** CFA® Program Curriculum, Volume 2, pp. 200-202.

---

14. (QID 106) A firm will maximize profits when:

A. marginal product returns start to diminish.

B. marginal revenue product equals the wage rate.

***C. the marginal revenue product curve crosses the demand curve.**

Explanation: LOS: Reading 21-a

Profit is maximized when marginal revenue product equals the wage rate, which is the equivalent to marginal revenue equals marginal cost.

The marginal revenue product curve always equals the demand curve, not just at profit maximization.

**Reference:** CFA® Program Curriculum, Volume 2, pp. 255-260.

15. (QID 107) Which of the following is least likely to be a factor that creates entry barriers to an industry?

A. Patent laws.

B. Economies of scale.

C. An inelastic demand curve.

---

16. (QID 108) Oligopolies are different to monopolistic competition markets because:

A. there are high barriers to entry in an oligopoly but not in a monopolistic competition market.

B. oligopolists are not competitive whereas monopolistic competition participants are competitive.

C. oligopolists produce identical products whereas in monopolistic competition the products are differentiated.

15. (QID 107) Which of the following is least likely to be a factor that creates entry barriers to an industry?

A. Patent laws.

B. Economies of scale.

***C. An inelastic demand curve.**

Explanation: LOS: Reading 19-a

The important factors are economies of scale and government licensing, patents and copyrights.

**Reference:** CFA® Program Curriculum, Volume 2, pp. 180-182.

---

16. (QID 108) Oligopolies are different to monopolistic competition markets because:

***A. there are high barriers to entry in an oligopoly but not in a monopolistic competition market.**

B. oligopolists are not competitive whereas monopolistic competition participants are competitive.

C. oligopolists produce identical products whereas in monopolistic competition the products are differentiated.

Explanation: LOS: Reading 20-a

Products can be either identical or differentiated in an oligopoly. Oligopolists are price searchers and are often highly competitive.

**Reference:** CFA® Program Curriculum, Volume 2, pp. 223-225.

17. (QID 109) The supply of labor curve is backward bending because:

A. the size of the adult population is increasing.

B. at high wage rates workers increase their demand for leisure.

C. at high wage rates the marginal benefit of working an extra hour diminishes so employees supply ever increasing levels of labor.

---

18. (QID 110) Which of the following might be considered as a problem in the calculation of unemployment?

A. Part-time workers are counted as being unemployed.

B. Unemployed workers are not included in the labor force.

C. Unpaid household work is not considered to be employment.

17. (QID 109) The supply of labor curve is backward bending because:

A. the size of the adult population is increasing.

***B. at high wage rates workers increase their demand for leisure.**

C. at high wage rates the marginal benefit of working an extra hour diminishes so employees supply ever increasing levels of labor.

Explanation: LOS: Reading 21-c

Initially as wage rates rise the quantity of labor supplied increases, but eventually at higher incomes workers value leisure more highly (the income effect) and the supply of labor starts to decline. Adult population changes will cause a shift in the supply curve.

**Reference:** CFA® Program Curriculum, Volume 2, pp. 262-264.

---

18. (QID 110) Which of the following might be considered as a problem in the calculation of unemployment?

A. Part-time workers are counted as being unemployed.

B. Unemployed workers are not included in the labor force.

***C. Unpaid household work is not considered to be employment.**

Explanation: LOS: Reading 22-c

Part-time workers are counted as being employed, unemployed workers are included in the labor force. However housework is not considered to be employment.

**Reference:** CFA® Program Curriculum, Volume 2, pp. 296-300.

19. (QID 111) An oligopoly is characterized by:

A. a few large producers who are not competitive since they are protected by high entry barriers.

B. a competitive market between a few large producers who are protected by high entry barriers.

C. a small number of producers who carry out interdependent policies, there are no significant entry barriers to the market.

---

20. (QID 112) In monopolistic competition there are:

A. low entry barriers and upward-sloping demand curves.

B. low entry barriers and downward-sloping demand curves.

C. high entry barriers and downward-sloping demand curves.

19. (QID 111) An oligopoly is characterized by:

A. a few large producers who are not competitive since they are protected by high entry barriers.

***B. a competitive market between a few large producers who are protected by high entry barriers.**

C. a small number of producers who carry out interdependent policies, there are no significant entry barriers to the market.

Explanation: LOS: Reading 20-a

An oligopoly is characterized by:

A1. High entry barriers.

A2. A small number of firms.

A3. Interdependence between the producers.

Oligopoly

A Market characterized by a small number of producers who often act together to control the supply of a particular good and its market price.

**Reference:** CFA® Program Curriculum, Volume 2, pp. 223-225.

---

20. (QID 112) In monopolistic competition there are:

A. low entry barriers and upward-sloping demand curves.

***B. low entry barriers and downward-sloping demand curves.**

C. high entry barriers and downward-sloping demand curves.

Explanation: LOS: Reading 20-a

In monopolistic competition firms produce differentiated goods. Therefore as their prices increase they will gradually lose customers, but not all their customers as in the case of price-taker markets, therefore demand curves are downward sloping. Monopolistic competition markets, as opposed to monopolies or oligopolies, have low entry barriers.

**Reference:** CFA® Program Curriculum, Volume 2, pp. 213-216.

21. (QID 113) Which of the following statements is least accurate regarding purely competitive markets?

A. They are markets with no entry barriers.

B. Each firm's marginal revenue is less than price.

C. They are markets where there are a large number of small firms.

---

22. (QID 114) The supply of capital from individuals is least likely to increase when:

A. incomes rise.

B. interest rates rise.

C. current income is low relative to future expected income.

21. (QID 113) Which of the following statements is least accurate regarding purely competitive markets?

A. They are markets with no entry barriers.

***B. Each firm's marginal revenue is less than price.**

C. They are markets where there are a large number of small firms.

Explanation: LOS: Reading 18-a

Purely competitive markets have no entry barriers and a large number of firms with a small market share and identical products. Marginal revenue equals price.

**Reference:** CFA® Program Curriculum, Volume 2, pp. 152-153.

---

22. (QID 114) The supply of capital from individuals is least likely to increase when:

A. incomes rise.

B. interest rates rise.

***C. current income is low relative to future expected income.**

Explanation: LOS: Reading 21-f

When current income is low relative to future expected income people tend to spend more and save less. The other two factors tend to increase the quantity of capital.

**Reference:** CFA® Program Curriculum, Volume 2, pp. 274-276.

23. (QID 115) Firms acting in collusion in an oligopoly would generally attempt to:

| Output | Prices |
|---|---|
| A. increase | increase |
| B. increase | decrease |
| C. decrease | increase |

27. (QID 139) If a monopoly uses price discrimination it is least likely to have the effect of:

A. minimizing the consumer surplus.

B. finding the single price that will maximize the quantity sold.

C. bringing the market demand curve close to the marginal revenue curve.

28. (QID 140) Firms acting in collusion in an oligopoly would generally attempt to:

| Output | Prices |
|---|---|
| A. increase | increase |
| B. increase | decrease |
| C. decrease | increase |

23. (QID 115) Firms acting in collusion in an oligopoly would generally attempt to:

| Output | Prices |
|---|---|
| A. increase | increase |
| B. increase | decrease |
| ***C. decrease** | **increase** |

Explanation: LOS: Reading 20-a

Collusion is usually with the intention of increasing economic profit for the participants by limiting output and raising pierces.

**Reference:** CFA® Program Curriculum, Volume 2, pp. 222-226.

---

24. (QID 139) If a monopoly uses price discrimination it is least likely to have the effect of:

A. minimizing the consumer surplus.

***B. finding the single price that will maximize the quantity sold.**

C. bringing the market demand curve close to the marginal revenue curve.

Explanation: LOS: Reading 19-c

Price discrimination has the effect of transferring the consumer surplus to the monopoly, bringing the market demand curve close to the marginal revenue curve and producing a higher quantity. By definition price discrimination is not a single-price monopoly so choice "finding the single price" is not accurate

**Reference:** CFA® Program Curriculum, Volume 2, pp. 193-198.

25. (QID 140) Firms acting in collusion in an oligopoly would generally attempt to:

| Output | Prices |
|---|---|
| A. increase | increase |
| B. increase | decrease |
| ***C. decrease** | **increase** |

Explanation: LOS: Reading 20-a

Collusion is usually with the intention of increasing economic profit for the participants by limiting output and raising pierces.

**Reference:** CFA® Program Curriculum, Volume 2, pp. 222-226.

# Study Session 06: Economics:

## Monetary and Fiscal Economics

This study session focuses on the monetary sector of an economy. It examines the functions of money and how it is created, highlighting the special role of the central bank within an economy. Supply and demand for resources, such as labor and capital, and goods are strongly interrelated, and this study session describes circumstances when this may lead to inflation and the transmission mechanisms between the monetary sector and the real part of the economy. Finally, the goals and implications of fiscal and monetary policy are explored by examining some of the main models of macroeconomic theory (Keynesian, classical, and monetarist).

**Reading 24: Money, Banks, and the Federal Reserve**

**Reading 25: Money, Interest, Real GDP, and the Price Level**

**Reading 26: Inflation**

**Reading 27: Fiscal Policy**

**Reading 28: Monetary Policy**

1. (QID 116) If a government believes in using fiscal policies to stabilize the economy, when there are signs that the economy is in an inflationary economic boom, the government is most likely to consider:

A. raising personal tax rates.

B. increasing defense spending.

C. borrowing to finance a larger budget deficit.

---

2. (QID 117) The supply of money in the U.S. is dependent on:

A. interest rates.

B. the Federal Reserve's monetary policy.

C. the net foreign investment into the country.

1. (QID 116) If a government believes in using fiscal policies to stabilize the economy, when there are signs that the economy is in an inflationary economic boom, the government is most likely to consider:

***A. raising personal tax rates.**

B. increasing defense spending.

C. borrowing to finance a larger budget deficit.

Explanation: LOS: Reading 26-d

The government is likely to adopt a restrictive fiscal policy which would involve increasing taxes and/or reducing government expenditure.

**Reference:** CFA® Program Curriculum, Volume 2, pp. 431-435.

---

2. (QID 117) The supply of money in the U.S. is dependent on:

A. interest rates.

***B. the Federal Reserve's monetary policy.**

C. the net foreign investment into the country.

Explanation: LOS: Reading 24-h

The role of a central bank, which is the Fed in the U.S., is to control money supply, through setting the reserve requirement, the discount rate and using open market operations.

**Reference:** CFA® Program Curriculum, Volume 2, pp. 369-371.

3. (QID 118) In the U.S. which of the following is least likely to be a depository institution?

A. A thrift institution.

B. Federal Reserve Bank.

C. A money market mutual fund.

---

4. (QID 119) Which of the following is an example of an instrument rule?

A. Set the federal funds rate at a level needed to achieve the target inflation rate.

B. Set the growth rate of the quantity of money at the targeted growth rate of potential GDP.

C. Expand the monetary base at the target inflation rate adjusted for the long-term aggregate GDP growth rate and the growth rate in velocity of the monetary base.

3. (QID 118) In the U.S. which of the following is least likely to be a depository institution?

A. A thrift institution.

***B. Federal Reserve Bank.**

C. A money market mutual fund.

Explanation: LOS: Reading 24-c

A depository institution is a firm that takes deposits from individuals and firms and makes loans to other individuals and firms. There are three types of depository institution in the U.S. - commercial banks, thrift institutions and money market mutual funds.

**Reference:** CFA® Program Curriculum, Volume 2, pp. 350-353.

---

4. (QID 119) Which of the following is an example of an instrument rule?

A. Set the federal funds rate at a level needed to achieve the target inflation rate.

B. Set the growth rate of the quantity of money at the targeted growth rate of potential GDP.

***C. Expand the monetary base at the target inflation rate adjusted for the long-term aggregate GDP growth rate and the growth rate in velocity of the monetary base.**

Explanation: LOS: Reading 27-d

The McCallum rule is an example of a new monetarist rule, it says expand the monetary base at the same rate as the target inflation rate adjusted for trend GDP and the growth in velocity of the monetary base.

**Reference:** CFA® Program Curriculum, Volume 2, pp. 451-452 and 467-468.

5. (QID 120) Which of the following statements regarding income taxes is least accurate? A rise in income tax rates will reduce:

A. the potential GDP.

B. the demand for labor.

C. the quantity of labor available.

---

6. (QID 121) Which of the following statements is least accurate regarding the tax multiplier?

A. When the marginal propensity to consume falls the multiplier rises.

B. The multiplier is a key factor in using fiscal policy to stabilize an economy.

C. The magnitude of the tax multiplier is less than the government purchases multiplier.

5. (QID 120) Which of the following statements regarding income taxes is least accurate? A rise in income tax rates will reduce:

A. the potential GDP.

***B. the demand for labor.**

C. the quantity of labor available.

Explanation: LOS: Reading 26-a

Income tax will not reduce the demand for labor directly but will reduce the supply of labor, reducing the full employment quantity of labor and potential GDP.

**Reference:** CFA® Program Curriculum, Volume 2, pp. 419-420.

---

6. (QID 121) Which of the following statements is least accurate regarding the tax multiplier?

***A. When the marginal propensity to consume falls the multiplier rises.**

B. The multiplier is a key factor in using fiscal policy to stabilize an economy.

C. The magnitude of the tax multiplier is less than the government purchases multiplier.

Explanation: LOS: Reading 26-d

A is not correct – when the marginal propensity to consume falls people save more of the reduction in taxes, reducing the effect of the tax change.

**Reference:** CFA® Program Curriculum, Volume 2, p. 432.

7. (QID 122) Demand-pull inflation is least likely to be accompanied by, in the short term:

A. an increase in money wage rates.

B. real GDP falling below potential GDP.

C. unemployment falling below its natural rate.

8. (QID 123) The crowding-out effect refers to:

A. financing high budget deficits pushes up interest rates which will reduce private investment.

B. individuals will spend more today if they think expenditure-related taxes will rise in the future.

C. the recognition by individuals that they must save more today to pay for higher taxes in the future if the government runs a budget deficit.

7. (QID 122) Demand-pull inflation is least likely to be accompanied by, in the short term:

A. an increase in money wage rates.

***B. real GDP falling below potential GDP.**

C. unemployment falling below its natural rate.

Explanation: LOS: Reading 25-b

If the aggregate demand curve shifts to the right, without a move in the supply curve, then prices will rise. This will lead to:

unemployment falling below its natural rate.

money wage rates starting to rise.

the supply curve shifting to the left.

prices rising further.

real GDP starting to decrease which will push real GDP above potential GDP.

**Reference:** CFA® Program Curriculum, Volume 2, pp. 385-388.

---

8. (QID 123) The crowding-out effect refers to:

***A. financing high budget deficits pushes up interest rates which will reduce private investment.**

B. individuals will spend more today if they think expenditure-related taxes will rise in the future.

C. the recognition by individuals that they must save more today to pay for higher taxes in the future if the government runs a budget deficit.

Explanation: LOS: Reading 26-b

The crowding-out effect refers to when a government tries to stimulate an economy by borrowing to finance a budget deficit. This will increase interest rates, which will reduce companies' and individuals' expenditure, particularly on investment, which will reduce the effectiveness of the government's policy.

**Reference:** CFA® Program Curriculum, Volume 2, pp. 426-427.

9. (QID 124) Which of thc following is least likely to act as an automatic stabilizer?

A. Net exports.

B. Needs-tested spending.

C. Progressive income tax.

10. (QID 125) Which of the following is not usually a major role of a central bank?:

A. Issuing currency.

B. Managing the exchange rate.

C. Regulating the banking system

9. (QID 124) Which of the following is least likely to act as an automatic stabilizer?

***A. Net exports.**

B. Needs-tested spending.

C. Progressive income tax.

Explanation: LOS: Reading 26-e

Automatic stabilizers stimulate demand during a recession and restrain demand during a boom without the government needing to change fiscal policy through legislation.

**Reference:** CFA® Program Curriculum, Volume 2, pp. 435-438.

---

10. (QID 125) Which of the following is not usually a major role of a central bank?:

A. Issuing currency.

***B. Managing the exchange rate.**

C. Regulating the banking system

Explanation: LOS: Reading 26-a

Issuing the currency is usually a major role; an exception is the Federal Reserve.which puts the money in circulation but the money is printed by the US Treasury. Regulating the banking system is frequently one of the major roles of a central bank.

Managing the exchange rate would not usually be a primary role of a central bank.

**Reference:** CFA® Program Curriculum, Volume 2, p. 479

11. (QID 126) If high rates of inflation resulting from an expansionary monetary policy are anticipated by decision makers then the unemployment rate and real GDP will:

| Unemployment | Real GDP |
|---|---|
| A. rise | fall |
| B. be unchanged | rise |
| C. be unchanged | be unchanged |

12. (QID 127) Which of the following would tend to increase the budget deficit during a recession?

A. An automatic stabilizer.

B. The crowding-out effect.

C. A fall in the exchange rate.

11. (QID 126) If high rates of inflation resulting from an expansionary monetary policy are anticipated by decision makers then the unemployment rate and real GDP will:

| Unemployment | Real GDP |
|---|---|
| A. rise | fall |
| B. be unchanged | rise |
| ***C. be unchanged** | **be unchanged** |

Explanation: LOS: Reading 25-b

Anticipated changes will only affect prices. Nominal GDP will rise but real GDP will be unchanged and unemployment unaffected.

**Reference:** CFA® Program Curriculum, Volume 2, pp. 391-392.

---

12. (QID 127) Which of the following would tend to increase the budget deficit during a recession?

***A. An automatic stabilizer.**

B. The crowding-out effect.

C. A fall in the exchange rate.

Explanation: LOS: Reading 26-e

An automatic stabilizer reduces taxes and increases government spending.

**Reference:** CFA® Program Curriculum, Volume 2, pp. 435-438.

13. (QID 128) The first price rise in cost-push inflation is triggered by a jump in wage rates, and therefore the short-run aggregate supply curve:

A. is unchanged.

B. shifts to the left.

C. shifts to the right.

---

14. (QID 129) If there is an increase in inflation which is unanticipated then the impact on profits and employment is most likely to be:

| Profits | Employment |
|---|---|
| A. lower | below full employment |
| B. lower | above full employment |
| C. higher | above full employment |

13. (QID 128) The first price rise in cost-push inflation is triggered by a jump in wage rates, and therefore the short-run aggregate supply curve:

A. is unchanged.

***B. shifts to the left.**

C. shifts to the right.

Explanation: LOS: Reading 25-b

Cost-put inflation is triggered by a rise in the price of labor or another resource; the first impact will be a move in the aggregate supply curve to the left as aggregate supply decreases.

**Reference:** CFA® Program Curriculum, Volume 2, pp. 388-390.

---

14. (QID 129) If there is an increase in inflation which is unanticipated then the impact on profits and employment is most likely to be:

| Profits | Employment |
|---|---|
| A. lower | below full employment |
| B. lower | above full employment |
| ***C. higher** | **above full employment** |

Explanation: LOS: Reading 25-c

The money wage rate will be too low which will increase profits. The real wage rate will fall so companies will try to hire more labor and increase production.

**Reference:** CFA® Program Curriculum, Volume 2, pp. 391-393.

15. (QID 130) The required reserve ratio is reduced to 15% giving a bank $1 billion of excess reserves. In the long term this will lead to a potential expansion in the money supply of:

A. $0.15 billion.

B. $0.87 billion.

C. $6.67 billion.

---

16. (QID 131) The major role of a central bank is usually to:

A. implement fiscal policy.

B. issue government securities.

C. maintain a favorable monetary environment.

15. (QID 130) The required reserve ratio is reduced to 15% giving a bank $1 billion of excess reserves. In the long term this will lead to a potential expansion in the money supply of:

A. $0.15 billion.

B. $0.87 billion.

***C. $6.67 billion.**

Explanation: LOS: Reading 24-e

The money supply will potentially expand by the excess reserves multiplied by the reciprocal of the required reserve ratio, this is:

$1 billion x 1/0.15 = $6.67 billion.

**Reference:** CFA® Program Curriculum, Volume 2, pp. 357-366.

---

16. (QID 131) The major role of a central bank is usually to:

A. implement fiscal policy.

B. issue government securities.

***C. maintain a favorable monetary environment.**

Explanation: LOS: Reading 24-d

Central banks are responsible for implementing monetary policy and thereby providing a favorable economic climate.

**Reference:** CFA® Program Curriculum, Volume 2, p. 355.

17. (QID 132) The Laffer curve illustrates that increasing tax rates:

A. increases the supply of labor.

B. ultimately reduces tax revenue.

C. decreases the demand for labor.

---

18. (QID 133) The short-term impact of a move by the Fed to reduce the quantity of money includes:

A. unchanged real interest rates.

B. an increase in the inflation rate.

C. an increase in short-term interest rates.

17. (QID 132) The Laffer curve illustrates that increasing tax rates:

A. increases the supply of labor.

***B. ultimately reduces tax revenue.**

C. decreases the demand for labor.

Explanation: LOS: Reading 26-a

The Laffer curve shows the relationship between tax rates (x-axis) and tax revenues (y-axis).

The slope starts off being upward sloping, then peaks and sloped downwards, so ultimately increasing tax rates decreases revenue as the quantity of employment falls is correct.

**Reference:** CFA® Program Curriculum, Volume 2, pp. 418-422.

---

18. (QID 133) The short-term impact of a move by the Fed to reduce the quantity of money includes:

A. unchanged real interest rates.

B. an increase in the inflation rate.

***C. an increase in short-term interest rates.**

Explanation: LOS: Reading 24-h

Both nominal and real interest rates will rise in the short term.

**Reference:** CFA® Program Curriculum, Volume 2, pp. 369-371.

19. (QID 134) In the U.S. commercial banks:

A. must hold reserves equal to 100% of their loans.

B. are permitted to hold reserves of less than 100% of their loans.

C. are permitted to hold reserves of less than 100% of their deposits.

---

20. (QID 135) An increase in the expected rate of inflation would lead to the following impact on the Phillips curves (PC):

| Short-run PC | Long-run PC |
|---|---|
| A. no change | shift to the right |
| B. shift upwards | no change |
| C. shift downwards | no change |

19. (QID 134) In the U.S. commercial banks:

A. must hold reserves equal to 100% of their loans.

B. are permitted to hold reserves of less than 100% of their loans.

***C. are permitted to hold reserves of less than 100% of their deposits.**

Explanation: LOS: Reading 24-d

A fractional reserve banking system means that banks only need to keep a fraction of their deposits as cash and other reserves. The rest are available to lend to customers.

**Reference:** CFA® Program Curriculum, Volume 2, p. 361.

---

20. (QID 135) An increase in the expected rate of inflation would lead to the following impact on the Phillips curves (PC):

| | Short-run PC | Long-run PC |
|---|---|---|
| A. | no change | shift to the right |
| ***B.** | **shift upwards** | **no change** |
| C. | shift downwards | no change |

Explanation: LOS: Reading 25-d

A rise in expected inflation will shift the short-run Phillips curve upwards, the LRPC is unaffected and the point of intersection is the new expected rate.

**Reference:** CFA® Program Curriculum, Volume 2, pp. 392-396.

21. (QID 136) When the Fed purchases U.S. securities this will tend to:

| Monetary base | Money supply |
|---|---|
| A. increase | increase |
| B. increase | decrease |
| C. decrease | increase |

---

22. (QID 137) The money multiplier is:

A. I. the ratio of currency to deposits.

B. II. the change in quantity of money for a change in the monetary base.

C. III. the average number of times a dollar of money is used annually to buy goods and services.

21. (QID 136) When the Fed purchases U.S. securities this will tend to:

| Monetary base | Money supply |
|---|---|
| ***A. increase** | **increase** |
| B. increase | decrease |
| C. decrease | increase |

Explanation: LOS: Reading 24-d

When the Fed purchases securities it adds to currency in circulation or deposits with banks thereby increasing the monetary base. This will lead to an increase in the money supply by a multiple decided by the actual money multiplier.

**Reference:** CFA® Program Curriculum, Volume 2, pp. 355-360.

---

22. (QID 137) The money multiplier is:

A. I. the ratio of currency to deposits.

***B. II. the change in quantity of money for a change in the monetary base.**

C. III. the average number of times a dollar of money is used annually to buy goods and services.

Explanation: LOS: Reading 24-f

The definition of the money multiplier is the change in quantity of money for a change in the monetary base so

II. is the correct choice.

III. is the velocity of money.

That leaves "the ratio of currency to deposits" as the correct choice.

**Reference:** CFA® Program Curriculum, Volume 2, pp. 365-366.

23. (QID 138) An increase in income taxes will shift:

A. the supply of labor curve to the left.

B. the supply of labor curve to the right.

C. the demand for labor curve to the left.

24. (QID 415) Which of the following is an example of a new monetarist feedback rule?

A. Set the discount rate at the ten-year average annual GDP growth rate less the four-year average annual growth in velocity of money.

B. Set the federal funds rate at the target inflation rate adjusted for the difference between the actual and target inflation rate and the difference between real GDP and potential GDP.

C. *Expand the monetary base at the target inflation rate adjusted for the long-term aggregate GDP growth rate and the growth rate in velocity of the monetary base.

23. (QID 138) An increase in income taxes will shift:

***A. the supply of labor curve to the left.**

B. the supply of labor curve to the right.

C. the demand for labor curve to the left.

Explanation: LOS: Reading 27-a

The supply curve shifts to the left as after-tax wage rates decline. The demand for labor is not affected.

**Reference:** CFA® Program Curriculum, Volume 2, pp. 436-438.

---

24. (QID 415) Which of the following is an example of a new monetarist feedback rule?

A. Set the discount rate at the ten-year average annual GDP growth rate less the four-year average annual growth in velocity of money.

B. Set the federal funds rate at the target inflation rate adjusted for the difference between the actual and target inflation rate and the difference between real GDP and potential GDP.

***C. *Expand the monetary base at the target inflation rate adjusted for the long-term aggregate GDP growth rate and the growth rate in velocity of the monetary base.**

Explanation: LOS: Reading 27-d

The McCallum rule is an example of a new monetarist rule, it says expand the monetary base at the same rate as the target inflation rate adjusted for trend GDP and the growth in velocity of the monetary base.

**Reference:** CFA® Program Curriculum, Volume 2, pp. 451-452 and 467-468.

25. (QID 416) The year-end price data for a country was:

| Year-end | Price level |
|---|---|
| 2006 | 110 |
| 2007 | 113 |
| 2008 | 117 |

The annual inflation rate in 2006 and the compound annual rate for the 2006-2008 period were closest to:

| 2007 inflation rate | 2006-2008 annual rate |
|---|---|
| A. 2.7% | 3.1% |
| B. 2.7% | 6.2% |
| C. 3.0% | 7.0% |

---

26. (QID 512) When the Fed lowers the federal funds rate which of the following is most likely to happen first?

A. Real GDP increases.

B. The inflation rate increases.

C. The US dollar exchange rate falls.

---

27. (QID 513) The primary goals of the Fed's monetary policy are most likely to include:

A. a strong US dollar.

B. stable corporate profits

C. moderate long-term interest rates.

25. (QID 416) The year-end price data for a country was:

| Year-end | Price level |
|---|---|
| 2006 | 110 |
| 2007 | 113 |
| 2008 | 117 |

The annual inflation rate in 2006 and the compound annual rate for the 2006-2008

period were closest to:

| | 2007 inflation rate | 2006-2008 annual rate |
|---|---|---|
| ***A.** | **2.7%** | **3.1%** |
| B. | 2.7% | 6.2% |
| C. | 3.0% | 7.0% |

Explanation: LOS: Reading 26-a

$$\text{Inflation rate} = \frac{\text{Price level this year - Price level last year}}{\text{Price level last year}} \times 100$$

$$\text{Inflation rate 2006} = \frac{113 \quad 110}{110} \times 100 = 2.7\%$$

$$\text{Inflation rate 2007} = \frac{117 \quad 113}{113} \times 100 = 3.5\%$$

**The compound annual rate is**

$$\sqrt{(1.027)(1.035)} \quad 1 = 3.1\%$$

**Reference:** CFA® Program Curriculum, Volume 2, p. 479.

26. (QID 512) When the Fed lowers the federal funds rate which of the following is most likely to happen first?

A. Real GDP increases.

B. The inflation rate increases.

***C. The US dollar exchange rate falls.**

Explanation: LOS: Reading 27-c

As interest rates fall the exchange rate is likely to fall almost immediately. The impact on inflation and real GDP take longer, often one to two years from the change in federal funds rate.

**Reference:** CFA® Program Curriculum, Volume 2, pp. 457-458.

---

27. (QID 513) The primary goals of the Fed's monetary policy are most likely to include:

A. a strong US dollar.

B. stable corporate profits

***C. moderate long-term interest rates.**

Explanation: LOS: Reading 27-a

The three main goals are 'maximum employment, stable prices and moderate long-term interest rates'

**Reference:** CFA® Program Curriculum, Volume 2, pp. 446-449.

# Study Session 7: Financial Introduction:

## Introductory Readings

Financial Accounting, 8th edition, Belverd E. Needles, Jr., and Marian Powers, (Houghton Mifflin, 2004)
"Measuring Business Income," Ch. 3
"Financial Reporting and Analysis," Ch. 5, pp. 246–258
"Inventories," Ch. 8
"Current Liabilities and the Time Value of Money," Ch. 9, pp. 412–426
"Contributed Capital," Ch. 12, pp. 543-553
"The Corporate Income Statement and the Statement of Stockholders' Equity," Ch.13, pp. 584-591

## Measuring Business Income

### Introduction

This section looks at the concept of net income which is used to measure a company's profitability. Candidates need to be familiar with the accrual basis of accounting and the matching principle and why they are used, rather than accounting simply on a cash basis.

### Accounting methods

Financial statements are prepared at the end of regular accounting periods to make comparisons between different accounting periods easier. A fiscal year refers to the twelve-month period used by a company (which in many cases is not the same as the calendar year).

Although revenues and expenses can be accounted for on a cash basis for tax purposes, this is generally regarded as unsatisfactory since revenues are often earned in a different period from which the payments are received, and expenses paid in a different period from which they are incurred. The **matching rule** states that revenues must be assigned to the periods when the services are performed or the goods are sold, and expenses must be assigned to the period in which they produce the revenue.

**Accrual accounting** refers to methods that accountants use to apply the matching rule, i.e. that revenues are recognized when they are earned and expenses when they are incurred rather than when they are actually paid. Accounts are likely to need adjustment. For example transactions may occur in one accounting period but the benefits may spread over more than one accounting period.

# Financial Reporting and Analysis

## Introduction

In this section Candidates learn the definition of each category or component on the balance sheet and income statement. We will refer to balance sheet and income statement items throughout the rest of the Financial Statement Analysis notes so it is essential you are comfortable with the structure, presentation and contents of financial statements.

## Balance Sheet

The major categories of a balance sheet are as follows:

| ASSETS | LIABILITIES |
|---|---|
| Current Assets | Current Liabilities |
| Investments | Long-term Liabilities |
| Property, Plant and Equipment | |
| Intangible Assets | **STOCKHOLDERS' EQUITY** |
| | Contributed Capital |
| | Retained Earnings |

**Current Assets** – cash and other assets which can reasonably be expected to be realized in cash or used within one year, or within the normal operating cycle of the business, whichever is longer.

**Investments** – assets that are not used in the normal operation of the business and are not expected to be converted into cash within one year.

**Property, Plant and Equipment** – long-term assets used in the continuing operation of the business. These assets are depreciated to allocate the cost of the assets over the period when they are used.

**Intangible Assets** – long-term assets with no physical substance – e.g. patents, goodwill.

**Current Liabilities** – obligations due to be paid or performed within one year, or within the normal operating cycle of the business, whichever is longer.

**Long-Term Liabilities** – debts that are due to be paid out in more than one year or beyond the normal operating cycle.

**Contributed Capital** – the par value of issued stock plus the amounts paid-in in excess of the par value.

**Retained Earnings** – earnings that have been retained by the company, rather than distributed to stockholders.

## Income statement

The components of a multi-step income statement are as follows:

| | |
|---|---|
| | Net Sales |
| – | Cost of Goods Sold |
| = | Gross Profit |
| – | Operating Expenses |
| = | Income from Operations |
| +/- | Other Revenue and Expenses |
| = | Income before Income Taxes |
| – | Income Taxes |
| = | Net Income |

**Net Sales** – gross proceeds from sales, less sales returned and discounts offered.

**Cost of Goods Sold** – amount paid for the goods that were sold.

**Operating Expenses** – costs other than the cost of goods sold, often broken down into selling expenses and general and administrative expenses.

**Other Revenue and Expenses** – revenues and expenses that are not a result of operating activities, these include interest income and interest expenses.

# Inventories

## Introduction

Inventory is another short-term asset appearing on the balance sheet and the cost of inventory will also affect the income statement. There are four methods of accounting for inventory and the candidate needs to understand the impact on the balance sheet and income statement of the method used. This Reading is covered in more detail in Study Session 9, Reading 39.

## Inventory

Inventory is a current asset and consists of goods held for sale in the normal course of business. The cost of inventory will include the costs of raw materials used, cost of labor and overhead costs. The cost of goods sold (COGS) is measured as the cost of goods available for sale less the value of inventory at the end of the accounting period. The valuation method used to value inventory is critical since it will decide the COGS and gross profit of the company and the value of inventory on the balance sheet.

## Inventory cost

Inventory cost is the price or consideration paid to acquire an asset. There are three components to inventory cost:

- Invoice price less purchase discounts.
- Freight or transportation including insurance costs when in transit.
- Applicable taxes and tariffs.

It could be argued that other costs, such as storage costs, should also be included in the cost of inventory. Allocation of these costs is difficult so they are usually expensed.

When assigning costs to items that are sold, different methods can be used. These methods make different assumptions on the order in which items are sold. The four most commonly used methods are shown below.

### Specific Identification Method

This method can be used when it is possible to match units left in inventory with a specific purchase. This might be used by an art dealer where there are high priced items for sale that are all unique.

### Average-Cost Method

Under this method inventory is priced at the average cost of items available for sale during the period.

### First-In, First-Out Method (FIFO)

This is based on the assumption that the cost of goods sold is associated with the earliest purchases in inventory. This means that the cost of goods held in inventory is associated with those that have been purchased most recently.

### Last-In, First-Out Method (LIFO)

The assumption under LIFO is that the cost of goods sold is associated with the most recently purchased, the cost of goods held in inventory are associated with those that have been purchased the earliest.

### Example Int-1 Calculating cost of inventory

On December 31st a company holds 200 units in inventory with an assigned total value of \$1,000, or \$5.00 per unit. On January 10th it purchases 30 additional units at a cost of \$5.50 per unit and on January 20th it purchases 70 additional units at a cost of \$6.00 per unit. 50 units are sold over the month so 250 units are left in inventory at the end of January.

Specific Identification Method

This requires additional information. If we are told that the specific cost of the 50 units sold was \$4.50 each, then

Cost of Goods Sold (COGS) $= 50 \times \$4.50 = \$225.00$

January 31st inventory = Costs of goods available for sale – COGS

= \$1,000 + (30 x \$5.50) + (70 x \$6.00) -- \$225 = \$1,360.00

Average-Cost Method

Average unit cost of goods available for sale

= Cost of goods available for sale/units available

= \$1,585/(200 + 30 + 70) = \$5.28

Cost of goods available = \$1,585.00

less January 31st inventory $= 250 \times \$5.28$

$= \$1{,}320.00$

COGS = \$265.00

First-In, First-Out Method (FIFO)

In this case the 50 units sold are those that were purchased first at a cost of \$5.00 per unit

Cost of goods available = \$1,585.00

less January 31st inventory $= (150 \times \$5.00) + (30 \times \$5.50) + (70 \times \$6.00)$

$= \$1{,}335.00$

COGS = \$250.00

Last-In, First-Out Method (LIFO)

In this case the 50 units sold are those that were purchased last at a cost of \$6.00 per unit.

Costs of goods available = \$1,585.00

less January 31st inventory $= (200 \times \$5.00) + (30 \times \$5.50) + (20 \times \$6.00)$

= \$1,285.00

COGS = \$300.00

## Effect of inventory accounting method

In the above example, where prices are rising, we can see that LIFO gives the highest COGS and FIFO the lowest COGS, so LIFO will give the lowest gross margin. For income statement items LIFO is generally considered the best method since it more closely follows the matching rule, the current value of costs is used. However, looking at the balance sheet, the inventory value recorded is higher under FIFO than LIFO. In this case FIFO could be considered a better method since inventory values are closer to current values.

When the replacement cost of inventory falls below the historic cost, perhaps due to a decline in price levels or obsolescence, then the inventory should be written down to the lower-of-cost-or-market. There are two methods for doing this:

### Item-by-Item Method

Cost and market values are computed for each item in inventory.

Major Category Method

Total cost and total market values are computed for each category of goods.

**Example Int-2 Calculating inventory values**

| Item-by-Item Method | | | | |
|---|---|---|---|---|
| | Quantity | Cost per Unit | Market Value per Unit | Lower of Cost or Market |
| Category 1 | | | | |
| Item a | 100 | $4.00 | $4.50 | $400.00 |
| Item b | 100 | $5.00 | $3.50 | $350.00 |
| Category 2 | | | | |
| Item c | 100 | $2.00 | $1.00 | $100.00 |
| Item d | 100 | $6.00 | $5.00 | $500.00 |
| | **Inventory at the lower of cost or market** | | | **$1,350.00** |

| Major Category Method | | | | |
|---|---|---|---|---|
| Category 1 | Quantity | Total Cost | Total Market Value | Lower of Cost or Market |
| Item a | 100 | $400.00 | $450.00 | |
| Item b | 100 | $500.00 | $350.00 | |
| Total | | $900.00 | $800.00 | $800.00 |
| Category 2 | | | | |
| Item c | 100 | $200.00 | $100.00 | |
| Item d | 100 | $600.00 | $500.00 | |
| Total | | $800.00 | $600.00 | $600.00 |
| | **Inventory at the lower of cost or market** | | | **$1,400.00** |

# Current Liabilities and the Time Value of Money

## Introduction

We now move on to look at the liability side of the balance sheet. Candidates need to be able to differentiate between current liabilities and long-term liabilities and know how to treat liabilities when the amount or likelihood of payment is uncertain.

## Liabilities

A liability is a legal obligation to make a future payment of assets, or perform a service in the future, as a result of a past transaction. Current liabilities are liabilities that are expected to be paid within a year, or within a normal operating cycle, whichever is longer. Long-term liabilities are due after one year or operating cycle. Generally, current liabilities are paid from the current assets or from the proceeds of current operations whereas long-term liabilities represent the financing of long-term assets.

Liabilities are usually valued at the amount of money need to pay the debt or the value of goods or services to be delivered. Whilst in some cases the amount is definitely known in other cases an estimate is made, perhaps based on past experience. An example is when a sale is made but there remains a liability to service the item sold.

Current liabilities can be broken down into:

### (i) Definitely Determinable Liabilities

- Accounts payable
- Bank loans and commercial paper
- Notes payable
- Accrued liabilities
- Dividends payable
- Sales and excise tax payable
- Current portion of long-term debt
- Payroll liabilities
- Unearned revenues

### (ii) Estimated Liabilities

The existence of a liability is clear but often the amount will not be known until later. These items include:

- Income taxes - a company's managers will usually only know the profits after the year-end so an estimated figure must be used.
- Property tax payable - these are usually paid to the local governments in the U.S., and the assessment dates are unlikely to match a firm's year-end. Therefore an estimated figure should be used.
- Product warranty liability - whilst a warranty or guarantee is outstanding on a product there is a liability and a firm should estimate how much the warranty is likely to cost.
- Vacation pay liability - not all employees will collect vacation pay so this should also be recorded as an estimated liability.

### (iii)Contingent liabilities

A contingent liability is not an existing liability but a potential liability in the sense that it depends on the outcome of a future event that arises because of a past transaction.

It should be entered in the accounts if it is both (i) probable and (ii) can be reasonably estimated. Potential liabilities that do not meet these conditions should be referred to in the notes to the accounts.

## Contributed Capital

## Introduction

Candidates are expected to know the breakdown of contributed capital and the difference between preferred stock and ordinary stock. We also look at payments to stockholders in the form of cash dividends or repurchase of stock and the impact on the balance sheet. Dividends are revisited in Study Session 13.

## Contributed capital

This is made up of three components:

1. Preferred Stock – par value, amount authorized and amount issued and outstanding.
2. Common Stock – par value, amount authorized and amount issued and outstanding.
3. Paid-in Capital in excess of par value.

## Accounting for dividends

There are three dates to consider:

1. Date of declaration – when the directors declare that a dividend is going to be paid, the issuer will record a cash dividend payable item as a liability.
2. Date of record – when ownership of the stock entitles the owner to receive the dividend. After this, and prior to payment, the stock is ex-dividend. No accounting entries are needed.
3. Date of payment – the date the dividend is paid, and the liability is settled.

## Common stock

This is the residual equity which means that the holders have the last claim on assets in the case that the company goes into liquidation. It is usually the only stock that carries voting rights. Dividends may be paid to stockholders which means that part of the stockholders' equity, usually earnings, is being paid out to stockholders.

## Preferred stock

This has preference over common stock, usually in terms of both dividends and claim on assets in the case of liquidation. Dividends are often quoted as a percentage of par value and in this sense the characteristics of preferred stock are similar to those of a fixed-income instrument. Different types of preferred stock are:

***Cumulative preferred stock*** – if a dividend is missed then it accumulates and must be paid before a dividend can be paid to common stock holders.

***Convertible preferred stock*** – can be exchanged into common stock.

**Callable preferred stock** – the issuer can redeem the stock at a pre-specified price.

### Stock issuance

Par value stock – the par value is credited to the Common Stock (or Preferred Stock) account and any surplus, or deficit, to the 'Paid-in Capital in Excess of Par Value' account, or debited to the 'Discount on Capital Stock' account respectively.
No-par stock – the proceeds of the issue are credited to the Common Stock account.

### Treasury stock

This is stock that has been bought back by the issuer, usually in the stock market, and not been resold or retired.
It is treated as stock that has been issued but is no longer outstanding, and therefore does not have voting rights, rights to dividends etc.

## The Corporate Income Statement and the Statement of Stockholders' Equity

### Introduction

Here we consider stock dividends and stock splits which are corporate actions that do not affect a company's income or asset value.

### Retained earnings

Retained earnings are the part of stockholders' equity that represents the stockholders' claim on assets generated by the firm's earnings. It is the profits (or losses) since inception less any dividends paid to stockholders or transfers to contributed capital.

### Accounting for stock dividends and stock splits

#### Stock dividends

This is a distribution of shares to existing common stockholders in proportion to the size of their holding. This does not involve a cash payment and leads only to a transfer of funds from retained earnings to the contributed capital account. The amount transferred is determined by the market value of the shares issued.

#### Stock splits

This is when a corporation increases the number of issued shares and reduces the par value accordingly. Again this does not involve a cash payment. The motivation is usually to reduce the market price and increase liquidity of the shares.

## Introduction Concept Check Questions

1. In a firm's financial statements expenses should be recorded:

   A. when they occur.

   B. when they are paid.

   C. once they can be reasonably estimated.

   D. in the same period that related revenues are recorded.

---

2. When inventory costs are increasing due to inflation, the decision to use LIFO rather than FIFO will lead to:

   A. lower net income and lower inventory balances.

   B. lower net income and higher inventory balances.

   C. higher net income and lower inventory balances.

   D. higher net income and higher inventory balances.

3. A stock dividend:

A. Has no impact on the financial statements.

B. Reduces the par value of stock outstanding.

C. Transfers an amount from retained earnings to contributed capital.

D. On the declaration date reduces stockholders' equity by the size of the dividend payable.

---

4. If Treasury stock is included in a firm's balance sheet as part of stockholders' equity it means that:

A. the firm has issued preferred shares.

B. the firm has repurchased its own stock.

C. the firm has invested in Treasury notes or Treasury bonds.

D. the firm has issued stock where the dividends are linked to Treasury bill yields.

## Introduction Concept Check Answers

1. In a firm's financial statements expenses should be recorded:

A. when they occur.

B. when they are paid.

C. once they can be reasonably estimated.

D. in the same period that related revenues are recorded.

**Correct Answer 1: D**

The matching rule says that related revenues and expenses should be recorded in the same accounting period.

---

2. When inventory costs are increasing due to inflation, the decision to use LIFO rather than FIFO will lead to:

A. lower net income and lower inventory balances.

B. lower net income and higher inventory balances.

C. higher net income and lower inventory balances.

D. higher net income and higher inventory balances.

**Correct Answer 2: A**

COGS will be higher under LIFO reducing net income. Ending inventory will be lower since it will include 'old' inventory bought at lower prices.

3. A stock dividend:

A. has no impact on the financial statements.

B. reduces the par value of stock outstanding.

C. transfers an amount from retained earnings to contributed capital.

D. on the declaration date reduces stockholders' equity by the size of the dividend payable.

**Correct Answer 3: C**

B refers to a stock split. D is not true since no cash is paid out.

---

4. If Treasury stock is included in a firm's balance sheet as part of stockholders' equity it means that:

A. the firm has issued preferred shares.

B. the firm has repurchased its own stock.

C. the firm has invested in Treasury notes or Treasury bonds.

D. the firm has issued stock where the dividends are linked to Treasury bill yields.

3.

**Correct Answer 4: B**

Treasury stock refers to repurchased stock. This is likely to have happened because the managers believed the stock was undervalued in the market or as a defense against a takeover.

# Study Session 07: Financial Reporting and Analysis: An Introduction

The readings in this study session discuss the general principles of the financial reporting system, underscoring the critical role of the analysis of financial reports in investment decision making.

The first reading introduces the range of information that an analyst may use in analyzing the financial performance of a company, including the principal financial statements (the income statement, balance sheet, cash flow statement, and statement of changes in owners' equity), notes to those statements, and management discussion and analysis of results. A general framework for addressing most financial statement analysis tasks is also presented.

A company's financial statements are the end-products of a process for recording the business transactions of the company. The second reading illustrates this process, introducing such basic concepts as the accounting equation and accounting accruals.

The presentation of financial information to the public by a company must conform to the governing set of financial reporting standards applying in the jurisdiction in which the information is released. The final reading in this study explores the role of financial reporting standard-setting bodies worldwide and the International Financial Reporting Standards framework promulgated by one key body, the International Accounting Standards Board. The movement towards worldwide convergence of financial reporting standards is also introduced.

**Note:** New rulings and/or pronouncements issued after the publication of the readings in Study Sessions 7 through 10 in financial statement analysis may cause some of the information in these readings to become dated. Candidates are expected to be familiar with the overall analytical framework contained in the study session readings, as well as the implications of alternative accounting methods for financial analysis and valuation, as provided in the assigned readings. For the purpose of Level I questions on financial statement analysis, when a ratio is defined and calculated differently in various texts, candidates should use the definitions given in the CFA Institute copyrighted readings by Robinson, et al. Variations in ratio definitions are part of the nature of practical financial analysis.

**Reading 29: Financial Statement Analysis: An Introduction**

**Reading 30: Financial Reporting Mechanics**

**Reading 31: Financial Reporting Standards**

1. (QID 139) The general ledger contains:

A. the same entries as the general journal, but in a different order.

B. the initial entries of transactions from which the general journal entries are derived.

C. the same entries as the general journal plus accruals and other adjustments made at the end of accounting periods.

---

2. (QID 140) If a manager is attempting to hide an expenditure for which he has paid cash he might record a fictitious:

A. pre-paid asset.

B. accrued expense.

C. pre-paid expense.

1. (QID 139) The general ledger contains:

***A. the same entries as the general journal, but in a different order.**

B. the initial entries of transactions from which the general journal entries are derived.

C. the same entries as the general journal plus accruals and other adjustments made at the end of accounting periods.

Explanation: LOS: Reading 29-g

The general ledger contains all the same entries as the general journal but they are stored by account, as opposed to by date in the general journal. The general journal, not the general ledger, is the first step in the accounting system flow.

**Reference:** CFA® Program Curriculum, Volume 3, pp. 66-67.

---

2. (QID 140) If a manager is attempting to hide an expenditure for which he has paid cash he might record a fictitious:

***A. pre-paid asset.**

B. accrued expense.

C. pre-paid expense.

Explanation: LOS: Reading 30-h

To keep the accounts in balance the reduction in cash could be balanced by a pre-paid asset in the accounts. This would avoid recording an expense in the accounts.

**Reference:** CFA® Program Curriculum, Volume 3, pp. 69-70.

3. (QID 141) An increase in earnings per share on the income statement is least likely to be explained by the firm:

A. reducing its interest costs.

B. increasing the prices of units sold.

C. increasing the number of shares outstanding.

---

4. (QID 142) A printing firm borrows $500,000 from its bank and spends $400,000 on inventory. It places $80,000 on six-month deposit and retains $20,000 in a checking account. The increase in current assets is:

A. $80,000.

B. $100,000

C. $500,000.

3. (QID 141) An increase in earnings per share on the income statement is least likely to be explained by the firm:

A. reducing its interest costs.

B. increasing the prices of units sold.

***C. increasing the number of shares outstanding.**

Explanation: LOS: Reading 29-b

Reducing interest costs, or increasing revenue through price increases will tend to increase profits and therefore earnings per share. Increasing the number of shares outstanding may reduce earnings per share unless the cash raised from the increase in shares is used to increase profits by a greater percentage.

**Reference:** CFA® Program Curriculum, Volume 3, pp. 11-13.

---

4. (QID 142) A printing firm borrows $500,000 from its bank and spends $400,000 on inventory. It places $80,000 on six-month deposit and retains $20,000 in a checking account. The increase in current assets is:

A. $80,000.

B. $100,000

***C. $500,000.**

Explanation: LOS: Reading 30-d

Current assets include cash, cash equivalents (which will become cash in a year or less) and inventory, so the current assets will increase by $500,000.

**Reference:** CFA® Program Curriculum, Volume 3, pp. 44-63.

5. (QID 143) Which of the following statements regarding the cash flow statement is least accurate?

A. The cash flow statement provides information on the sources and use of cash.

B. Firms are required to provide a reconciliation between cash flow and income statement items.

C. The total cash flow in a year is equal to the change in cash and cash equivalents recorded in the beginning and end-year balance sheets.

6. (QID 144) The balance sheet is least likely to be used for information on a firm's:

A. liquidity.

B. profitability.

C. owners' equity.

5. (QID 143) Which of the following statements regarding the cash flow statement is least accurate?

A. The cash flow statement provides information on the sources and use of cash.

***B. Firms are required to provide a reconciliation between cash flow and income statement items.**

C. The total cash flow in a year is equal to the change in cash and cash equivalents recorded in the beginning and end-year balance sheets.

Explanation: LOS: Reading 29-b

An analyst can reconcile items on the cash flow statement against income statement and balance sheet items, but a firm is not required to provide the reconciliation.

**Reference:** CFA® Program Curriculum, Volume 3, pp. 15-17.

---

6. (QID 144) The balance sheet is least likely to be used for information on a firm's:

A. liquidity.

***B. profitability.**

C. owners' equity.

Explanation: LOS: Reading 29-b

The balance sheet contains information on a firm's ability to meet its short-term and total obligations (liquidity and solvency respectively). It also reports the total value of assets and liabilities, the difference is owners' equity. Profitability is usually measured using the income statement.

**Reference:** CFA® Program Curriculum, Volume 3, pp. 13-15.

7. (QID 145) Which of the following is a requirement of presentation under International Financial Reporting Standards (IFRS)?

A. Assets and liabilities for related items should be offset against each other.

B. Current and noncurrent assets should normally be combined unless an IFRS requires other wise.

C. The previous year's data should normally be provided for items in the financial statements.

---

8. (QID 146) Ahead of a major expansion program a firm raises an additional $600 million from an issue of new common stock. It also raises $500 million from the issue of long-term bonds. The profit made by the company in the same year was $20 million and it paid out dividends of $8 million. This will lead to an overall increase in stockholders' equity over the year of:

A. $612 million.

B. $620 million.

C. $1,112 million.

7. (QID 145) Which of the following is a requirement of presentation under International Financial Reporting Standards (IFRS)?

A. Assets and liabilities for related items should be offset against each other.

B. Current and noncurrent assets should normally be combined unless an IFRS requires other wise.

***C. The previous year's data should normally be provided for items in the financial statements.**

Explanation: LOS: Reading 31-f

Assets and liabilities cannot be offset against each other unless permitted or required by IFRS. Current and noncurrent assets should normally be separated. Comparative data should be provided for the previous year for items in the financial statements so "The previous year's data" is correct.

**Reference:** CFA® Program Curriculum, Volume 3, pp. 111-112.

---

8. (QID 146) Ahead of a major expansion program a firm raises an additional $600 million from an issue of new common stock. It also raises $500 million from the issue of long-term bonds. The profit made by the company in the same year was $20 million and it paid out dividends of $8 million. This will lead to an overall increase in stockholders' equity over the year of:

***A. $612 million.**

B. $620 million.

C. $1,112 million.

Explanation: LOS: Reading 30-d

Retained profits will increase by $20 million, less dividends paid of $8 million, which equals $12 million. This, plus the increase in paid-up equity of $600 million, will be the increase in stockholders' equity. The bond issue will increase liabilities but not stockholders' equity.

**Reference:** CFA® Program Curriculum, Volume 3, pp. 38-44.

9. (QID 147) A manufacturing company borrows short-term from a bank to purchase inventory, and also receives interest on a long-term bond investment. These are likely to be classified as which types of activity?

| Borrows from bank | Interest on bond |
|---|---|
| A. Operating | Financing |
| B. Operating | Investing |
| C. Financing | Financing |

---

10. (QID 148) The following information is provided on a company

| | |
|---|---|
| Retained earnings at end of year | $1,450 million |
| Retained earnings at beginning of year | $1,325 million |
| Contributed capital at end of year | $1,250 million |
| Total assets at end of year | $3,750 million |
| Dividends paid over year | $75 million |

Total liabilities at end of year are:

A. $975 million.

B. $1,050 million.

C. $1,175 million.

9. (QID 147) A manufacturing company borrows short-term from a bank to purchase inventory, and also receives interest on a long-term bond investment. These are likely to be classified as which types of activity?

| Borrows from bank | Interest on bond |
|---|---|
| A. Operating | Financing |
| ***B. Operating** | **Investing** |
| C. Financing | Financing |

Explanation: LOS: Reading 30-a

Short-term borrowing to finance operating activities would usually be classified as an operating activity. Interest received on a bond, where holding bond investments is not the main business of the company, would be classified as an investing activity.

**Reference:** CFA® Program Curriculum, Volume 3, pp. 34-35.

---

10. (QID 148) The following information is provided on a company

| | |
|---|---|
| Retained earnings at end of year | $1,450 million |
| Retained earnings at beginning of year | $1,325 million |
| Contributed capital at end of year | $1,250 million |
| Total assets at end of year | $3,750 million |
| Dividends paid over year | $75 million |

Total liabilities at end of year are:

A. $975 million.

***B. $1,050 million.**

C. $1,175 million.

Explanation: LOS: Reading 30-c

Liabilities = Assets – Owners' Equity

= $3,750 million – ($1,450 million + $1,250 million) = $1,050 million

**Reference:** CFA® Program Curriculum, Volume 3, pp. 38-41.

11. (QID 149) Which of the following is most likely to be classified as a financing activity?

A. Repurchase of own stock.

B. Receipt of dividends from an investment.

C. Giving credit to a customer.

12. (QID 150) Under International Accounting Standards (IAS) which of the following is not required to be included in the financial statements:

A. an internal audit report.

B. a statement of changes in stockholders' equity.

C. notes of significant accounting policies.

11. (QID 149) Which of the following is most likely to be classified as a financing activity?

***A. Repurchase of own stock.**

B. Receipt of dividends from an investment.

C. Giving credit to a customer.

Explanation: LOS: Reading 30-a

Financing activities relate to issuing or repaying capital, so repurchase of its own stock would be classified as a financing activity.

Reference CFA® Program Curriculum, Volume 3, pp. 34-35.

---

12. (QID 150) Under International Accounting Standards (IAS) which of the following is not required to be included in the financial statements:

***A. an internal audit report.**

B. a statement of changes in stockholders' equity.

C. notes of significant accounting policies.

Explanation: LOS: Reading 31-d

The required information includes

" a balance sheet

" an income statement

" a statement of changes in equity

" a cash flow statement

" notes of significant accounting policies and other explanatory notes

The report from the external, rather than internal, auditor would normally be included.

**Reference:** CFA® Program Curriculum, Volume 3, p. 110.

13. (QID 151) Which of the following is least likely to be identified as a main objective of the International Organization of Securities Commissions (IOSCO)?

A. Protecting investors.

B. Reducing systematic risk.

C. Ensuring harmonization of accounting standards globally.

---

14. (QID 152) The following information is provided on a company:

| | |
|---|---|
| Retained earnings at beginning of year | $220 million |
| Estimated income for year | $35 million |
| Estimated revenue for year | $345 million |
| Repurchase of stock over year | $60 million |
| Estimated dividends paid over year | $20 million |

The estimated retained earnings at end of year are:

A. $155 million.

B. $215 million.

C. $255 million.

13. (QID 151) Which of the following is least likely to be identified as a main objective of the International Organization of Securities Commissions (IOSCO)?

A. Protecting investors.

B. Reducing systematic risk.

***C. Ensuring harmonization of accounting standards globally.**

Explanation: LOS: Reading 31-b

Note: One of the choices describe the three core objectives of IOSCO, the other is reducing systematic risk.

Although IOSCO assists in achieving harmonization of accounting standards it is not a core objective.

**Reference:** CFA® Program Curriculum, Volume 3, pp. 97-98.

---

14. (QID 152) The following information is provided on a company:

| | |
|---|---|
| Retained earnings at beginning of year | $220 million |
| Estimated income for year | $35 million |
| Estimated revenue for year | $345 million |
| Repurchase of stock over year | $60 million |
| Estimated dividends paid over year | $20 million |

The estimated retained earnings at end of year are:

A. $155 million.

***B. $215 million.**

C. $255 million.

Explanation: LOS: Reading 30-c

Estimated retained earnings at end of year

= retained earnings at beginning of year + net income – dividends paid

= $220 million + $35 million - $20 million = £215 million

The repurchase of stock affects paid-up equity rather than retained earnings.

**Reference:** CFA® Program Curriculum, Volume 3, pp. 38-44.

15. (QID 153) When a company has recognized revenue in the financial statements but has not billed the customer or received payment from the customer this gives rise to:

| Revenue | Asset/liability |
|---|---|
| A. accrued revenue | asset |
| B. deferred revenue | liability |
| C. deferred revenue | asset |

16. (QID 154) The International Accounting Standards Board (IASB) was established in order to

A. harmonize accounting standards worldwide.

B. review disclosure standards for publicly owned companies.

C. provide an alternative set of accounting standards to U.S. GAAP.

15. (QID 153) When a company has recognized revenue in the financial statements but has not billed the customer or received payment from the customer this gives rise to:

| Revenue | Asset/liability |
|---|---|
| ***A. accrued revenue** | **asset** |
| B. deferred revenue | liability |
| C. deferred revenue | asset |

Explanation: LOS: Reading 30-e

When a company has recognized revenue in the financial statements but has not billed the customer or received cash this gives rise to unbilled or accrued revenue which is an asset.

**Reference:** CFA® Program Curriculum, Volume 3, pp. 63-66.

---

16. (QID 154) The International Accounting Standards Board (IASB) was established in order to

***A. harmonize accounting standards worldwide.**

B. review disclosure standards for publicly owned companies.

C. provide an alternative set of accounting standards to U.S. GAAP.

Explanation: LOS: Reading 31-b

The IASB was set up to coordinate the accounting standards followed by companies worldwide.

**Reference:** CFA® Program Curriculum, Volume 3, p. 97.

17. (QID 155) Company ABC purchases 100,000 units of inventory at a total cost of $500,000. It pays a deposit of 10% of the cost; the remainder of the cost will be paid in 20 days' time. As a result of this transaction assets will increase by:

A. $500,000.

B. $450,000.

C. $50,000.

---

18. (QID 156) The method by which a company calculates depreciation is usually described in its:

A. balance sheet.

B. auditor's report.

C. notes to the financial statements.

17. (QID 155) Company ABC purchases 100,000 units of inventory at a total cost of $500,000. It pays a deposit of 10% of the cost; the remainder of the cost will be paid in 20 days' time. As a result of this transaction assets will increase by:

A. $500,000.

***B. $450,000.**

C. $50,000.

Explanation: LOS: Reading 30-d

The accounting entries will be an increase in inventory of $500,00 and a reduction in cash of $50,000, so a net increase in assets of $450,000. Accounts payable, a liability, will increase by the same amount, $450,000.

**Reference:** CFA® Program Curriculum, Volume 3, pp. 48-56.

---

18. (QID 156) The method by which a company calculates depreciation is usually described in its:

A. balance sheet.

B. auditor's report.

***C. notes to the financial statements.**

Explanation: LOS: Reading 29-c

A company's accounting policies, including how depreciation is calculated, would usually be included in the notes to the financial statements.

Reference CFA® Program Curriculum, Volume 3, pp. 17-18.

19. (QID 157) A travel company records deferred revenue on its balance sheet. This might be explained by:

A. customers are paying in cash for holidays before they travel.

B. the company is recording revenue before the customers have committed to purchase holidays through the company.

C. customers are committing to purchase holidays before the revenue is recorded in the accounts.

---

20. (QID 158) The basis of accounting that allocates cash flows to time periods which are different to when they occur is called:

A. cash basis.

B. accrual basis.

C. matching basis.

19. (QID 157) A travel company records deferred revenue on its balance sheet. This might be explained by:

***A. customers are paying in cash for holidays before they travel.**

B. the company is recording revenue before the customers have committed to purchase holidays through the company.

C. customers are committing to purchase holidays before the revenue is recorded in the accounts.

Explanation: LOS: Reading 30-e

Deferred revenue is unearned revenue, when companies receive cash before they earn the related revenue. This is a liability on the balance sheet.

**Reference:** CFA® Program Curriculum, Volume 3, pp. 63-66.

---

20. (QID 158) The basis of accounting that allocates cash flows to time periods which are different to when they occur is called:

A. cash basis.

***B. accrual basis.**

C. matching basis.

Explanation: LOS: Reading 30-e

Under the cash basis a firm recognizes revenues when they are received and expenses when they are paid. Under the accrual basis it recognizes revenue when it provides substantially all of the services that it expects to perform and under the matching principle expenses are recognized in the same period as the related revenues.

**Reference:** CFA® Program Curriculum, Volume 3, pp. 63-66.

21. (QID 159) Equity valuation is usually part of which step in the financial analysis framework?

A. Follow-up.

B. Processing the data.

C. Analysis of the processed data.

22. (QID 160) The role of the International Accounting Standards Board (IASB) is most accurately described as:

A. ensuring that differences between tax and financial statement accounting standards are minimized.

B. providing accounting standards which can form a solid base for harmonization of accounting practices.

C. ensuring that countries that adopt International Financial Reporting Standards (IFRS) comply with the standards.

21. (QID 159) Equity valuation is usually part of which step in the financial analysis framework?

A. Follow-up.

***B. Processing the data.**

C. Analysis of the processed data.

Explanation: LOS: Reading 29-f

Processing the data about a company includes computing ratios, and performing a valuation of a company's equity.

**Reference:** CFA® Program Curriculum, Volume 3, pp. 24-28.

---

22. (QID 160) The role of the International Accounting Standards Board (IASB) is most accurately described as:

A. ensuring that differences between tax and financial statement accounting standards are minimized.

***B. providing accounting standards which can form a solid base for harmonization of accounting practices.**

C. ensuring that countries that adopt International Financial Reporting Standards (IFRS) comply with the standards.

Explanation: LOS: Reading 31-b

The IASB is not a regulatory body but aims to establish a comprehensive, generally accepted basis of accounting that can be adopted across different countries as part of the harmonization process.

**Reference:** CFA® Program Curriculum, Volume 3, p. 99.

23. (QID 161) When a company has incurred salary costs that have not been paid by the end of the accounting period this gives rise to:

| Expense | Asset/liability |
|---|---|
| A. accrued expense | asset |
| B. accrued expense | liability |
| C. deferred expense | asset |

24. (QID 193) The Statement of Changes in Owners' Equity would be least likely to include information on:

A. net assets.

B. net income.

C. dividends distributed.

25. (QID 194) Accruals appear in financial statements when:

A. a company uses a cash-based accounting method.

B. there is uncertainty whether revenue is going to be realized or an expense paid.

C. there is a difference between the timing of cash movements and the recognition of a revenue or expense.

23. (QID 161) When a company has incurred salary costs that have not been paid by the end of the accounting period this gives rise to:

| Expense | Asset/liability |
|---|---|
| A. accrued expense | asset |
| ***B. accrued expense** | **liability** |
| C. deferred expense | asset |

Explanation: LOS: Reading 30-e

This is an example of an expense which has been incurred but not yet paid, this is an accrued expense and a liability since it must be paid in the future.

**Reference:** CFA® Program Curriculum, Volume 3, pp. 65-68.

---

24. (QID 193) The Statement of Changes in Owners' Equity would be least likely to include information on:

***A. net assets.**

B. net income.

C. dividends distributed.

Explanation: LOS: Reading 29-b

The Statement of Changes in Owners' Equity contains information on the composition and changes in owners' equity over the reporting period. This would include information on new shares issued and retained income. It would not explicitly include information on net assets; this would be in the balance sheet.

**Reference:** CFA® Program Curriculum, Volume 3, p. 17.

25. (QID 194) Accruals appear in financial statements when:

A. a company uses a cash-based accounting method.

B. there is uncertainty whether revenue is going to be realized or an expense paid.

***C. there is a difference between the timing of cash movements and the recognition of a revenue or expense.**

Explanation: LOS: Reading 30-e

Accrual accounting requires that revenue is recognized when it is earned and expenses when they are incurred. This may be before or after the cash is received or paid which gives rise to accrual entries.

**Reference:** CFA® Program Curriculum, Volume 3, pp. 63-65.

# Study Session 08: Financial Reporting and Analysis:

## The Income Statement, Balance Sheet, and Cash Flow Statement

Each reading in this study session focuses on one of the three major financial statements: the balance sheet, the income statement, and the statement of cash flows. For each financial statement, the chapter details its purpose, construction, pertinent ratios, and common-size analysis. Understanding these concepts allows a financial analyst to evaluate trends in performance over several measurement periods and to compare the performance of different companies over the same period(s). Additional analyst tools such as the earnings per share calculation are also described.

**Reading 32: Understanding the Income Statement**

**Reading 33: Understanding the Balance Sheet**

**Reading 34: Understanding the Cash Flow Statement**

1. (QID 162) A firm decides to use the completed contract method as opposed to the percentage-of-completion method to account for a major construction project that it is working on. Until the contract is completed this will have the following impact on its financial statements:

A. increase revenues.

B. reduce cash flows.

C. reduce stockholders' equity.

---

2. (QID 163) A U.S. firm must reflect the effects of conversion of an outstanding convertible on earnings per share:

A. in all cases.

B. only if the conversion leads to dilution of earnings per share.

C. only if the combined effect of conversion of all common stock equivalents outstanding leads to dilution of earnings per share.

1. (QID 162) A firm decides to use the completed contract method as opposed to the percentage-of-completion method to account for a major construction project that it is working on. Until the contract is completed this will have the following impact on its financial statements:

A. increase revenues.

B. reduce cash flows.

***C. reduce stockholders' equity.**

Explanation: LOS: Reading 32-b

Under the completed contract method the firm recognizes revenues and expenses only at the end of the contract, which reduces stockholders' equity. The percentage-of-completion method recognizes revenues, costs and income in proportion to the percentage of work completed. Cash flow under both methods will be the same.

**Reference:** CFA® Program Curriculum, Volume 3, pp. 142-146.

---

2. (QID 163) A U.S. firm must reflect the effects of conversion of an outstanding convertible on earnings per share:

A. in all cases.

***B. only if the conversion leads to dilution of earnings per share.**

C. only if the combined effect of conversion of all common stock equivalents outstanding leads to dilution of earnings per share.

Explanation: LOS: Reading 32-i

Firms must recognize the potential effects of conversion on earnings per share and each outstanding common stock equivalent must be considered separately to see if it is dilutive or antidilutive.

**Reference:** CFA® Program Curriculum, Volume 3, pp. 166-174.

3. (QID 164) A common-size income statement:

   A. calculates all entries as a percentage of sales.

   B. calculates all entries as a percentage of net income.

   C. is an income statement that has been restated to use the same accounting principles as it has used in previous years.

4. (QID 165) Which of the following will lead to the largest increase in cash flow from operations?

   A. A decrease in accounts receivable and a decrease in inventories.

   B. An increase in accounts receivable and a decrease in inventories.

   C. A decrease in accounts receivable and an increase in inventories.

3. (QID 164) A common-size income statement:

***A. calculates all entries as a percentage of sales.**

B. calculates all entries as a percentage of net income.

C. is an income statement that has been restated to use the same accounting principles as it has used in previous years.

Explanation: LOS: Reading 32-j

Common-size statements normalize balance sheets, income statements and cash flow statements and are used to analyze trends within a company and also to compare different sized companies. Common-size income statements calculate all entries as a percentage of sales.

**Reference:** CFA® Program Curriculum, Volume 3, pp. 174-177.

---

4. (QID 165) Which of the following will lead to the largest increase in cash flow from operations?

***A. A decrease in accounts receivable and a decrease in inventories.**

B. An increase in accounts receivable and a decrease in inventories.

C. A decrease in accounts receivable and an increase in inventories.

Explanation: LOS: Reading 34-f

A decrease in accounts receivable means that the amount owing from customers has declined, and a decrease in inventories means that additional inventory has been sold.

**Reference:** CFA® Program Curriculum, Volume 3, pp. 257-263.

5. (QID 166) An online travel company sells discounted hotel rooms to customers on behalf of major hotel chains. Once a sale has been completed the hotel chain bears the contractual obligation to provide the room described to the customer. The travel company reports the value of the rooms sold as revenue and the cost of purchasing accommodation from the hotels as a cost of goods sold. Under U.S. GAAP:

A. net reporting is more appropriate since the hotel chains are primary obligors under the contracts.

B. gross reporting is preferred since it gives a better indication of the volume of business being conducted by the company.

C. net reporting should always be used when the pricing is being controlled by another party, in this case the hotel chains.

---

6. (QID 167) Free cash flow to the firm is:

A. cash flow from operations plus cash flow from investments.

B. cash available to providers of a firm's capital after making all the required cash outlays.

C. cash available to providers of a firm's capital after making all the required and discretionary cash outlays.

5. (QID 166) An online travel company sells discounted hotel rooms to customers on behalf of major hotel chains. Once a sale has been completed the hotel chain bears the contractual obligation to provide the room described to the customer. The travel company reports the value of the rooms sold as revenue and the cost of purchasing accommodation from the hotels as a cost of goods sold. Under U.S. GAAP:

***A. net reporting is more appropriate since the hotel chains are primary obligors under the contracts.**

B. gross reporting is preferred since it gives a better indication of the volume of business being conducted by the company.

C. net reporting should always be used when the pricing is being controlled by another party, in this case the hotel chains.

Explanation: LOS: Reading 32-b

Under U.S. GAAP gross revenues should be reported by the travel company only after taking into consideration whether the travel company is the main obligor under the contract, bears inventory risk and credit risk, can choose supplier and price. In this case the company is acting as agent, it does not hold inventory and is not the main obligor under the contract so net reporting is appropriate.

**Reference:** CFA® Program Curriculum, Volume 3, pp. 148-150.

---

6. (QID 167) Free cash flow to the firm is:

A. cash flow from operations plus cash flow from investments.

***B. cash available to providers of a firm's capital after making all the required cash outlays.**

C. cash available to providers of a firm's capital after making all the required and discretionary cash outlays.

Explanation: LOS: Reading 34-i

Free cash flow is cash flow that is available for discretionary spending after making all the required cash outlays. Free cash flow to firm is available to pay all providers of capital.

**Reference:** CFA® Program Curriculum, Volume 3, pp. 279-280.

7. (QID 168) A company that is going through a rapid growth phase often has:

A. positive operating cash flows as cash collections increase.

B. negative operating cash flows as inventories and receivables increase.

C. negative operating cash flows since it has heavy capital expenditure commitments.

8. (QID 169) A company uses IAS GAAP for their cash flow classification for interest and dividend payments and receipts. Which of the following statements is most accurate?

A. Total cash flows will be lower than if the company had used U.S. GAAP.

B. The company's cash flow from financing may be lower than if the company had used U.S. GAAP.

C. The company's cash flow from investing may be lower than if the company had used U.S. GAAP.

7. (QID 168) A company that is going through a rapid growth phase often has:

A. positive operating cash flows as cash collections increase.

***B. negative operating cash flows as inventories and receivables increase.**

C. negative operating cash flows since it has heavy capital expenditure commitments.

Explanation: LOS: Reading 34-a

The major impact of heavy capital expenditure would be on investing cash flows, although the interest cost would affect operating cash flows. The major impact on operating cash flows is that as the business expands the money tied up in working capital rises. This is because inventory levels expand as sales increase and the receivables from clients are also likely to increase.

**Reference:** CFA® Program Curriculum, Volume 3, pp. 247-255.

---

8. (QID 169) A company uses IAS GAAP for their cash flow classification for interest and dividend payments and receipts. Which of the following statements is most accurate?

A. Total cash flows will be lower than if the company had used U.S. GAAP.

***B. The company's cash flow from financing may be lower than if the company had used U.S. GAAP.**

C. The company's cash flow from investing may be lower than if the company had used U.S. GAAP.

Explanation: LOS: Reading 34-c

Interest and dividends paid may have been classified as cash flow from financing (CFF), thereby reducing CFF.

Interest and dividends received could have been classified as cash flow from investing so "The company's cash flow from financing" is not correct.

**Reference:** CFA® Program Curriculum, Volume 3, pp. 246-247.

9. (QID 170) On January 1st 2008 a company had 15,000,000 of common stock and $3,000,000 of 8% preferred stock outstanding. On October 1st the company issued and sold 5,000,000 new shares of common stock. The company did not have any common stock equivalents outstanding. If net income for the year was $23,000,000, the company's basic earnings per share in 2007 were closest to:

A. $1.14.

B. $1.40.

C. $1.42.

---

10. (QID 171) The balance sheet is useful because it:

A. reports all of the assets and liabilities of a firm.

B. provides information to creditors on assets that are available as collateral for debt.

C. is less influenced by the choice of accounting policies than the income statement or statement of cash flows.

9. (QID 170) On January 1st 2008 a company had 15,000,000 of common stock and $3,000,000 of 8% preferred stock outstanding. On October 1st the company issued and sold 5,000,000 new shares of common stock. The company did not have any common stock equivalents outstanding. If net income for the year was $23,000,000, the company's basic earnings per share in 2007 were closest to:

A. $1.14.

***B. $1.40.**

C. $1.42.

Explanation: LOS: Reading 32-h

$$\text{earnings per share} = \frac{\text{net income} - \text{preferred dividends}}{\text{weighted average number of shares outstanding}}$$

$$= \frac{\$23{,}000{,}000 - \$240{,}000}{16{,}250{,}000} = \$1.40$$

**Reference:** CFA® Program Curriculum, Volume 3, pp. 166-168.

---

10. (QID 171) The balance sheet is useful because it:

A. reports all of the assets and liabilities of a firm.

***B. provides information to creditors on assets that are available as collateral for debt.**

C. is less influenced by the choice of accounting policies than the income statement or statement of cash flows.

Explanation: LOS: Reading 33-a

The balance sheet is not correct since, for example, brand names and customer lists, if internally generated, will not be included.

A report of the market value is not correct since, for example, assets may be priced at cost or adjusted for depreciation and the value does not reflect market value.

Choice of accounting policies is not correct since the statement of cash flows is generally least affected by the choice of accounting policies.

**Reference:** CFA® Program Curriculum, Volume 3, pp. 190-195.

11. (QID 172) Which of the following is least likely to be a condition for recognizing revenue for the sale of a good according to the principles set out by the International Accounting Standards Board (IASB)?

A. The buyer has paid for the goods.

B. The buyer has taken on the risks associated with ownership of the good.

C. The costs incurred as a result of the transaction are decided.

---

12. (QID 173) Under IFRS and U.S. GAAP when an acquirer has purchased another company giving rise to goodwill being recorded, should the goodwill then be amortized or tested for impairment?

| IFRS | U.S. GAAP |
|---|---|
| A. impairment | impairment |
| B. impairment | amortization |
| C. amortization | impairment |

11. (QID 172) Which of the following is least likely to be a condition for recognizing revenue for the sale of a good according to the principles set out by the International Accounting Standards Board (IASB)?

***A. The buyer has paid for the goods.**

B. The buyer has taken on the risks associated with ownership of the good.

C. The costs incurred as a result of the transaction are decided.

Explanation: LOS: Reading 32-b

Revenue is recognized when the following conditions are satisfied:

" the seller has transferred to the buyer the significant risks and rewards of ownership

" managerial involvement and effective control of the goods has been transferred

" the revenue can be reliably measured

" it is probable the economic proceeds of the transaction will pass to the seller

" the costs associated with the transactions can be reliably estimated.

These can all occur independently of cash changing hands.

**Reference:** CFA® Program Curriculum, Volume 3, pp. 140-141.

---

12. (QID 173) Under IFRS and U.S. GAAP when an acquirer has purchased another company giving rise to goodwill being recorded, should the goodwill then be amortized or tested for impairment?

| | IFRS | U.S. GAAP |
|---|---|---|
| ***A.** | **impairment** | **impairment** |
| B. | impairment | amortization |
| C. | amortization | impairment |

Explanation: LOS: Reading 33-e

Under both IFRS and U.S. GAAP goodwill should be checked for impairment annually. If the goodwill number overstates its economic value (usually in terms of future cash flows generated) then it is impaired (recognized as a noncash expense). Amortization is no longer permitted.

**Reference:** CFA® Program Curriculum, Volume 3, pp. 215-217.

13. (QID 174) Which of the following is an example of a complex capital structure?

A. The company has preferred shares outstanding.

B. The company has issued options to employees.

C. The company has performed a stock split in the current accounting period.

---

14. (QID 175) When available-for-sale securities are held by a firm, an unrealized gain is:

| | Income statement | Balance sheet |
|---|---|---|
| A. | recognized | recognized |
| B. | recognized | not recognized |
| C. | not recognized | recognized |

13. (QID 174) Which of the following is an example of a complex capital structure?

A. The company has preferred shares outstanding.

***B. The company has issued options to employees.**

C. The company has performed a stock split in the current accounting period.

Explanation: LOS: Reading 32-h

A complex capital structure means that dilutive securities such as options, warrants or convertibles are outstanding.

**Reference:** CFA® Program Curriculum, Volume 3, pp. 165-166.

---

14. (QID 175) When available-for-sale securities are held by a firm, an unrealized gain is:

| Income statement | Balance sheet |
|---|---|
| A. recognized | recognized |
| B. recognized | not recognized |
| ***C. not recognized** | **recognized** |

Explanation: LOS: Reading 33-c

The unrealized gain is not recognized on the income statement, but is deferred as a valuation gain in stockholders' equity, reported in comprehensive income.

**Reference:** CFA® Program Curriculum, Volume 3, pp. 217-219.

15. (QID 176) Which of the following statements is least accurate regarding Treasury stock? The purchase of Treasury stock:

A. reduces stockholders' equity.

B. is antidilutive, and leads to an increase in earnings per share.

C. reduces the cash paid out in dividends since there are fewer shares outstanding.

---

16. (QID 177) A company had 60,000 shares outstanding on January 1st and issues a 50% stock dividend on June 30th. The weighted average number of shares outstanding over the years ending December 31st is:

A. 75,000.

B. 90,000.

C. 120,000.

15. (QID 176) Which of the following statements is least accurate regarding Treasury stock? The purchase of Treasury stock:

A. reduces stockholders' equity.

***B. is antidilutive, and leads to an increase in earnings per share.**

C. reduces the cash paid out in dividends since there are fewer shares outstanding.

Explanation: LOS: Reading 33-h

When a company buys back its own stock it is referred to as Treasury stock. This will reduce cash and stockholders' equity as it is a reduction in the number of shares outstanding. Treasury stock does not receive dividends and is not included in the number of shares in an earnings per share calculation, so "is antidilutive, and leads to an increase in earnings per share" is the best choice.

**Reference:** CFA® Program Curriculum, Volume 3, p. 220-226.

---

16. (QID 177) A company had 60,000 shares outstanding on January 1st and issues a 50% stock dividend on June 30th. The weighted average number of shares outstanding over the years ending December 31st is:

A. 75,000.

***B. 90,000.**

C. 120,000.

Explanation: LOS: Reading 32-h

30,000 additional shares will be issued. Since the shares are given to existing shareholders and no cash is paid the shares outstanding are adjusted for the complete year.

**Reference:** CFA® Program Curriculum, Volume 3, pp. 166-168.

17. (QID 178) Using different revenue and expense recognition methods will have no impact on the:

A. reported income statement.

B. reported operating cash flow.

C. assets and liabilities reported in the balance sheet.

---

18. (QID 179) If a firm's accounts receivable increase and accounts payable decrease then it will have a:

A. positive impact on operating cash flow as customers owe a smaller amount of money to the firm and the firm owes more money to suppliers than in the previous accounting period.

B. negative impact on operating cash flow as customers owe a larger amount of money to the firm and the firm owes less money to suppliers than in the previous accounting period.

C. negative impact on operating cash flow as customers owe a smaller amount of money to the firm and the firm owes more money to suppliers than in the previous accounting period.

17. (QID 178) Using different revenue and expense recognition methods will have no impact on the:

A. reported income statement.

***B. reported operating cash flow.**

C. assets and liabilities reported in the balance sheet.

Explanation: LOS: Reading 34-e

The income statement and balance sheet will be different depending on which revenue recognition method is used. The advantage of looking at cash flow is that the cash flow is the same regardless of the method used (assuming tax treatment is the same).

**Reference:** CFA® Program Curriculum, Volume 3, pp. 271-285.

---

18. (QID 179) If a firm's accounts receivable increase and accounts payable decrease then it will have a:

A. positive impact on operating cash flow as customers owe a smaller amount of money to the firm and the firm owes more money to suppliers than in the previous accounting period.

***B. negative impact on operating cash flow as customers owe a larger amount of money to the firm and the firm owes less money to suppliers than in the previous accounting period.**

C. negative impact on operating cash flow as customers owe a smaller amount of money to the firm and the firm owes more money to suppliers than in the previous accounting period.

Explanation: LOS: Reading 34-a

When receivables increase it indicates that sales have been higher than cash collections, so more money is owed by customers. A decline in payables means that the firm has paid more in cash to suppliers than the value of goods received so it owes less money to suppliers. Both of these factors will lead to a smaller operating cash flow.

**Reference:** CFA® Program Curriculum, Volume 3, pp. 257-263.

19. (QID 180) The gross profit margin of a company has increased steadily, this could be explained by a:

A. decline in interest expense as a percentage of sales.

B. decline in raw material costs as a percentage of sales.

C. decline in sales, general and administrative expense as a percentage of sales.

---

20. (QID 181) Which of the following would be least likely to be included in comprehensive income?

A. Purchase of Treasury stock.

B. Pension liability adjustment.

C. Unrealized gains on securities.

19. (QID 180) The gross profit margin of a company has increased steadily, this could be explained by a:

A. decline in interest expense as a percentage of sales.

***B. decline in raw material costs as a percentage of sales.**

C. decline in sales, general and administrative expense as a percentage of sales.

Explanation: LOS: Reading 32-j

Gross profit is sales minus cost of goods sold and therefore would be a decline in raw material costs

Gross Profit would not be affected the other choices.

**Reference:** CFA® Program Curriculum, Volume 3, pp. 178-179.

---

20. (QID 181) Which of the following would be least likely to be included in comprehensive income?

***A. Purchase of Treasury stock.**

B. Pension liability adjustment.

C. Unrealized gains on securities.

Explanation: LOS: Reading 33-h

Comprehensive income is net income plus all other changes in stockholders' equity resulting from transactions with non-business owners. Therefore the purchase of Treasury stock would not be in comprehensive income, although it reduces stockholders' equity.

**Reference:** CFA® Program Curriculum, Volume 3, pp. 220-224.

21. (QID 182) If a company declares a total dividend of $6 million and increases dividend payables by $4 million in an accounting period, under U.S. GAAP, it will:

A. increase the investing cash flow by $4 million.

B. decrease the investing cash flow by $2 million.

C. decrease the financing cash flow by $2 million.

---

22. (QID 183) The treasury stock method for calculating diluted earnings per share assumes that:

A. any dilutive securities held by the firm's treasury can be excluded from the diluted earnings per share calculation.

B. any convertible bonds outstanding are converted at the beginning of the period and the interest savings are added to the firm's interest income.

C. any options and warrants outstanding are exercised at the beginning of the period and the proceeds used to purchase common stock for the firm's treasury.

21. (QID 182) If a company declares a total dividend of $6 million and increases dividend payables by $4 million in an accounting period, under U.S. GAAP, it will:

A. increase the investing cash flow by $4 million.

B. decrease the investing cash flow by $2 million.

***C. decrease the financing cash flow by $2 million.**

Explanation: LOS: Reading 34-a

Payment of dividends is included in financing cash flows. The dividends paid out are $6 million less $4 million which equals $2 million.

Reference CFA® Program Curriculum, Volume 3, pp. 265-266.

---

22. (QID 183) The treasury stock method for calculating diluted earnings per share assumes that:

A. any dilutive securities held by the firm's treasury can be excluded from the diluted earnings per share calculation.

B. any convertible bonds outstanding are converted at the beginning of the period and the interest savings are added to the firm's interest income.

***C. any options and warrants outstanding are exercised at the beginning of the period and the proceeds used to purchase common stock for the firm's treasury.**

Explanation: LOS: Reading 32-h

The treasury stock method is a way of calculating earnings per share using the hypothetical assumption that any options are exercised at the beginning of the period (or date of issue if later) and the company uses the proceeds to repurchase their own stock.

**Reference:** CFA® Program Curriculum, Volume 3, pp. 166-173.

23. (QID 184) If a firm makes a provision for a write down of assets that are going to be sold as part of a restructuring of its operations, this would normally be classified under U.S. GAAP as:

A. an extraordinary item.

B. an unusual or infrequent item.

C. a loss from discontinued operations.

---

24. (QID 223) Jones Construction takes on a new project which it anticipates will take two years to complete. It agrees a total contract price of \$4,000,000 and its expected operating costs are \$3,000,000. In the first year it incurs costs of \$1,800,000 and receives payments of \$2,000,000. If it is using the percentage-of-completion method to recognize revenue then the operating income recorded in the first year will be:

A. \$200,000.

B. \$600,000.

C. \$1,800,000.

---

25. (QID 224) If a firm makes a provision for a write down of assets that are going to be sold as part of a restructuring of its operations, this would normally be classified under U.S. GAAP as:

A. an extraordinary item.

B. an unusual or infrequent item.

C. a loss from discontinued operations.

23. (QID 184) If a firm makes a provision for a write down of assets that are going to be sold as part of a restructuring of its operations, this would normally be classified under U.S. GAAP as:

A. an extraordinary item.

***B. an unusual or infrequent item.**

C. a loss from discontinued operations.

Explanation: LOS: Reading 32-g

Restructuring costs are usually classed as nonrecurring items. Extraordinary items must be both unusual in nature and infrequent in occurrence.

**Reference:** CFA® Program Curriculum, Volume 3, p. 163.

---

24. (QID 223) Jones Construction takes on a new project which it anticipates will take two years to complete. It agrees a total contract price of $4,000,000 and its expected operating costs are $3,000,000. In the first year it incurs costs of $1,800,000 and receives payments of $2,000,000. If it is using the percentage-of-completion method to recognize revenue then the operating income recorded in the first year will be:

A. $200,000.

***B. $600,000.**

C. $1,800,000.

Explanation: LOS: Reading 32-b

The revenue in the first year is:

$1,800,000 x $4,000,000 = $2,400,000

------------

$3,000,000

Costs = $1,800,000

Operating income = $2,400,000 - $1,800,000 = $600,000

**Reference:** CFA® Program Curriculum, Volume 3, pp. 142-146.

25. (QID 224) If a firm makes a provision for a write down of assets that are going to be sold as part of a restructuring of its operations, this would normally be classified under U.S. GAAP as:

A. an extraordinary item.

***B. an unusual or infrequent item.**

C. a loss from discontinued operations.

Explanation: LOS: Reading 32-g

Restructuring costs are usually classed as nonrecurring items. Extraordinary items must be both unusual in nature and infrequent in occurrence.

**Reference:** CFA® Program Curriculum, Volume 3, p. 163.

# Study Session 09: Financial Reporting and Analysis:

## Inventories, Long-Term Assets, Deferred Taxes, and On and Off Balance Sheet Debt

The readings in this study session examine specific categories of assets and liabilities that are particularly susceptible to the impact of alternative accounting policies and estimates. Analysts must understand the effects of alternative policies on financial statements and ratios, and be able to execute appropriate adjustments to enhance comparability between companies. In addition, analysts must be alert to differences between a company's reported financial statements and economic reality.

The description and measurement of inventories require careful attention because the investment in inventories is frequently the largest current asset for merchandizing and manufacturing companies. For these companies, the measurement of inventory cost (i.e., cost of goods sold) is a critical factor in determining gross profit and other measures of company profitability. Long-term operating assets are often the largest category of assets on a company's balance sheet. The analyst needs to scrutinize management's choices with respect to recognizing expenses associated with the operating assets because of the potentially large impact such choices can have on reported earnings.

A company's accounting policies (such as depreciation choices) can cause differences in taxes reported in financial statements and taxes reported on tax returns. The reading "Analysis of Income Taxes" discusses several issues that arise relating to deferred taxes.

Both on- and off-balance-sheet debt affect a company's liquidity and solvency, and have consequences for its long-term growth and viability. The notes of the financial statements must be carefully reviewed to ensure that all potential liabilities (e.g., leasing arrangements and other contractual commitments) are appropriately evaluated for their conformity to economic reality. Adjustments to the financial statements may be required to achieve comparability when evaluating several companies, and may also be required to improve credit and investment decision-making.

**Reading 35: Analysis of Inventories**

**Reading 36: Analysis of Long-Lived Assets:**

**Part I—The Capitalization Decision**

**Reading 37: Analysis of Long-Lived Assets:**

**Part II—Analysis of Depreciation and Impairment**

**Reading 38: Analysis of Income Taxes**

**Reading 39: Analysis of Financing Liabilities**

**Reading 40: Leases and Off-Balance-Sheet Debt**

1. (QID 185) If a firm decides to capitalize rather than expense the cost of assets this will mean:

| Return on assets | Long-term the return on assets |
|---|---|
| A. less volatile | lower |
| B. less volatile | higher |
| C. more volatile | lower |

2. (QID 186) If prices of a product held in inventory are falling the use of LIFO rather than FIFO for inventory accounting will lead to:

| Working capital | Net income |
|---|---|
| A. lower | lower |
| B. lower | higher |
| C. higher | higher |

1. (QID 185) If a firm decides to capitalize rather than expense the cost of assets this will mean:

| Return on assets | Long-term the return on assets |
|---|---|
| ***A. less volatile** | **lower** |
| B. less volatile | higher |
| C. more volatile | lower |

Explanation: LOS: Reading 36-a

Capitalization will lead to higher reported assets that will increase the denominator of return on assets so the return on assets will be lower. Earnings will be less volatile than if assets were expensed. Expensing would lead to larger fluctuations in earnings.

**Reference:** CFA® Program Curriculum, Volume 3, pp. 331-336.

---

2. (QID 186) If prices of a product held in inventory are falling the use of LIFO rather than FIFO for inventory accounting will lead to:

| Working capital | Net income |
|---|---|
| A. lower | lower |
| B. lower | higher |
| ***C. higher** | **higher** |

Explanation: LOS: Reading 35-c

COGS will be lower under LIFO in a period of falling prices leading to higher net income and higher tax payments. Working capital will be higher since the higher inventory value will outweigh the lower cash balance due to higher tax payments.

**Reference:** CFA® Program Curriculum, Volume 3, pp. 295-300.

3. (QID 187) Which of the following statements is least accurate regarding accelerated depreciation methods?

A. I. Accelerated depreciation methods depreciate an asset in proportion to its actual use.

B. II. Accelerated depreciation methods are sometimes used to reduce the tax burden immediately after an asset is purchased.

C. III. Accelerated depreciation methods are appropriate if the benefits from using an asset are highest when it is relatively new.

---

4. (QID 188) Impairment of an asset must be recognized in a firm's accounts when:

A. I. there has been a decrease in the market value of the asset.

B. II. there has been an increase in the replacement cost of the asset.

C. III. the carrying value of the asset is higher than the expected future cash flows from the use of the asset plus its disposal value.

3. (QID 187) Which of the following statements is least accurate regarding accelerated depreciation methods?

***A. I. Accelerated depreciation methods depreciate an asset in proportion to its actual use.**

B. II. Accelerated depreciation methods are sometimes used to reduce the tax burden immediately after an asset is purchased.

C. III. Accelerated depreciation methods are appropriate if the benefits from using an asset are highest when it is relatively new.

Explanation: LOS: Reading 36-d

I. is not correct since the units of production method depreciates assets in proportion to their use, and thus becomes a variable cost.

Accelerated depreciation reduces the value of an asset by the largest amount in the early years regardless of when it is getting the most use.

**Reference:** CFA® Program Curriculum, Volume 3, pp. 347-352.

---

4. (QID 188) Impairment of an asset must be recognized in a firm's accounts when:

A. I. there has been a decrease in the market value of the asset.

B. II. there has been an increase in the replacement cost of the asset.

***C. III. the carrying value of the asset is higher than the expected future cash flows from the use of the asset plus its disposal value.**

Explanation: LOS: Reading 36i

I. does not automatically lead to a write down if the value of the asset can be recovered through future cash flows.

II. is not correct; replacement cost does not impact on the value of an asset in the balance sheet.

**Reference:** CFA® Program Curriculum, Volume 3, pp. 402-406.

5. (QID 189) If a company issues a zero-coupon bond an analyst should:

   A. reduce cash flow from operations.

   B. increase cash flow from investing.

   C. increase cash flow from operations.

---

6. (QID 190) Which inventory accounting method usually gives a valuation of inventory that is closest to its economic value?

   A. FIFO.

   B. LIFO.

   C. Lower of cost or market.

5. (QID 189) If a company issues a zero-coupon bond an analyst should:

***A. reduce cash flow from operations.**

B. increase cash flow from investing.

C. increase cash flow from operations.

Explanation: LOS: Reading 38-A

Cash flow from operations is overstated since the full repayment of maturity value is treated as a financing cash flow whereas it represents interest repayments, which should be classified as an operating cash flow.

**Reference:** CFA® Program Curriculum, Volume 3, pp. 430-433.

---

6. (QID 190) Which inventory accounting method usually gives a valuation of inventory that is closest to its economic value?

***A. FIFO.**

B. LIFO.

C. Lower of cost or market.

Explanation: LOS: Reading 35-b

Since FIFO leaves the most recently purchased goods in inventory the valuation will usually be the closest to current values.

**Reference:** CFA® Program Curriculum, Volume 3, pp. 295-300.

7. (QID 191) Lessors usually prefer to classify leases as finance leases rather than operating leases because:

A. I. they can report larger sales revenue immediately.

B. II. they can report a larger net cash flow immediately.

C. III. over the term of the lease the total net income will be higher.

---

8. (QID 192) Which of the following statements concerning patents in the U.S. is most accurate?

A. I. The value of a patent is constant throughout its life.

B. II. The acquisition costs of buying patents from outside entities can be capitalized.

C. III. Legal costs associated with developing patents internally must be expensed, other costs are capitalized.

7. (QID 191) Lessors usually prefer to classify leases as finance leases rather than operating leases because:

***A. I. they can report larger sales revenue immediately.**

B. II. they can report a larger net cash flow immediately.

C. III. over the term of the lease the total net income will be higher.

Explanation: LOS: Reading 40-b

II. is not correct since operating cash flow is positive but investing cash low is negative by the same amount.

III. is not correct since the total net income would be the same whichever method is used.

**Reference:** CFA® Program Curriculum, Volume 3, pp. 458-464.

---

8. (QID 192) Which of the following statements concerning patents in the U.S. is most accurate?

A. I. The value of a patent is constant throughout its life.

***B. II. The acquisition costs of buying patents from outside entities can be capitalized.**

C. III. Legal costs associated with developing patents internally must be expensed, other costs are capitalized.

Explanation: LOS: Reading 36-f

I. is not correct since patents can often become worthless if competition enters the market or the product becomes out of date.

III. is not correct since costs for internally generated patents should be expensed except for the legal costs, which can be capitalized.

**Reference:** CFA® Program Curriculum, Volume 3, pp. 340-347.

9. (QID 193) A company included amortization of goodwill in its financial statements whereas amortization of goodwill is not recognized as an expense for tax purposes. This leads to the reporting of:

A. a deferred tax asset.

B. a deferred tax liability.

C. neither a deferred tax asset nor a deferred tax liability.

---

10. (QID 194) A company buys a piece of machinery for $50,000 and it estimates the life of the machine to be four years after which it will have a salvage value of $10,000. Using the double-declining-balance method of depreciation the depreciation charge in the third year will be:

A. $2,500.

B. $6,250.

C. $12,500.

9. (QID 193) A company included amortization of goodwill in its financial statements whereas amortization of goodwill is not recognized as an expense for tax purposes. This leads to the reporting of:

A. a deferred tax asset.

B. a deferred tax liability.

***C. neither a deferred tax asset nor a deferred tax liability.**

Explanation: LOS: Reading 37-f

Permanent differences in tax treatment do not give rise to deferred tax items since they will not reverse in the future.

**Reference:** CFA® Program Curriculum, Volume 3, p. 397.

---

10. (QID 194) A company buys a piece of machinery for $50,000 and it estimates the life of the machine to be four years after which it will have a salvage value of $10,000. Using the double-declining-balance method of depreciation the depreciation charge in the third year will be:

***A. $2,500.**

B. $6,250.

C. $12,500.

Explanation: LOS: Reading 36-d

Depreciation expense will be:

Year 1 ½ x ($50,000 ) = $25,000

Year 2 ½ x ($50,000 - $25,000) = $12,500

Year 3 ½ x ($50,000 - $37,500) = $6,250 but this is reduced to $2,500 since the machinery has already reached its salvage value.

**Reference:** CFA® Program Curriculum, Volume 3, pp. 348-352.

11. (QID 195) If a firm decides to capitalize rather than expense the cost of assets this will lead to:

A. lower cash flow from operations.

B. higher cash flow from operations.

C. no impact on cash flow from operations.

12. (QID 196) Which of the following costs related to the acquisition of a long-lived asset must generally be expensed in the U.S?

A. Installation costs.

B. Freight and delivery costs.

C. Related research and development costs.

11. (QID 195) If a firm decides to capitalize rather than expense the cost of assets this will lead to:

A. lower cash flow from operations.

***B. higher cash flow from operations.**

C. no impact on cash flow from operations.

Explanation: LOS: Reading 36-b

Cash flow from operations will be higher since the cost will be recorded in the cash flow from investments.

**Reference:** CFA® Program Curriculum, Volume 3, pp. 331-336..

---

12. (QID 196) Which of the following costs related to the acquisition of a long-lived asset must generally be expensed in the U.S?

A. Installation costs.

B. Freight and delivery costs.

***C. Related research and development costs.**

Explanation: LOS: Reading 36-a

Research and development costs in the U.S. should be treated as an expense when they occur.

**Reference:** CFA® Program Curriculum, Volume 3, pp. 337-341.

13. (QID 197) A firm sells its product on account and allows customers to pay in installments over future time periods. In the financial reports it recognizes revenue at the time of sale but on a tax basis it recognizes revenues when it receives the cash. This will give rise to:

A. a deferred tax asset.

B. a deferred tax liability.

C. neither a deferred tax asset nor a deferred tax liability.

---

14. (QID 200) The average age of Manufacturers Corporation's machinery is lower than other companies in the same industry. Which of the following is the least likely to explain this?

A. The company has just made major write downs of impaired assets.

B. The company uses a shorter depreciation life for machinery than its competitors.

C. The company has just acquired another manufacturing company and is making use of its machinery, at the time of acquisition the depreciation on this machinery was set at zero.

13. (QID 197) A firm sells its product on account and allows customers to pay in installments over future time periods. In the financial reports it recognizes revenue at the time of sale but on a tax basis it recognizes revenues when it receives the cash. This will give rise to:

A. a deferred tax asset.

***B. a deferred tax liability.**

C. neither a deferred tax asset nor a deferred tax liability.

Explanation: LOS: Reading 37-a

The firm's internal accounts will show a higher carrying value, due to accounts receivable, than that shown on a tax basis. A deferred tax liability will account for the difference. Whether the deferred tax liability gets larger or smaller over different periods will depend on whether sales are increasing or decreasing.

**Reference:** CFA® Program Curriculum, Volume 3, pp. 385-391.

---

14. (QID 200) The average age of Manufacturers Corporation's machinery is lower than other companies in the same industry. Which of the following is the least likely to explain this?

***A. The company has just made major write downs of impaired assets.**

B. The company uses a shorter depreciation life for machinery than its competitors.

C. The company has just acquired another manufacturing company and is making use of its machinery, at the time of acquisition the depreciation on this machinery was set at zero.

Explanation: LOS: Reading 36-e

$$\text{average age} = \frac{\text{accumul. depreciation}}{\text{depreciat. expense}}$$

Impairment of assets would lead to lower current depreciation charges; this will lead to a higher average asset life.

The other choices will lead to lower average age.

**Reference:** CFA® Program Curriculum, Volume 3, pp. 352-356.

15. (QID 199) Manufacturers Corporation provides the following data:

| | |
|---|---|
| Machinery and Equipment | 2008 |
| Gross Investment | $345 million |
| Accumulated Depreciation | $165 million |
| Depreciation Expense | $ 26 million (straight-line method) |

The average age of the machinery is closest to:

A. 6.3 years.

B. 6.9 years.

C. 13.3 years.

---

16. (QID 198) Lessees, when they are expanding companies, generally prefer to classify leases as operating rather than finance leases since it leads to all of the following except:

A. higher reported assets.

B. higher return on equity.

C. lower reported leverage.

15. (QID 199) Manufacturers Corporation provides the following data:

Machinery and Equipment 2008

Gross Investment $345 million

Accumulated Depreciation $165 million

Depreciation Expense $ 26 million (straight-line method)

The average age of the machinery is closest to:

***A. 6.3 years.**

B. 6.9 years.

C. 13.3 years.

Explanation: LOS: Reading 36-e

$$\text{average age} = \frac{\text{accumul. depreciation}}{\text{depreciat. expense}} = \frac{165}{26} = 6.3 \text{ years}$$

**Reference:** CFA® Program Curriculum, Volume 3, pp. 352-356.

---

16. (QID 198) Lessees, when they are expanding companies, generally prefer to classify leases as operating rather than finance leases since it leads to all of the following except:

***A. higher reported assets.**

B. higher return on equity.

C. lower reported leverage.

Explanation: LOS: Reading 38-f

A is not correct; with an operating lease both reported assets and liabilities will be lower.

**Reference:** CFA® Program Curriculum, Volume 3, pp. 445-457.

17. (QID 201) A company decides to use the sum-of-years'-digits depreciation method to depreciate a piece of machinery that it is purchasing for $35,000. It estimates that the machinery has a depreciable life of six years and a salvage value of $8,000. The net book value of the machinery at the end of the third year is closest to:

A. $10,370.

B. $15,714.

C. $19,286.

---

18. (QID 202) Which of the following statements is most accurate regarding cash flow impact for a lessee of a finance lease?

A. Total cash outflow each year is the same as the lease payment.

B. All of the rental payments are treated as cash flow from operations.

C. The rental payments are partly allocated as cash flow from operations and partly as cash flow from investing.

17. (QID 201) A company decides to use the sum-of-years'-digits depreciation method to depreciate a piece of machinery that it is purchasing for $35,000. It estimates that the machinery has a depreciable life of six years and a salvage value of $8,000. The net book value of the machinery at the end of the third year is closest to:

A. $10,370.

***B. $15,714.**

C. $19,286.

Explanation: LOS: Reading 37-a

Original cost minus salvage value = $27,000

Sum-of-years' digits = 21

| | rate | depreciation expense | accumulation depreciation | net book value |
|---|---|---|---|---|
| Year 0 | | | | $35,000 |
| Year 1 | 6/21 | $7,714 | $7,714 | $27,286 |
| Year 2 | 5/21 | $6,429 | $14,143 | $20,857 |
| Year 3 | 4/21 | $5,143 | $19,286 | $15,714 |

**Reference:** CFA® Program Curriculum, Volume 3, p. 373.

---

18. (QID 202) Which of the following statements is most accurate regarding cash flow impact for a lessee of a finance lease?

***A. Total cash outflow each year is the same as the lease payment.**

B. All of the rental payments are treated as cash flow from operations.

C. The rental payments are partly allocated as cash flow from operations and partly as cash flow from investing.

Explanation: LOS: Reading 38-f

There is no cash outflow at the beginning of the lease, other than lease payments, since the asset is not purchased.

The rental payments are partly allocated to cash flow from operations and partly to cash flow from financing.

**Reference:** CFA® Program Curriculum, Volume 3, pp. 445-457.

19. (QID 203) In a period of rising prices and stable inventory quantities, cash flows will usually be:

A. lower under LIFO than FIFO.

B. higher under LIFO than FIFO.

C. the same whether LIFO or FIFO is used.

---

20. (QID 204) A company is a producer of coffee and provides the following financial data:

| $ million | 2007 | 2008 |
|---|---|---|
| Inventories (year end) | 185 | 205 |
| COGS | 1,560 | 1,750 |

The company uses FIFO for inventory accounting. Assuming that the major constituent of inventory is coffee, and coffee prices rose by 30% over the period, the COGS under LIFO in 2007 is approximately:

A. $1,805.5 million.

B. $1,811.5 million.

C. $1,935.0 million.

19. (QID 203) In a period of rising prices and stable inventory quantities, cash flows will usually be:

A. lower under LIFO than FIFO.

***B. higher under LIFO than FIFO.**

C. the same whether LIFO or FIFO is used.

Explanation: LOS: Reading 35-c

COGS will be higher under LIFO leading to lower pretax income and lower tax being paid. This will lead to higher cash flows.

**Reference:** CFA® Program Curriculum, Volume 3, pp. 295-300.

---

20. (QID 204) A company is a producer of coffee and provides the following financial data:

| $ million | 2007 | 2008 |
|---|---|---|
| Inventories (year end) | 185 | 205 |
| COGS | 1,560 | 1,750 |

The company uses FIFO for inventory accounting. Assuming that the major constituent of inventory is coffee, and coffee prices rose by 30% over the period, the COGS under LIFO in 2007 is approximately:

***A. $1,805.5 million.**

B. $1,811.5 million.

C. $1,935.0 million.

Explanation: LOS: Reading 35-e

COGS under LIFO

= COGS under FIFO + (Beginning Inventory under FIFO x r)

where r is the inflation rate for the goods being produced.

= 1750 + (185 x 0.30)

= 1805.5

**Reference:** CFA® Program Curriculum, Volume 3, pp. 309-318.

21. (QID 205) A company constructs a new factory and finances the factory partly from borrowings and partly using retained earnings. In line with U.S. accounting rules, during the construction period the firm should:

A. expense the interest costs associated with the borrowing.

B. only capitalize the interest costs associated with the borrowing.

C. capitalize the interest costs associated with the borrowing and the cost of the equity used.

---

22. (QID 206) Bond covenants are used to

A. protect investors in the bond.

B. clarify the relationship between bond holder and the bond issuer.

C. protect equity investors from bond holders exercising a claim on a firm's assets.

21. (QID 205) A company constructs a new factory and finances the factory partly from borrowings and partly using retained earnings. In line with U.S. accounting rules, during the construction period the firm should:

A. expense the interest costs associated with the borrowing.

***B. only capitalize the interest costs associated with the borrowing.**

C. capitalize the interest costs associated with the borrowing and the cost of the equity used.

Explanation: LOS: Reading 36-a

Although somewhat inconsistent, only interest costs are capitalized.

**Reference:** CFA® Program Curriculum, Volume 3, pp. 337-340.

---

22. (QID 206) Bond covenants are used to

***A. protect investors in the bond.**

B. clarify the relationship between bond holder and the bond issuer.

C. protect equity investors from bond holders exercising a claim on a firm's assets.

Explanation: LOS: Reading 38-b

Covenants are to protest creditors', in this case the bond holders', interests by limiting the debtor's activities if it could weaken the creditors' position.

**Reference:** CFA® Program Curriculum, Volume 3, pp. 434-435.

23. (QID 207) The following information is given regarding a company's activities:

* Tax rate is 30%.

* The only expense is depreciation.

* A new machine is purchased at a cost of $10,000.

* Annual revenues of $40,000 are generated from the new machine.

* The company, in its financial reports, depreciates the machine by using the straight-line method over four years and the salvage value is estimated to be $2,000.

* For tax purposes the machine is depreciated using the straight-line method over two years with the same salvage value.

The deferred tax expense in year 2 will be:

A. $ 600.

B. $ 1,200.

C. $10,800.

---

24. (QID 417) A company has been recognizing impairment of its asset base (which is held for use) but following a change in regulation in its industry it wishes to reverse the impairment write-down.

This is permitted

A. Under U.S. GAAP only.

B. Under IAS GAAP only.

C. Under U.S. and IAS GAAP.

23. (QID 207) The following information is given regarding a company's activities:

* Tax rate is 30%.

* The only expense is depreciation.

* A new machine is purchased at a cost of $10,000.

* Annual revenues of $40,000 are generated from the new machine.

* The company, in its financial reports, depreciates the machine by using the straight-line method over four years and the salvage value is estimated to be $2,000.

* For tax purposes the machine is depreciated using the straight-line method over two years with the same salvage value.

The deferred tax expense in year 2 will be:

***A. $ 600.**

B. $ 1,200.

C. $10,800.

Explanation: LOS: Reading 38-f

Tax reporting – straight-line depreciation over two years

| | Year 1 | Year 2 |
|---|---|---|
| Revenue | $40,000 | $40,000 |
| Depreciation | $ 4,000 | $ 4,000 |
| Taxable income | $36,000 | $36,000 |
| Taxes payable | $10,800 | $10,800 |

**Financial statement reporting - straight-line depreciation over 4 years**

| | Year 1 | Year 2 |
|---|---|---|
| Revenue | $40,000 | $40,000 |
| Depreciation | $ 2,000 | $ 2,000 |
| Pre tax income | $38,000 | $38,000 |
| Tax expense | $11,400 | $11,400 |
| of which | | |
| Taxes payable | $10,800 | $10,800 |
| Deferred tax expense | $ 600 | $ 600 |

**Reference:** CFA® Program Curriculum, Volume 3, pp. 425-470.

24. (QID 417) A company has been recognizing impairment of its asset base (which is held for use) but following a change in regulation in its industry it wishes to reverse the impairment write-down.

This is permitted

A. Under U.S. GAAP only.

***B. Under IAS GAAP only.**

C. Under U.S. and IAS GAAP.

Explanation: LOS: Reading 36-i

Reversal of impairments are not permitted for held in use assets under U.S. GAAP, they are permitted under international accounting standards.

**Reference:** CFA® Program Curriculum, Volume 3, p. 373.

# Study Session 10: Financial Reporting and Analysis: Techniques, Applications, and International Standards Convergence

The readings in this study session discuss financial analysis techniques, financial statement analysis applications, and the international convergence of accounting standards.

The first reading presents the most frequently used tools and techniques used to evaluate companies, including common size analysis, cross-sectional analysis, trend analysis, and ratio analysis. The second reading then shows the application of financial analysis techniques to major analyst tasks including the evaluation of past and future financial performance, credit risk, and the screening of potential equity investments. The reading also discusses analyst adjustments to reported financials. Such adjustments are often needed to put companies' reported results on a comparable basis.

This study session concludes with a reading on convergence of international and U.S. accounting standards. Although there has been much progress in harmonizing accounting standards globally, as this reading discusses, there are still significant variations between generally accepted accounting principles from one country to another.

1. (QID 208) Which of the following ratios would be most useful in evaluating a company's internal liquidity?

A. Interest coverage.

B. Debt-to-equity ratio.

C. Defensive interval ratio.

---

2. (QID 209) A retail analyst follows a top-down approach to projecting a retail company's sales. The first step in his analysis is most likely to be to consider the impact of which of the following?

A. The projected rise in consumer spending.

B. The competitive factors in the retail sector.

C. The sensitivity of the company's sales to economic growth.

1. (QID 208) Which of the following ratios would be most useful in evaluating a company's internal liquidity?

A. Interest coverage.

B. Debt-to-equity ratio.

***C. Defensive interval ratio.**

Explanation: LOS: Reading 39-d

The defensive interval ratio measures how long a company can pay its daily expenditures using its existing liquid assets (cash + short-term marketable securities + receivables). This is a measure of a company's liquidity. Interest coverage and debt-to-equity ratios measure solvency and asset turnover measures activity.

**Reference:** CFA® Program Curriculum, Volume 3, pp. 506-509.

---

2. (QID 209) A retail analyst follows a top-down approach to projecting a retail company's sales. The first step in his analysis is most likely to be to consider the impact of which of the following?

***A. The projected rise in consumer spending.**

B. The competitive factors in the retail sector.

C. The sensitivity of the company's sales to economic growth.

Explanation: LOS: Reading 42-b

The first step in a top-down approach is to assess the economic environment and other macro factors. The impact of these is then considered on the industry and finally the analyst moves down to company analysis. Therefore "The projected rise in consumer spending" is the best choice.

**Reference:** CFA® Program Curriculum, Volume 3, pp. 581-583.

3. (QID 210) Common-size statements are least likely to be used for cross-sectional analysis because they allow analysts:

A. to identify trends in a company's performance.

B. to compare companies which are operating in different countries.

C. to identify companies with different capital structures.

4. (QID 211) Credit analysis of a bond issuer is least likely to involve:

A. valuation of the issuing firm.

B. projecting cash flows to see if they are sufficient to cover interest payments.

C. assessing the risk the issuer cannot repay interest or principal on the bond.

3. (QID 210) Common-size statements are least likely to be used for cross-sectional analysis because they allow analysts:

***A. to identify trends in a company's performance.**

B. to compare companies which are operating in different countries.

C. to identify companies with different capital structures.

Explanation: LOS: Reading 39-a

Cross-sectional analysis compares a ratio from one company against one from another company, or against the overall sector, for a specific period. Common-size statements allow for comparison of different-sized companies and ones operating in different currencies.

**Reference:** CFA® Program Curriculum, Volume 3, pp. 490-496.

---

4. (QID 211) Credit analysis of a bond issuer is least likely to involve:

***A. valuation of the issuing firm.**

B. projecting cash flows to see if they are sufficient to cover interest payments.

C. assessing the risk the issuer cannot repay interest or principal on the bond.

Explanation: LOS: Reading 39-f

Credit analysis is assessing the risk that a counterparty or debtor will not be able to make promised payments. The valuation of the issuing firm would be of primary interest to equity, rather than credit, analysts.

**Reference:** CFA® Program Curriculum, Volume 3, pp. 532-535.

5. (QID 212) ABC Corporation provides you with the following information:

| **Income Statement** $ million | | **Balance Sheet** Average over period | | $ million | |
|---|---|---|---|---|---|
| Sales | 150 | Cash | 90 | Accounts Payable | 30 |
| COGS | (75) | Accounts Receivable | 10 | S. Term bank notes | 25 |
| Gross Profit | 75 | Inventory | 70 | Long-Term Debt | 60 |
| SGA Expenses | (20) | Property, P & E | 150 | | |
| Op. Profit | 55 | Depreciation | (70) | Common Stock | 50 |
| Interest expense | (15) | Investment | 30 | Retained Earnings | 115 |
| Tax | (10) | | | | |
| **Net Income** | **30** | **Total Assets** | **280** | **Total Liabilities & Equity** | **280** |

Inventory turnover is closest to:

A. 0.93.

B. 1.07.

C. 2.14.

5. (QID 212) ABC Corporation provides you with the following information:

| Income Statement<br>$ million | | Balance Sheet<br>Average over period | | $ million | |
|---|---|---|---|---|---|
| Sales | 150 | Cash | 90 | Accounts Payable | 30 |
| COGS | (75) | Accounts Receivable | 10 | S. Term bank notes | 25 |
| Gross Profit | 75 | Inventory | 70 | Long-Term Debt | 60 |
| SGA Expenses | (20) | Property, P & E | 150 | | |
| Op. Profit | 55 | Depreciation | (70) | Common Stock | 50 |
| Interest expense | (15) | Investment | 30 | Retained Earnings | 115 |
| Tax | (10) | | | | |
| **Net Income** | **30** | **Total Assets** | **280** | **Total Liabilities & Equity** | **280** |

Inventory turnover is closest to:

A. 0.93.

***B. 1.07.**

C. 2.14.

Explanation: LOS: Reading 39-c

$$\text{Inventory turnover} = \frac{\text{COGS}}{\text{average inventory}} = \frac{75}{70} = 1.07$$

**Reference:** CFA® Program Curriculum, Volume 3, pp. 499-505.

6. (QID 213) The payables turnover ratio, assuming there is no change in inventory levels over the year, of ABC Corporation is closest to (see question 5 for financial data):

| Income Statement $ million | | Balance Sheet Average over period | | $ million | |
|---|---|---|---|---|---|
| Sales | 150 | Cash | 90 | Accounts Payable | 30 |
| COGS | (75) | Accounts Receivable | 10 | S. Term bank notes | 25 |
| Gross Profit | 75 | Inventory | 70 | Long-Term Debt | 60 |
| SGA Expenses | (20) | Property, P & E | 150 | | |
| Op. Profit | 55 | Depreciation | (70) | Common Stock | 50 |
| Interest expense | (15) | Investment | 30 | Retained Earnings | 115 |
| Tax | (10) | | | | |
| **Net Income** | **30** | **Total Assets** | **280** | **Total Liabilities & Equity** | **280** |

A. 0.4.

B. 2.5.

C. 5.0.

6. (QID 213) The payables turnover ratio, assuming there is no change in inventory levels over the year, of ABC Corporation is closest to (see question 5 for financial data):

| Income Statement $ million | | Balance Sheet Average over period | | $ million | |
|---|---|---|---|---|---|
| Sales | 150 | Cash | 90 | Accounts Payable | 30 |
| COGS | (75) | Accounts Receivable | 10 | S. Term bank notes | 25 |
| Gross Profit | 75 | Inventory | 70 | Long-Term Debt | 60 |
| SGA Expenses | (20) | Property, P & E | 150 | | |
| Op. Profit | 55 | Depreciation | (70) | Common Stock | 50 |
| Interest expense | (15) | Investment | 30 | Retained Earnings | 115 |
| Tax | (10) | | | | |
| **Net Income** | **30** | **Total Assets** | **280** | **Total Liabilities & Equity** | **280** |

A. 0.4.

***B. 2.5.**

C. 5.0.

Explanation: LOS: Reading 39-c

$$\text{payables turnover ratio} = \frac{\text{COGS}}{\text{average trade payables}} = \frac{75}{30} = 2.5$$

**Reference:** CFA® Program Curriculum, Volume 3, pp. 499-505.

7. (QID 214) The return on total invested capital of ABC Corporation is closest to (see question 5 for financial data) is closest to:

A. 12.0%.

B. 13.3%.

C. 22.0%.

8. (QID 215) The total asset turnover of ABC Corporation is closest to (see question 5 for financial data):

A. 0.54.

B. 0.71.

C. 1.87.

7. (QID 214) The return on total invested capital of ABC Corporation is closest to (see question 5 for financial data) is closest to:

A. 12.0%.

B. 13.3%.

***C. 22.0%.**

Explanation: LOS: Reading 39-c

Return on total invested capital

$$= \frac{\text{EBIT}}{\text{average total invested capital}}$$

$$= \frac{55}{85 + 165} = 22.0\%$$

**Reference:** CFA® Program Curriculum, Volume 3, pp. 513-517.

---

8. (QID 215) The total asset turnover of ABC Corporation is closest to (see question 5 for financial data):

***A. 0.54.**

B. 0.71.

C. 1.87.

Explanation: LOS: Reading 39-c

$$= \frac{150}{280} = 0.54$$

**Reference:** CFA® Program Curriculum, Volume 3, pp. 499-505.

9. (QID 216) Which of the following is most accurate regarding whether LIFO and FIFO can be used for inventory accounting under U.S. GAAP and International Financial Reporting Standards (IFRS)?

| U.S. GAAP | IFRS |
|---|---|
| A. FIFO only | LIFO only |
| B. LIFO only | FIFO only |
| C. LIFO or FIFO | FIFO only |

10. (QID 217) If a firm has an interest coverage ratio of 3, the company will just be able to pay its interest costs from current earnings if earnings before interest and tax decline by:

A. 20.00%.

B. 33.33%.

C. 66.66%.

9. (QID 216) Which of the following is most accurate regarding whether LIFO and FIFO can be used for inventory accounting under U.S. GAAP and International Financial Reporting Standards (IFRS)?

| U.S. GAAP | IFRS |
|---|---|
| A. FIFO only | LIFO only |
| B. LIFO only | FIFO only |
| ***C. LIFO or FIFO** | **FIFO only** |

Explanation: LOS: Reading 42-e

Under IFRS the use of LIFO is prohibited. Under U.S. GAP both measures can be used.

**Reference:** CFA® Program Curriculum, Volume 3, pp. 599-602.

---

10. (QID 217) If a firm has an interest coverage ratio of 3, the company will just be able to pay its interest costs from current earnings if earnings before interest and tax decline by:

A. 20.00%.

B. 33.33%.

***C. 66.66%.**

Explanation: LOS: Reading 39-c

$$\text{interest coverage} = \frac{\text{EBIT}}{\text{interest expense}}$$

If the interest cover falls to 1, EBIT will fall to a third of its original value i.e. decline by 66.67%.

**Reference:** CFA® Program Curriculum, Volume 3, pp. 509-513.

11. (QID 218) When a company increases the dividend pay out ratio, it is most likely to lead to the sustainable potential growth rate of the company:

A. falling.

B. rising.

C. rising or falling depending on the ROE relative to the cost of capital.

---

12. (QID 219) If a manufacturing company has a very low total asset turnover compared to its competitors this could be explained by:

A. I. the company is using older, and in many cases fully depreciated, machinery.

B. II. the company has too much capital invested in assets for the size of its revenue.

C. III. the company uses operating leases rather than outright purchase for its machinery.

11. (QID 218) When a company increases the dividend pay out ratio, it is most likely to lead to the sustainable potential growth rate of the company:

***A. falling.**

B. rising.

C. rising or falling depending on the ROE relative to the cost of capital.

Explanation: LOS: Reading 39-f

Sustainable potential growth rate = retention rate x ROE

If the dividend pay out ratio increases the retention rate will fall, reducing the future growth rate.

**Reference:** CFA® Program Curriculum, Volume 3, p. 529.

---

12. (QID 219) If a manufacturing company has a very low total asset turnover compared to its competitors this could be explained by:

***A. I. the company is using older, and in many cases fully depreciated, machinery.**

B. II. the company has too much capital invested in assets for the size of its revenue. ✓

C. III. the company uses operating leases rather than outright purchase for its machinery.

Explanation: LOS: Reading 39-c

total asset turnover = net sales/average total net assets

I. is not correct since using old machinery would reduce total net assets and increase the asset turnover.

III. is not correct since it would imply that the asset value was potentially lower than its competitors.

**Reference:** CFA® Program Curriculum, Volume 3, pp. 499-505.

13. (QID 220) Which of the following is a characteristic of a firm that would be least likely to reduce credit risk? The firm:

A. has stable profit margins.

B. is operating in a niche market.

C. has high operational efficiency.

---

14. (QID 221) South Inc.'s breakdown of current assets and liabilities is as follows:

| Current Assets | ($ '000) | CurrentLiabilities | ('000) |
|---|---|---|---|
| Cash and cash equivalents | 40 | Short term debt | 25 |
| Receivables | 650 | Accounts payable | 420 |
| Inventories | 350 | Taxes payable | 120 |
| Other current assets | 70 | Other current liabilities | 45 |
| Total | 1110 | Total | 610 |

The quick ratio is closest to:

A. 0.07.

B. 1.13.

C. 1.55.

13. (QID 220) Which of the following is a characteristic of a firm that would be least likely to reduce credit risk? The firm:

A. has stable profit margins.

***B. is operating in a niche market.**

C. has high operational efficiency.

Explanation: LOS: Reading 42-c

A firm that is diversified, both in terms of products and clients, would generally be considered lower risk. Also a larger company would have better purchasing power with its suppliers so better be able to withstand a downturn.

**Reference:** CFA® Program Curriculum, Volume 3, pp. 591-594.

---

14. (QID 221) South Inc.'s breakdown of current assets and liabilities is as follows:

| Current Assets | ($ '000) | CurrentLiabilities | ('000) |
|---|---|---|---|
| Cash and cash equivalents | 40 | Short term debt | 25 |
| Receivables | 650 | Accounts payable | 420 |
| Inventories | 350 | Taxes payable | 120 |
| Other current assets | 70 | Other current liabilities | 45 |
| Total | 1110 | Total | 610 |

The quick ratio is closest to:

A. 0.07.

***B. 1.13.**

C. 1.55.

Explanation: LOS: Reading 39-c

$$\text{Quick ratio} = \frac{\text{cash + market securities + receivables}}{\text{current liabilities}}$$

$$= \frac{690}{610} = 1.13$$

**Reference:** CFA® Program Curriculum, Volume 3, pp. 506-509.

15. (QID 419) An increase in a firm's marketing costs would be least likely to affect:

A. gross margins.

B. return on assets.

C. operating margins.

16. (QID 223) When a company uses both operating and finance leases an analyst should add the present value of which type of lease to the assets and liabilities in the balance sheet?

| Assets | Liabilities |
|---|---|
| A. capital only | capital only |
| B. operating only | operating only |
| C. no adjustment | operating only |

15. (QID 419) An increase in a firm's marketing costs would be least likely to affect:

***A. gross margins.**

B. return on assets.

C. operating margins.

Explanation: LOS: Reading 39-c

Gross profit is sales minus cost of goods sold and therefore gross margins would not be affected by an increase in marketing costs. Marketing costs are an operating cost and there for would impact on operating and net margins, and return on assets.

**Reference:** CFA® Program Curriculum, Volume 3, pp. 513-517.

---

16. (QID 223) When a company uses both operating and finance leases an analyst should add the present value of which type of lease to the assets and liabilities in the balance sheet?

| Assets | Liabilities |
|---|---|
| A. capital only | capital only |
| ***B. operating only** | **operating only** |
| C. no adjustment | operating only |

Explanation: LOS: Reading 42-e

Finance leases will already be recorded on the balance sheet so there is no need to make an adjustment. However an operating lease is a form of off-balance sheet financing so both the assets and liabilities should be adjusted.

**Reference:** CFA® Program Curriculum, Volume 3, pp. 606-613.

17. (QID 224) A firm's fixed charge coverage has risen from five to seven times. This is least likely to be explained by:

A. the firm has refinanced and reduced the interest rate it pays on its debt.

B. the firm has issued new equity and reduced the debt on the balance sheet.

C. the firm has changed its policy and has started using operating lease arrangements to acquire the use of fixed assets.

---

18. (QID 225) The cash conversion cycle is:

A. the average time period between a sale being recorded and cash being collected from customers.

B. cost of goods sold divided by cash plus marketable securities.

C. the average time period between the outlay of cash and the collection of related cash.

17. (QID 224) A firm's fixed charge coverage has risen from five to seven times. This is least likely to be explained by:

A. the firm has refinanced and reduced the interest rate it pays on its debt.

B. the firm has issued new equity and reduced the debt on the balance sheet.

***C. the firm has changed its policy and has started using operating lease arrangements to acquire the use of fixed assets.**

Explanation: LOS: Reading 39-c

Fixed charge coverage is EBIT plus lease payments divided by interest payments plus lease payments. Profit Margins is not the best choice. Two choices would reduce interest expense and increase fixed financial cost coverage.

Using more operating leases will increase the lease expense which would not explain the increase in fixed financial cost coverage (given the original coverage was five, the percentage change in denominator will be more than the percentage change in numerator).

**Reference:** CFA® Program Curriculum, Volume 3, pp. 509-513.

---

18. (QID 225) The cash conversion cycle is:

A. the average time period between a sale being recorded and cash being collected from customers.

B. cost of goods sold divided by cash plus marketable securities.

***C. the average time period between the outlay of cash and the collection of related cash.**

Explanation: LOS: Reading 39-c

The cash conversion cycle is the number of days that cash is tied up in inventory and then waiting for payment by customers, less the time that the company has before it must pay suppliers.

**Reference:** CFA® Program Curriculum, Volume 3, pp. 513-517.

19. (QID 226) The gross profit margin of a company has increased steadily, this could be explained by:

A. a decline in sales, general and administrative expense as a percentage of sales.

B. a decline in interest expense as a percentage of sales.

C. a decline in raw material costs as a percentage of sales.

20. (QID 227) The following financial information is given for a company:

Net profit margin = 3%

Operating profit margin = 10%

Asset turnover = 1.5

Financial leverage = 1.8

Interest burden = 0.8

The return on equity is closest to:

A. 3.6%.

B. 6.5%.

C. 8.1%.

19. (QID 226) The gross profit margin of a company has increased steadily, this could be explained by:

A. a decline in sales, general and administrative expense as a percentage of sales.

B. a decline in interest expense as a percentage of sales.

***C. a decline in raw material costs as a percentage of sales.**

Explanation: LOS: Reading 39-d

Gross profit is sales minus cost of goods sold and therefore would be a decline in raw material costs

Gross Profit would not be affected the other choices.

**Reference:** CFA® Program Curriculum, Volume 3, pp. 513-517.

---

20. (QID 227) The following financial information is given for a company:

Net profit margin = 3%

Operating profit margin = 10%

Asset turnover = 1.5

Financial leverage = 1.8

Interest burden = 0.8

The return on equity is closest to:

A. 3.6%.

B. 6.5%.

***C. 8.1%.**

Explanation: LOS: Reading 39-e

Return on equity

= net profit margin x asset turnover x financial leverage

= 0.03 x 1.5 x 1.8

= 8.1%

**Reference:** CFA® Program Curriculum, Volume 3, pp. 520-525.

21. (QID 228) Under International Financial Reporting Standards (IFRS) when an acquirer of another company pays less than the fair value of its net identifiable assets then:

A. negative goodwill is recognized.

B. a gain is recorded in the accounts.

C. the difference in value is accounted for as an extraordinary item.

---

22. (QID 229) Under International Financial Reporting Standards (IFRS) when a company receives a dividend, and when it pays a dividend, these activities are classified as follows:

| Dividends received | Dividends paid |
|---|---|
| A. investing | financing |
| B. operating | operating |
| C. operating or investing | operating or financing |

21. (QID 228) Under International Financial Reporting Standards (IFRS) when an acquirer of another company pays less than the fair value of its net identifiable assets then:

A. negative goodwill is recognized.

***B. a gain is recorded in the accounts.**

C. the difference in value is accounted for as an extraordinary item.

Explanation: LOS: Reading 43-b

The value of the assets and liabilities acquired should be reassessed and if the company is still paying less than their fair value a gain is recognized. Extraordinary items are not permitted under IFRS.

**Reference:** CFA® Program Curriculum, Volume 3, pp. 627-631.

---

22. (QID 229) Under International Financial Reporting Standards (IFRS) when a company receives a dividend, and when it pays a dividend, these activities are classified as follows:

| Dividends received | Dividends paid |
|---|---|
| A. investing | financing |
| B. operating | operating |
| ***C. operating or investing** | **operating or financing** |

Explanation: LOS: Reading 43-d

IFRS allows flexibility over classification of dividends paid and received, dividends received can be classified as operating or investing, and dividends paid as operating or financing. Under U.S. GAAP dividends received are an operating item and dividends paid a financing item.

**Reference:** CFA® Program Curriculum, Volume 3, pp. 636-637.

23. (QID 230) Under International Financial Reporting Standards (IFRS) impairment of goodwill:

A. is charged directly to stockholders' equity and does not impact on the income statement.

B. is charged as a valuation allowance against the acquired assets.

C. leads to a reduction in net income in the period when the impairment is recognized.

---

24. (QID 418) Which of the following would be a warning sign that a company is using aggressive financial reporting methods?

A. long useful lives for depreciating assets.

B. frequent use of finance leases as the lessee.

C. higher operating cash flow growth rate than earnings growth rate.

23. (QID 230) Under International Financial Reporting Standards (IFRS) impairment of goodwill:

A. is charged directly to stockholders' equity and does not impact on the income statement.

B. is charged as a valuation allowance against the acquired assets.

***C. leads to a reduction in net income in the period when the impairment is recognized.**

Explanation: LOS: Reading 43-b

Impairment reduces income in the year it is recorded, reduces the value of net asset and reduces stockholder's equity. Under IFRS goodwill must be checked annually for impairment, amortization is not permitted.

**Reference:** CFA® Program Curriculum, Volume 3, pp. 627-631.

---

24. (QID 418) Which of the following would be a warning sign that a company is using aggressive financial reporting methods?

***A. long useful lives for depreciating assets.**

B. frequent use of finance leases as the lessee.

C. higher operating cash flow growth rate than earnings growth rate.

Explanation: LOS: Reading 40-g

If long useful lives are being used it would reduce the annual depreciation expense leading to higher profits in the short term. Excessive use of operating, rather than finance leases and relatively low operating cash flows compared to earnings would be seen as warning signs.

**Reference:** CFA® Program Curriculum, Volume 3, pp. 556-558.

25. (QID 222) South Inc.'s breakdown of current assets and liabilities is as follows:

| Current Assets | ($ '000) | CurrentLiabilities | ('000) |
|---|---|---|---|
| Cash and cash equivalents | 40 | Short term debt | 25 |
| Receivables | 650 | Accounts payable | 420 |
| Inventories | 350 | Taxes payable | 120 |
| Other current assets | 70 | Other current liabilities | 45 |
| Total | 1110 | Total | 610 |

South Inc.'s net annual sales for the same period were $6,825,000 and receivables were unchanged from the previous year (ref. Question 14). The days of sales outstanding for the year is closest to:

A. 34.3 days.

B. 34.8 days.

C. 38.3 days.

---

26. (QID 277) A company provides the following information:

| | 2007 | 2008 |
|---|---|---|
| Return on equity | 8.9% | 9.4% |
| Return on total assets | 4.5% | 4.2% |
| Total asset turnover | 1.5 | 1.7 |

The numbers could be explained by:

| Financial leverage | Net profit margin |
|---|---|
| A. increased | increased |
| B. increased | decreased |
| C. decreased | increased |

25. (QID 222) South Inc.'s breakdown of current assets and liabilities is as follows:

| Current Assets | ($ '000) | CurrentLiabilities | ('000) |
|---|---|---|---|
| Cash and cash equivalents | 40 | Short term debt | 25 |
| Receivables | 650 | Accounts payable | 420 |
| Inventories | 350 | Taxes payable | 120 |
| Other current assets | 70 | Other current liabilities | 45 |
| Total | 1110 | Total | 610 |

South Inc.'s net annual sales for the same period were $6,825,000 and receivables were unchanged from the previous year (ref. Question 14). The days of sales outstanding for the year is closest to:

A. 34.3 days.

***B. 34.8 days.**

C. 38.3 days.

Explanation: LOS: Reading 39-c

receivables turnover

$$= \frac{\text{net annual sales}}{\text{average receivables}}$$

$$= \frac{6,825,000}{650,000} = 10.5$$

average receivables collection period

$$= \frac{365}{\text{receivables turnover}}$$

$$= 34.8 \text{ days}$$

**Reference:** CFA® Program Curriculum, Volume 3, pp. 499-505.

26. (QID 277) A company provides the following information:

| | 2007 | 2008 |
|---|---|---|
| Return on equity | 8.9% | 9.4% |
| Return on total assets | 4.5% | 4.2% |
| Total asset turnover | 1.5 | 1.7 |

The numbers could be explained by:

| Financial leverage | Net profit margin |
|---|---|
| A. increased | increased |
| ***B. increased** | **decreased** |
| C. decreased | increased |

Explanation: LOS: Reading 39-e

Return on equity = return on assets x financial leverage. Return on equity has increased when return on assets fell, so financial leverage must have increased.

Return on assets = net profit margin x total asset turnover. If return on assets fell and total asset turnover increased in must be because net profit margins fell.

**Reference:** CFA® Program Curriculum, Volume 3, pp. 517-525.

# Study Session 11: Corporate Finance

This study session covers the principles that corporations use to make their investing and financing decisions. Capital budgeting is the process of making decisions about which long-term projects the corporation should accept for investment, and which it should reject. Both the expected return of a project and the financing cost should be taken into account. The cost of capital, or the rate of return required for a project, must be developed using economically sound methods.

Corporate managers are concerned with liquidity and solvency, and use financial statements to evaluate performance as well as to develop and communicate future plans. The final reading in this study session is on corporate governance practices, which can expose the firm to a heightened risk of ethical lapses. Although these practices may not be inherently unethical, they create the potential for conflicts of interest to develop between shareholders and managers, and the extent of that conflict affects the firm's valuation.

1. (QID 231) Which of the following cash flows should not be included in capital budgeting cash flow analysis?

A. Sunk costs.

B. Externalities.

C. Opportunity costs.

---

2. (QID 232) The net operating cycle for a company has been getting longer. This is most likely to be explained by:

A. the company is increasing its inventory turnover.

B. the company has been delaying payment to its suppliers.

C. the company is taking longer to collect on its credit accounts.

1. (QID 231) Which of the following cash flows should not be included in capital budgeting cash flow analysis?

***A. Sunk costs.**

B. Externalities.

C. Opportunity costs.

Explanation: LOS: Reading 44-b

Sunk costs should not be included since they will not affect future cash flows or impact on incremental cash flows.

**Reference:** CFA® Program Curriculum, Volume 4, p. 9.

---

2. (QID 232) The net operating cycle for a company has been getting longer. This is most likely to be explained by:

A. the company is increasing its inventory turnover.

B. the company has been delaying payment to its suppliers.

***C. the company is taking longer to collect on its credit accounts.**

Explanation: LOS: Reading 46-b

The net operating cycle or cash conversion cycle is

= number of days of receivables + number of days of inventory – number of days of payables

The company is taking longer to collect on its credit accounts means that it is collecting receivables more slowly so its net operating cycle or cash conversion cycle is getting longer.

**Reference:** CFA® Program Curriculum, Volume 4, pp. 87-93.

3. (QID 233) Patricia Rice, an independent member of the board of Ashburton Pet Foods, proposes an amendment to the articles of association. She proposes that the board can independently, without first seeking management's approval, hire external consultants when it sees fit. She also requests that an appropriate budget is allocated for this purpose.

Which statement is most accurate?

A. The proposal is unjustified because it would undermine the authority of the management.

B. The proposal only makes sense if management approval is sought first and the required expertise relates to auditing matters.

C. The proposal conforms to modern corporate governance practices specifically when the required expertise relates to financial matters and/or reputational concerns.

---

4. (QID 234) ABC Corp. has a 6% ten-year bond outstanding, which is trading at a yield to maturity of 8%. The company's marginal tax rate is 40%. The component cost of debt for ABC Corp. is closest to:

A. 3.6%.

B. 4.8%.

C. 8.0%.

3. (QID 233) Patricia Rice, an independent member of the board of Ashburton Pet Foods, proposes an amendment to the articles of association. She proposes that the board can independently, without first seeking management's approval, hire external consultants when it sees fit. She also requests that an appropriate budget is allocated for this purpose.

Which statement is most accurate?

A. The proposal is unjustified because it would undermine the authority of the management.

B. The proposal only makes sense if management approval is sought first and the required expertise relates to auditing matters.

***C. The proposal conforms to modern corporate governance practices specifically when the required expertise relates to financial matters and/or reputational concerns.**

Explanation: LOS: Reading 48-b

Rice's proposal is perfectly valid and in line with modern corporate governance practices.

**Reference:** CFA® Program Curriculum, Volume 4, p. 164.

---

4. (QID 234) ABC Corp. has a 6% ten-year bond outstanding, which is trading at a yield to maturity of 8%. The company's marginal tax rate is 40%. The component cost of debt for ABC Corp. is closest to:

A. 3.6%.

***B. 4.8%.**

C. 8.0%.

Explanation: LOS: Reading 45-f

The cost of debt is the required return of investors in the bond, which is the yield to marurity, less tax savings which is:

$$\text{cost of debt} = k_d(1-T) = 8\% \times (1.00 - 0.40) = 4.8\%$$

**Reference:** CFA® Program Curriculum, Volume 4, pp. 43-44.

5. (QID 235) ABC Corp. issued nonconvertible, noncallable preferred stock last year at an issue price of $100; it pays a dividend of $5 per annum. The stock is now trading at $110. The company's marginal tax rate is 40%. The cost of preferred stock for ABC Corp is closest to:

A. 2.7%.

B. 3.0%.

C. 4.5%.

---

6. (QID 236) The beta of ABC's common stock is 1.1, the dividend paid is $3.50, and the stock price is $82.00. The expected market return is 12% and the risk-free rate is 6%. The cost of equity is closest to:

A. 6.6%.

B. 12.6%.

C. 13.2%.

5. (QID 235) ABC Corp. issued nonconvertible, noncallable preferred stock last year at an issue price of $100; it pays a dividend of $5 per annum. The stock is now trading at $110. The company's marginal tax rate is 40%. The cost of preferred stock for ABC Corp is closest to:

A. 2.7%.

B. 3.0%.

***C. 4.5%.**

Explanation: LOS: Reading 45-g

The cost of preferred stock is the dividend divided by the price. There is no adjustment for tax, since a preferred dividend is not a tax deductible expense.

The cost is $5/$110 = 4.5%

**Reference:** CFA® Program Curriculum, Volume 4, pp. 46-47.

---

6. (QID 236) The beta of ABC's common stock is 1.1, the dividend paid is $3.50, and the stock price is $82.00. The expected market return is 12% and the risk-free rate is 6%. The cost of equity is closest to:

A. 6.6%.

***B. 12.6%.**

C. 13.2%.

Explanation: LOS: Reading 45-h

Using CAPM to calculate the cost of equity gives:

$$k_e = k_{RF} + \beta(k_M - k_{RF}) = 6\% + 1.1(12\% - 6\%) = 12.6\%$$

**Reference:** CFA® Program Curriculum, Volume 4, pp. 48-49.

7. (QID 237) Proforma analysis will typically involve forecasting a financing deficit or surplus, this is because:

A. there is a combination of sales-driven and fixed burdens estimates.

B. total assets will generally grow at a significantly different rate to sales.

C. items on the income statement are fixed, but there are no fixed items on the balance sheet.

---

8. (QID 238) When calculating cash flows for capital budgeting cash flow analysis, which of the following statements is most accurate?

A. Interest payments should not be included since the cost of capital includes the cost of debt.

B. Gross interest payments should be included since the cost of capital includes the cost of debt.

C. Interest payments reflecting long-term debt should be included since the cost of capital includes the cost of debt.

7. (QID 237) Proforma analysis will typically involve forecasting a financing deficit or surplus, this is because:

***A. there is a combination of sales-driven and fixed burdens estimates.**

B. total assets will generally grow at a significantly different rate to sales.

C. items on the income statement are fixed, but there are no fixed items on the balance sheet.

Explanation: LOS: Reading 47-b

If all accounts were sales driven there would not be a problem, but some items such as interest will be based on fixed long-term debt creating the financing deficit or surplus.

**Reference:** CFA® Program Curriculum, Volume 4, pp. 145-149.

---

8. (QID 238) When calculating cash flows for capital budgeting cash flow analysis, which of the following statements is most accurate?

***A. Interest payments should not be included since the cost of capital includes the cost of debt.**

B. Gross interest payments should be included since the cost of capital includes the cost of debt.

C. Interest payments reflecting long-term debt should be included since the cost of capital includes the cost of debt.

Explanation: LOS: Reading 44-b

The weighted cost of capital includes the cost of debt so the cash flow available for bond and equity holders should be used, i.e. before interest payments.

**Reference:** CFA® Program Curriculum, Volume 4, p. 8.

9. (QID 239) When two projects are mutually exclusive then:

A. it is better to use the internal rate of return method to evaluate the projects since it is widely accepted in industry.

B. it is better to use the net present value method to evaluate the projects since it is based on the assumption that the projects' cash flows are reinvested at the cost of capital.

C. it is better to use the internal rate of return method to evaluate the projects since it is based on the assumption that the projects' cash flows are reinvested at the cost of capital.

---

10. (QID 240) A firm reports the following financial information:

| | |
|---|---|
| Operating profit margin | = 30% |
| Tax retention rate | = 80% |
| Financial leverage multiplier | = 3.5 |
| Interest expense rate | = 0.2 |

Under the DuPont system the return on equity is closest to:

A. 16.8%.

B. 26.3%.

C. there is insufficient information to calculate the return on equity.

9. (QID 239) When two projects are mutually exclusive then:

A. it is better to use the internal rate of return method to evaluate the projects since it is widely accepted in industry.

***B. it is better to use the net present value method to evaluate the projects since it is based on the assumption that the projects' cash flows are reinvested at the cost of capital.**

C. it is better to use the internal rate of return method to evaluate the projects since it is based on the assumption that the projects' cash flows are reinvested at the cost of capital.

Explanation: LOS: Reading 44-e

If a company is evaluating mutually exclusive projects the crossover rate is critical in deciding which project to pursue. The cost of capital should be used since this better reflects the reinvestment options available to the company. The cost of capital is used in the NPV method.

**Reference:** CFA® Program Curriculum, Volume 4, pp. 17-22.

---

10. (QID 240) A firm reports the following financial information:

| | |
|---|---|
| Operating profit margin | = 30% |
| Tax retention rate | = 80% |
| Financial leverage multiplier | = 3.5 |
| Interest expense rate | = 0.2 |

Under the DuPont system the return on equity is closest to:

A. 16.8%.

B. 26.3%.

***C. there is insufficient information to calculate the return on equity.**

Explanation: LOS: Reading 47-a

The total asset turnover is needed to calculate the return on equity.

**Reference:** CFA® Program Curriculum, Volume 4, pp. 132-141.

11. (QID 241) The quick ratio of a firm is lower than the industry average whereas its current ratio is higher than the industry average. This is most likely to be explained by the firm having, relative to the industry average, high:

A. cash levels.

B. receivables.

C. inventory levels.

---

12. (QID 242) A $1,000,000 project has the following cash flows, $500,000 at the end of the first year, $400,000 at the end of the second year and $300,000 at the end of each year thereafter. If the cost of capital is 10%, the discounted payback period is closest to:

A. 2.00 years.

B. 2.33 years.

C. 2.95 years.

11. (QID 241) The quick ratio of a firm is lower than the industry average whereas its current ratio is higher than the industry average. This is most likely to be explained by the firm having, relative to the industry average, high:

A. cash levels.

B. receivables.

***C. inventory levels.**

Explanation: LOS: Reading 49-c

$$\text{Current ratio} = \frac{\text{current assets}}{\text{current liabilities}}$$

$$\text{Quick ratio} = \frac{\text{(cash + marketable securities + receivables)}}{\text{current liabilities}}$$

If the quick ratio is lower and the current ratio is higher, it looks as if the inventory (usually the main difference between the two ratios) is proportionately high for the company.

**Reference:** CFA® Program Curriculum, Volume 4, pp. 499-505.

---

12. (QID 242) A $1,000,000 project has the following cash flows, $500,000 at the end of the first year, $400,000 at the end of the second year and $300,000 at the end of each year thereafter. If the cost of capital is 10%, the discounted payback period is closest to:

A. 2.00 years.

B. 2.33 years.

***C. 2.95 years.**

Explanation: LOS: Reading 44-d

The discounted payback period is the number of years that it will take for the costs of the project to be recovered based on cash flows discounted at the cost of capital.

The discounted values of the cash flows in the first three years are: $454,545.50, $330,578.50 and $225,394.40 respectively. Payback will occur $214,876.00/$225,394.40 into the third year, i.e. 95% of the way through the year.

**Reference:** CFA® Program Curriculum, Volume 4, pp. 14-15.

13. (QID 243) Southeast Inc.'s existing operations have a beta of 0.9 and its cost of capital is 14%. The risk-free rate is 6%. It is considering investing in a new project that has a beta of 1.4, the company's assets would then be split between 75% in the original business and 25% in the new project. The company will remain debt free. If the new project does not alter the valuation of the company the new cost of capital for the company is closest to:

A. 15.1%.

B. 16.2%.

C. 18.5%.

---

14. (QID 244) A company is forecasting its short-term cash flows, which of the following items is a cash outflow?

A. tax refunds.

B. debt repayments.

C. maturing investments.

13. (QID 243) Southeast Inc.'s existing operations have a beta of 0.9 and its cost of capital is 14%. The risk-free rate is 6%. It is considering investing in a new project that has a beta of 1.4, the company's assets would then be split between 75% in the original business and 25% in the new project. The company will remain debt free. If the new project does not alter the valuation of the company the new cost of capital for the company is closest to:

***A. 15.1%.**

B. 16.2%.

C. 18.5%.

Explanation: LOS: Reading 45-j

The market return is given by applying CAPM to the original business:

$$k_s = k_{RF} + \beta(k_M - k_{RF})$$

$$14\% = 6\% + 0.9(k_M - 6\%)$$

$$k_M = 14.9\%$$

**The required return for the new business is**
**6% + 1.4 (14.9% – 6%) = 18.46%**

**The weighted-average required return**
$= (0.75 \times 14\%) + (0.25 \times 18.46\%) = 15.1\%$

This is the same as the cost of capital.

**Reference:** CFA® Program Curriculum, Volume 4, pp. 62-65.

---

14. (QID 244) A company is forecasting its short-term cash flows, which of the following items is a cash outflow?

A. tax refunds.

***B. debt repayments.**

C. maturing investments.

Explanation: LOS: Reading 46-c

Debt repayments will involve cash outflows to the parties that the company has borrowed from. The other items are cash inflows.

**Reference:** CFA® Program Curriculum, Volume 4, pp. 94-95.

15. (QID 245) Evaluation of a project is least likely to involve which of the following steps?

A. Estimating the risk associated with the cash flows.

B. Discounting the cash flows back at the risk-free rate.

C. Comparing the cost of the project to the present value of the cash flows.

16. (QID 246) A company provides the following information

| | |
|---|---|
| Credit sales | \$125 million |
| Cost of goods sold | \$ 80 million |
| Accounts receivable | \$ 15 million |
| Beginning Inventory | \$ 16 million |
| Ending Inventory | \$ 22 million |
| Accounts payable | \$ 13 million |

The operating cycle and net operating cycle are closest to:

| Operating cycle | Net operating cycle |
|---|---|
| A. 144.2 | 84.9 |
| B. 108.2 | 48.9 |
| C. 108.2 | 53.1 |

15. (QID 245) Evaluation of a project is least likely to involve which of the following steps?

A. Estimating the risk associated with the cash flows.

***B. Discounting the cash flows back at the risk-free rate.**

C. Comparing the cost of the project to the present value of the cash flows.

Explanation: LOS: Reading 44-a

The cash flows should be discounted back at the cost of capital (which takes into account the risk of the project).

**Reference:** CFA® Program Curriculum, Volume 4, pp. 8-9.

---

16. (QID 246) A company provides the following information

| | |
|---|---|
| Credit sales | $125 million |
| Cost of goods sold | $ 80 million |
| Accounts receivable | $ 15 million |
| Beginning Inventory | $ 16 million |
| Ending Inventory | $ 22 million |
| Accounts payable | $ 13 million |

The operating cycle and net operating cycle are closest to:

| Operating cycle | Net operating cycle |
|---|---|
| A. 144.2 | 84.9 |
| B. 108.2 | 48.9 |
| ***C. 108.2** | **53.1** |

Explanation: LOS: Reading 46-a

Operating cycle

= number of days of receivables + number of days of inventory

= (15/125) x 365 + (22/80) x 365 = 43.8 + 100.38 = 144.18 days

Net operating cycle or cash conversion cycle

= number of days of receivables + number of days of inventory – number of days of payables

To calculate number of days of payables, we need to calculate purchases

= $80 million + ( $22 - $16) million = $86 million

= 144.18 days - (13/86) x 365 = 144.18 – 55.18 = 89.00 days

**Reference:** CFA® Program Curriculum, Volume 4, pp. 85-93.

17. (QID 247) A company gives credit term to it customers and changes the terms from 2/10 net 30 to 2/10 net 20. This is most likely to reduce:

A. cash positions.

B. the average days payable.

C. the average days of receivables.

---

18. (QID 248) Multiple internal rates of return (IRRs) for a project can occur if:

A. the cash flows decline each year of the life of the project.

B. the internal rate of return is a multiple of the crossover rate.

C. the project requires additional capital expenditure during its life.

17. (QID 247) A company gives credit term to it customers and changes the terms from 2/10 net 30 to 2/10 net 20. This is most likely to reduce:

A. cash positions.

B. the average days payable.

***C. the average days of receivables.**

Explanation: LOS: Reading 46-d

2/20 net 30 means a 2% discount for paying within 10 days and the net amount is due on the 30th day. Reducing the credit terms to 20 days will lead to cash being collected more quickly than before so "the average days of receivables" is the correct choice.

**Reference:** CFA® Program Curriculum, Volume 4, pp. 118-119.

---

18. (QID 248) Multiple internal rates of return (IRRs) for a project can occur if:

A. the cash flows decline each year of the life of the project.

B. the internal rate of return is a multiple of the crossover rate.

***C. the project requires additional capital expenditure during its life.**

Explanation: LOS: Reading 44-e

A nonconventional project is one which requires cash outflows during or at the end of the life of the project. In this case multiple IRRs will occur.

**Reference:** CFA® Program Curriculum, Volume 4, pp. 22-25.

19. (QID 249) Matt Owusu-Abeyie has just sold the company he founded, Ashburton Pet Foods, to the publiC. He has been asked to serve on the board of Ashburton Pet Foods for the next 10 years. Owusu-Abeyie's long-term participation on the board is least likely to lead to:

A. the share price declining significantly when he retires.

B. making it difficult for Owusu-Abeyie to undo any mistakes he made in the company.

C. impairing Owusu-Abeyie's willingness to act in the best interests of shareowners.

20. (QID 250) Which of the following methods is the least appropriate to calculate the cost of retained earnings?

A. Efficient frontier.

B. Risk premium approach.

C. Dividend discount model.

19. (QID 249) Matt Owusu-Abeyie has just sold the company he founded, Ashburton Pet Foods, to the publiC. He has been asked to serve on the board of Ashburton Pet Foods for the next 10 years. Owusu-Abeyie's long-term participation on the board is least likely to lead to:

***A. the share price declining significantly when he retires.**

B. making it difficult for Owusu-Abeyie to undo any mistakes he made in the company.

C. impairing Owusu-Abeyie's willingness to act in the best interests of shareowners.

Explanation: LOS: Reading 48-d

The departure of a long-term board member might signify a rejuvenation of the company and may generate enthusiasm in the market.

**Reference:** CFA® Program Curriculum, Volume 4, pp. 162-163.

---

20. (QID 250) Which of the following methods is the least appropriate to calculate the cost of retained earnings?

***A. Efficient frontier.**

B. Risk premium approach.

C. Dividend discount model.

Explanation: LOS: Reading 45-h

The efficient frontier provides the optimal mix of securities from a risk-return point of view and is dependent on the input of expected return data for the securities.

**Reference:** CFA® Program Curriculum, Volume 4, pp. 48-53.

21. (QID 251) The average accounting rate of return (AAR) is least likely to be criticized as a method for evaluating projects because the AAR:

A. does not incorporate the time value of money.

B. does not incorporate the required rate of return.

C. does not consider the income over the complete life of a project.

---

22. (QID 252) TeleNorth is a publicly-listed telecommunications company which is a privatized partially state-owned entity in the Republic of NorcorreA. The Norcorrean government holds 'golden shares' that carry super-voting rights. Which one of the following statements is most appropriate from a corporate governance point of view?

A. As a state-owned enterprise, TeleNorth can only appoint a classified board.

B. Proxy voting is only permitted at the discretion of golden sharesholders, i.e. the government.

C. The separation of voting rights from economic rights may reduce investors' enthusiasm for the shares.

21. (QID 251) The average accounting rate of return (AAR) is least likely to be criticized as a method for evaluating projects because the AAR:

A. does not incorporate the time value of money.

B. does not incorporate the required rate of return.

***C. does not consider the income over the complete life of a project.**

Explanation: LOS: Reading 44-d

Criticisms of the AAR include the following:

" it is based on net income rather than cash flows,

" it does not look at the timing of income, and

" it does not distinguish between profitable and unprofitable projects

(relative to a required return).

It does however look at the average income over the life of a project so "does not consider the income over the complete life of a project" is the best choice.

**Reference:** CFA® Program Curriculum, Volume 4, pp. 15-16.

---

22. (QID 252) TeleNorth is a publicly-listed telecommunications company which is a privatized partially state-owned entity in the Republic of NorcorreA. The Norcorrean government holds 'golden shares' that carry super-voting rights. Which one of the following statements is most appropriate from a corporate governance point of view?

A. As a state-owned enterprise, TeleNorth can only appoint a classified board.

B. Proxy voting is only permitted at the discretion of golden sharesholders, i.e. the government.

***C. The separation of voting rights from economic rights may reduce investors' enthusiasm for the shares.**

Explanation: LOS: Reading 48-g

A state-owned enterpriseis incorrect from a corporate governance view because a company is free to choose any type of board as long as it satisfactorily protects the long-term interests of the shareowners. The other two choices are in violation of shareowner rights leaving "The separation of voting rights" as the correct choice.

**Reference:** CFA® Program Curriculum, Volume 4, pp. 179-182.

23. (QID 253) A company prohibits itself from offering shares at discounted prices to management, board members and other insiders prior to a public offering of its securities. This practice is:

A. preferred by investors because it demonstrates that the company aligns itself with the investors' interests.

B. not preferred by the capital markets regulatory body because it might encourage an opportunity for insiders' trading.

C. not preferred from a corporate governance point of view because it might encourage the executives to give compensation to themselves from short-term share transactions.

---

24. (QID 305) The cost of a project is $150 million and the following cash flows are anticipated, the cost of capital is 10%.

| Year | Net Cash Flow ($ million) |
|---|---|
| 0 | -150 |
| 1 | 25 |
| 2 | 50 |
| 3 | 55 |
| 4 | 40 |
| 5 | 60 |
| Total | |

The implied decision to accept or reject the project, and the Profitability Index (PI) is closest to:

| Accept/reject | PI |
|---|---|
| A. Reject | 0.13 |
| B. Reject | 0.53 |
| C. Accept | 1.13 |

23. (QID 253) A company prohibits itself from offering shares at discounted prices to management, board members and other insiders prior to a public offering of its securities. This practice is:

***A. preferred by investors because it demonstrates that the company aligns itself with the investors' interests.**

B. not preferred by the capital markets regulatory body because it might encourage an opportunity for insiders' trading.

C. not preferred from a corporate governance point of view because it might encourage the executives to give compensation to themselves from short-term share transactions.

Explanation: LOS: Reading 48-g

This is a preferred practice from a corporate governance point of view, which indicates it is beneficial for the long-term interests of the investors.

**Reference:** CFA® Program Curriculum, Volume 4, pp. 169-171.

24. (QID 305) The cost of a project is $150 million and the following cash flows are anticipated, the cost of capital is 10%.

| Year | Net Cash Flow ($ million) |
|---|---|
| 0 | -150 |
| 1 | 25 |
| 2 | 50 |
| 3 | 55 |
| 4 | 40 |
| 5 | 60 |
| Total | |

The implied decision to accept or reject the project, and the Profitability Index (PI) is closest to:

| Accept/reject | PI |
|---|---|
| A. Reject | 0.13 |
| B. Reject | 0.53 |
| ***C. Accept** | **1.13** |

Explanation: LOS: Reading 44-d

First of all calculate the present values of the cash flows:

| Year | Net Cash Flow ($ million) | Discounted Net Cash Flow ($ million) |
|---|---|---|
| 0 | -150 | -150.0 |
| 1 | 25 | 22.7 |
| 2 | 50 | 41.3 |
| 3 | 55 | 41.3 |
| 4 | 40 | 27.3 |
| 5 | 60 | 37.3 |
| Total | | 19.9 |

PI = PV of future cash flows/Initial investment

= 1 + NPV/ Initial investment

= 1 + 19.9/150

= 1.13

This is greater than 1, so the project is expected to add to shareholder value.

**Reference:** CFA® Program Curriculum, Volume 4, p. 17.

# Study Session 12: Portfolio Management

As the first discussion within the CFA curriculum on portfolio management, this study session provides the critical framework and context for subsequent Level I study sessions covering equities, fixed income, derivatives, and alternative investments. Furthermore, this study session provides the underlying theories and tools for portfolio management at Levels II and III.

The first reading discusses the asset allocation decision and the portfolio management process—they are an integrated set of steps undertaken in a consistent manner to create and maintain an appropriate portfolio (combination of assets) to meet clients' stated goals. The last two readings focus on the design of a portfolio and introduces the capital asset pricing model (CAPM), a centerpiece of modern financial economics that relates the risk of an asset to its expected return.

**Reading 49: The Asset Allocation Decision**

**Reading 50: An Introduction to Portfolio Management**

**Reading 51: An Introduction to Asset Pricing Models**

1. (QID 254) The Capital Asset Pricing Model simplies says that an investor should:

A. calculate the variance of a multiple asset portfolio.

B. adjust the beta of a portfolio to take advantage of anticipated market moves.

C. select different optimal portfolios on the efficient frontier to match the risk tolerance of each client.

---

2. (QID 255) An investor has stated that his objective is to build a sizeable investment portfolio to meet his retirement needs in ten years' time. He is looking to invest primarily in shares and he expects returns to be generated by capital gains and reinvestment of the dividends paid into the portfolio. His return objective is best described in terms of:

A. total return.

B. current income.

C. capital appreciation.

1. (QID 254) The Capital Asset Pricing Model simplies says that an investor should:

A. calculate the variance of a multiple asset portfolio.

***B. adjust the beta of a portfolio to take advantage of anticipated market moves.**

C. select different optimal portfolios on the efficient frontier to match the risk tolerance of each client.

Explanation: LOS: Reading 51-d

CAPM states that the expected return of an asset or portfolio is a function of its market risk or beta risk.

**Reference:** CFA® Program Curriculum, Volume 4, pp. 259-263.

---

2. (QID 255) An investor has stated that his objective is to build a sizeable investment portfolio to meet his retirement needs in ten years' time. He is looking to invest primarily in shares and he expects returns to be generated by capital gains and reinvestment of the dividends paid into the portfolio. His return objective is best described in terms of:

***A. total return.**

B. current income.

C. capital appreciation.

Explanation: LOS: Reading 49-c

Total return refers to achieving returns through a combination of capital gain and reinvestment of income.

**Reference:** CFA® Program Curriculum, Volume 4, pp. 202-206.

3. (QID 256) There are two stocks, A and B, in a portfolio and 70% of the portfolio is invested in stock A and 20% in B, the remaining 10% is invested in cash equivalents. The expected return on stock A is 15% and stock B is 12%, cash returns are 5%. The beta of stock A is 1.3 and the beta of stock B is 0.9. The expected return of the portfolio is closest to:

A. 12.9%.

B. 13.4%.

C. 15.8%.

---

4. (QID 257) When adding an asset to a multi-asset portfolio in order to estimate the standard deviation of the combined portfolio, it is most important to consider:

A. the average standard deviation of the assets' returns in the portfolio.

B. the unsystematic risk of each asset and how it will be diversified away in the combined portfolio.

C. the covariance between the asset's returns and the returns of the other assets in the portfolio.

3. (QID 256) There are two stocks, A and B, in a portfolio and 70% of the portfolio is invested in stock A and 20% in B, the remaining 10% is invested in cash equivalents. The expected return on stock A is 15% and stock B is 12%, cash returns are 5%. The beta of stock A is 1.3 and the beta of stock B is 0.9. The expected return of the portfolio is closest to:

A. 12.9%.

***B. 13.4%.**

C. 15.8%.

Explanation: LOS: Reading 50-c

The expected return is:

(0.7 x 15%) + (0.2 x 12%) + (0.1 x 5%) = 13.4%

**Reference:** CFA® Program Curriculum, Volume 4, pp. 226-227.

---

4. (QID 257) When adding an asset to a multi-asset portfolio in order to estimate the standard deviation of the combined portfolio, it is most important to consider:

A. the average standard deviation of the assets' returns in the portfolio.

B. the unsystematic risk of each asset and how it will be diversified away in the combined portfolio.

***C. the covariance between the asset's returns and the returns of the other assets in the portfolio.**

Explanation: LOS: Reading 50-e

The components of the formula for portfolio standard deviation are the weighted average (where weights are squared) and the weighted covariances between each pair of assets in the portfolio. Once the number of assets in the portfolio starts to rise the number of covariance terms is significantly larger than the variance terms.

**Reference:** CFA® Program Curriculum, Volume 4, pp. 234-244.

5. (QID 258) The optimal portfolio for an investor is best described as:

A. I. the point where the securities market line is tangent to the efficient frontier.

B. II. the point on the efficient frontier that has the highest return per unit of risk.

C. III. the point where his/her highest utility curve is tangential to the efficient frontier.

---

6. (QID 259) It is least accurate to say that combining two assets in a portfolio will:

A. diversify some of the risk if the assets are not perfectly correlated.

B. provide a return that is the weighted average of the individual returns.

C. always reduce the risk of the portfolio to less than the risk of either asset.

5. (QID 258) The optimal portfolio for an investor is best described as:

A. I. the point where the securities market line is tangent to the efficient frontier.

B. II. the point on the efficient frontier that has the highest return per unit of risk.

***C. III. the point where his/her highest utility curve is tangential to the efficient frontier.**

Explanation: LOS: Reading 50-g

Choice I. describe the market portfolio which will only be optimal for investors who can tolerate exactly the risk of the market portfolio.

Choice II. may be a portfolio that is too risky for the investor.

The utility curves represent the trade off between risk and return; the optimal portfolio will be where the highest utility curve touches the efficient frontier.

**Reference:** CFA® Program Curriculum, Volume 4, pp. 243-244.

---

6. (QID 259) It is least accurate to say that combining two assets in a portfolio will:

A. diversify some of the risk if the assets are not perfectly correlated.

B. provide a return that is the weighted average of the individual returns.

***C. always reduce the risk of the portfolio to less than the risk of either asset.**

Explanation: LOS: Reading 50-e

"always reduce the risk" is not correct

– the risk will not be reduced to less than either asset unless the correlation is low or negative, e.g. if the correlation is 1 then the risk is the weighted average of the risks of the two assets.

**Reference:** CFA® Program Curriculum, Volume 4, pp. 234-241.

7. (QID 260) A U.S. investor is a taxpayer with a long investment time horizon. His objective is to maintain the purchasing power of his portfolio. Based on historic data up to 2004 which of the following is likely to represent the most appropriate investment policy?

A. The portfolio should only be invested in long-term bonds and municipal bonds.

B. Common stocks and long-term bonds should make up the largest portion of his portfolio.

C. The portfolio should be equally divided between common stocks, bonds and Treasury bills.

---

8. (QID 263) Which of the following statements is most accurate regarding Markowitz's efficient frontier? It contains the portfolios that have the

A. minimum rate of return for any given level of beta risk.

B. maximum rate of return for any given level of standard deviation of returns.

C. minimum rate of return for any given level of standard deviation of returns.

7. (QID 260) A U.S. investor is a taxpayer with a long investment time horizon. His objective is to maintain the purchasing power of his portfolio. Based on historic data up to 2004 which of the following is likely to represent the most appropriate investment policy?

A. The portfolio should only be invested in long-term bonds and municipal bonds.

***B. Common stocks and long-term bonds should make up the largest portion of his portfolio.**

C. The portfolio should be equally divided between common stocks, bonds and Treasury bills.

Explanation: LOS: Reading 49-c

Common stocks and long-term bonds are both asset classes that have produced after-tax returns that are significantly higher than inflation. Treasury bills are generally not considered attractive for long-term investment since historically they have lost value in real terms.

This is the best answer based on the data in the source text which covers the period 1981 to 2004.

**Reference:** CFA® Program Curriculum, Volume 4, pp. 216-219.

---

8. (QID 263) Which of the following statements is most accurate regarding Markowitz's efficient frontier? It contains the portfolios that have the

A. minimum rate of return for any given level of beta risk.

***B. maximum rate of return for any given level of standard deviation of returns.**

C. minimum rate of return for any given level of standard deviation of returns.

Explanation: LOS: Reading 50-f

The efficient frontier plots portfolio returns against total risk as represented by standard deviation. It represents the portfolios that offer the highest return for any given level of risk.

**Reference:** CFA® Program Curriculum, Volume 4, pp. 243-244.

9. (QID 262) The Security Market Line (SML) relates the expected return on an asset to its:

A. beta.

B. variance.

C. standard deviation.

---

10. (QID 261) The following data is provided on the expected return of an asset under different scenarios:

| Probability | Return |
|---|---|
| 0.20 | 12% |
| 0.60 | 15% |
| 0.20 | 18% |

The standard deviation of the returns is closest to:

A. 1.9%.

B. 2.3%.

C. 3.6%.

9. (QID 262) The Security Market Line (SML) relates the expected return on an asset to its:

***A. beta.**

B. variance.

C. standard deviation.

Explanation: LOS: Reading 51-d

The Security Market Line (SML) plots the required return from an asset against its systematic or beta risk.

**Reference:** CFA® Program Curriculum, Volume 4, pp. 259-263.

---

10. (QID 261) The following data is provided on the expected return of an asset under different scenarios:

| Probability | Return |
|---|---|
| 0.20 | 12% |
| 0.60 | 15% |
| 0.20 | 18% |

The standard deviation of the returns is closest to:

***A. 1.9%.**

B. 2.3%.

C. 3.6%.

Explanation: LOS: Reading 50-c

The expected return is

(0.20 x 12%) + (0.60 x 15%) + (0.20 x 18%) = 15%.

$$\sigma^2 = 0.2(0.12 - 0.15)^2 + 0.2(0.18 - 0.15)^2 = 0.00036$$
$$\sigma = 0.01897 \text{ or } 1.9\%$$

**Reference:** CFA® Program Curriculum, Volume 4, pp. 226-227.

11. (QID 264) The Capital Market Line:

A. is an efficient frontier.

B. is used to estimate the beta of a stock.

C. reflects the trade off between expected return and beta risk in a market.

---

12. (QID 265) Studies show that a portfolio investing in 18 randomly selected stocks in the U.S. stock market will diversify away approximately:

A. 90% of the systematic risk.

B. 60% of the unsystematic risk.

C. 90% of the unsystematic risk.

11. (QID 264) The Capital Market Line:

***A. is an efficient frontier.**

B. is used to estimate the beta of a stock.

C. reflects the trade off between expected return and beta risk in a market.

Explanation: LOS: Reading 51-b

The CML connects the risk-free asset with the market portfolio. It therefore is a set of portfolios offering the highest return for any given level of risk (standard deviation).

**Reference:** CFA® Program Curriculum, Volume 4, pp. 259-263.

---

12. (QID 265) Studies show that a portfolio investing in 18 randomly selected stocks in the U.S. stock market will diversify away approximately:

A. 90% of the systematic risk.

B. 60% of the unsystematic risk.

***C. 90% of the unsystematic risk.**

Explanation: LOS: Reading 51-c

Systematic risk cannot be diversified away but unsystematic risk can be largely eliminated with a relatively small number of stocks.

**Reference:** CFA® Program Curriculum, Volume 4, pp. 255-256.

13. (QID 266) If the standard deviations of returns of two assets are 3.2% and 4.5%, and the covariance between the assets is 6.8, then the correlation coefficient between the returns is closest to:

A. 0.03.

B. 0.22.

C. 0.47.

---

14. (QID 267) Analysis of portfolio performance shows that:

A. individual security selection is the largest contributor to performance.

B. the most important decision is to select the normal long-term asset allocation correctly.

C. there is no consistent pattern as to whether asset allocation or stock selection is the major contributor to performance.

13. (QID 266) If the standard deviations of returns of two assets are 3.2% and 4.5%, and the covariance between the assets is 6.8, then the correlation coefficient between the returns is closest to:

A. 0.03.

B. 0.22.

***C. 0.47.**

Explanation: LOS: Reading 50-d

$$r_{xy} = \frac{\text{covariance}_{xy}}{\sigma_x \sigma_y} = \frac{6.8}{3.2 \times 4.5} = 0.47$$

**Reference:** CFA® Program Curriculum, Volume 4, pp. 232-233.

---

14. (QID 267) Analysis of portfolio performance shows that:

A. individual security selection is the largest contributor to performance.

***B. the most important decision is to select the normal long-term asset allocation correctly.**

C. there is no consistent pattern as to whether asset allocation or stock selection is the major contributor to performance.

Explanation: LOS: Reading 49-e

Around 90% of the investment returns come from the long-term asset allocation of the portfolio.

**Reference:** CFA® Program Curriculum, Volume 4, pp. 214-226.

15. (QID 268) The returns of two assets X and Y have perfect negative correlation. When the two assets are combined in a portfolio, which of the following statements is the most accurate?

A. I. The return of the portfolio will always be zero.

B. II. The risk/return trade off will always be suboptimal.

C. III. The risk of the portfolio can be completely eliminated.

---

16. (QID 269) If the market risk premium is 4%, the risk-free rate is 6%, and a stock has a beta of 1.1 and standard deviation of 3%, then the expected return from the stock is:

A. 10.4%.

B. 11.0%.

C. 15.0%.

15. (QID 268) The returns of two assets X and Y have perfect negative correlation. When the two assets are combined in a portfolio, which of the following statements is the most accurate?

A. I. The return of the portfolio will always be zero.

B. II. The risk/ return trade off will always be suboptimal.

***C. III. The risk of the portfolio can be completely eliminated.**

Explanation: LOS: Reading 50-e

The returns of the portfolio will only be zero in a few cases, e.g. the returns of the assets are perfectly inversely related and they are equally weighted, so I. is not correct.

The risk/return tradeoffs will be optimal on the upper part of the efficient frontier representing all possible combinations of the assets so II. is not correct.

Risk will be diversified away and can be completely eliminated if the weightings are calculated based on the relative standard deviations of the two assets, so III. is correct.

**Reference:** CFA® Program Curriculum, Volume 4, pp. 228-241.

---

16. (QID 269) If the market risk premium is 4%, the risk-free rate is 6%, and a stock has a beta of 1.1 and standard deviation of 3%, then the expected return from the stock is:

***A. 10.4%.**

B. 11.0%.

C. 15.0%.

Explanation: LOS: Reading 51-d

Using CAPM, the return:

$$R_x = R_f + \beta[E(R_m) - R_f] = 6\% + (1.1 \times 4\%) = 10.4\%$$

**Reference:** CFA® Program Curriculum, Volume 4, pp. 259-263.

17. (QID 270) Investors are generally risk-averse means that:

A. investors prefer not to take on any risk.

B. there is an inverse relationship between return and risk.

C. for a given level of return investors prefer a lower risk investment.

---

18. (QID 271) If the correlation coefficient between the returns of two assets is 0.8 and the variance of the returns of the two assets is 0.0018 and 0.0026, the covariance of the returns is closest to:

A. 4.60.

B. 17.09.

C. 17.30.

17. (QID 270) Investors are generally risk-averse means that:

A. investors prefer not to take on any risk.

B. there is an inverse relationship between return and risk.

***C. for a given level of return investors prefer a lower risk investment.**

Explanation: LOS: Reading 50-a

Risk aversion simply means that investors wish to be compensated for taking on risk and therefore for a given level of return they prefer a lower risk investment.

**Reference:** CFA® Program Curriculum, Volume 4, pp. 224-225.

---

18. (QID 271) If the correlation coefficient between the returns of two assets is 0.8 and the variance of the returns of the two assets is 0.0018 and 0.0026, the covariance of the returns is closest to:

A. 4.60.

B. 17.09.

***C. 17.30.**

Explanation: LOS: Reading 50-d

Important:

(Remember to take the square root of the variance to get the standard deviation.)

$$r_{xy} = \frac{\text{covariance}_{xy}}{\sigma_x \sigma y}$$

$$\text{cov} = 0.8 \times 4.24 \times 5.1 = 17.30$$

**Reference:** CFA® Program Curriculum, Volume 4, pp. 232-233.

19. (QID 272) Which of the following is the least appropriate example of an investment constraint that will have an impact on an investor's policy statement?

A. Time horizon.

B. Liquidity requirements.

C. Capital appreciation requirements.

---

20. (QID 273) Which of the following would be a factor that would have a direct impact on an investor's risk tolerance?

A. His total net worth.

B. A high rate of income tax.

C. A preference for ethical investments.

19. (QID 272) Which of the following is the least appropriate example of an investment constraint that will have an impact on an investor's policy statement?

A. Time horizon.

B. Liquidity requirements.

***C. Capital appreciation requirements.**

Explanation: LOS: Reading 49-d

Capital appreciation is an objective rather than a constraint.

**Reference:** CFA® Program Curriculum, Volume 4, pp. 206-212.

---

20. (QID 273) Which of the following would be a factor that would have a direct impact on an investor's risk tolerance?

***A. His total net worth.**

B. A high rate of income tax.

C. A preference for ethical investments.

Explanation: LOS: Reading 49-b

"total net worth" has a direct impact on risk tolerance.

The other choices all constraints on the way a portfolio of investments would be managed but do not directly affect the risk tolerance of the investor.

**Reference:** CFA® Program Curriculum, Volume 4, pp. 202-206.

21. (QID 274) Which of the following is least likely to be an assumption of capital market theory?

A. Investors are averse to buying and selling securities.

B. All investors have the same time horizon when they invest.

C. There are no transaction costs in buying and selling securities.

---

22. (QID 275) The slope of an efficient frontier decreases steadily as an investor moves up the frontier because:

A. the portfolios become increasingly efficient as you move up the frontier.

B. as an investor continues to take on more risk the incremental return diminishes.

C. an investor has to be rewarded for taking on additional risk by being given rapidly increasingly higher returns.

21. (QID 274) Which of the following is least likely to be an assumption of capital market theory?

***A. Investors are averse to buying and selling securities.**

B. All investors have the same time horizon when they invest.

C. There are no transaction costs in buying and selling securities.

Explanation: LOS: Reading 51-a

It is not assumed that investors are averse to buying and selling securities. It is assumed they will do the transactions required to invest at a point on the efficient frontier.

**Reference:** CFA® Program Curriculum, Volume 4, pp. 250-251.

---

22. (QID 275) The slope of an efficient frontier decreases steadily as an investor moves up the frontier because:

A. the portfolios become increasingly efficient as you move up the frontier.

***B. as an investor continues to take on more risk the incremental return diminishes.**

C. an investor has to be rewarded for taking on additional risk by being given rapidly increasingly higher returns.

Explanation: LOS: Reading 50-f

Adding equal increments of additional risk (horizontal axis) leads to smaller incremental returns (vertical axis).

**Reference:** CFA® Program Curriculum, Volume 4, pp. 243-244.

23. (QID 276) The characteristic line:

A. is a regression line used to estimate a stock's systematic risk.

B. is a regression line used to estimate a stock's standard deviation.

C. indicates the required rate of return of a stock given its systematic risk.

---

24. (QID 335) Two assets have zero correlation. If a portfolio is invested with 30% in the first asset that has a variance of 12, and 70% in the second asset that has a variance of 8, the variance of the combined portfolio is closest to:

A. 2.2.

B. 5.0.

C. 6.7.

---

25. (QID 336) The characteristic line:

A. is a regression line used to estimate a stock's systematic risk.

B. indicates the required rate of return of a stock given its systematic risk

C. indicates the required rate of return of a stock given its standard deviation

23. (QID 276) The characteristic line:

***A. is a regression line used to estimate a stock's systematic risk.**

B. is a regression line used to estimate a stock's standard deviation.

C. indicates the required rate of return of a stock given its systematic risk.

Explanation: LOS: Reading 51-d

Systematic risk is often calculated by using regression analysis to examine the return of an asset against the return of the market. The slope of the line is the beta which measures systematic risk.

**Reference:** CFA® Program Curriculum, Volume 4, pp. 267-271.

---

24. (QID 335) Two assets have zero correlation. If a portfolio is invested with 30% in the first asset that has a variance of 12, and 70% in the second asset that has a variance of 8, the variance of the combined portfolio is closest to:

A. 2.2.

***B. 5.0.**

C. 6.7.

Explanation: LOS: Reading 50-c

Variance is given by:

$$\sigma^2_{port} = w_1^2\sigma_1^2 + w_2^2\sigma_2^2 + 2r_{12}w_1w_2\sigma_1\sigma_2$$
$$= (0.3)^2 12 + (0.7)^2 8$$
$$= 1.08 + 3.92$$
$$= 5$$

**Reference:** CFA® Program Curriculum, Volume 4, pp. 234-237.

25. (QID 336) The characteristic line:

***A. is a regression line used to estimate a stock's systematic risk.**

B. indicates the required rate of return of a stock given its systematic risk

C. indicates the required rate of return of a stock given its standard deviation

Explanation: LOS: Reading 51-d

Systematic risk is often calculated by using regression analysis to examine the return of an asset against the return of the market. The slope of the line is the beta which measures systematic risk.

**Reference:** CFA® Program Curriculum, Volume 4, pp. 263-267.

# Study Session 13: Equity Investments: Securities Markets

This study session addresses how securities are bought and sold and what constitutes a well-functioning securities market. The reading on market indexes gives an understanding of how indexes are constructed and calculated and the biases inherent in each of the weighting schemes used.

Some of the most interesting and important work in the investment field during the past several decades revolves around the efficient market hypothesis (EMH) and its implications for active versus passive equity portfolio management. The readings on this subject provide an understanding of the EMH and the seemingly persistent anomalies to the theory, an understanding that is necessary to judge the value of fundamental or technical security analysis.

**Reading 52: Organization and Functioning of Securities Markets**

**Reading 53: Security-Market Indexes**

**Reading 54: Efficient Capital Markets**

**Reading 55: Market Efficiency and Anomalies**

1. (QID 277) If a market is internally efficient it means that:

A. I. transaction costs are minimal.

B. II. stock prices reflect all information from public and private sources.

C. III. investors direct money to the companies that can make the best use of the funds.

---

2. (QID 278) In the primary market Treasury bonds are sold:

A. by private placement.

B. by Federal Reserve auction.

C. on a best efforts basis by a consortium of investment banks.

1. (QID 277) If a market is internally efficient it means that:

***A. I. transaction costs are minimal.**

B. II. stock prices reflect all information from public and private sources.

C. III. investors direct money to the companies that can make the best use of the funds.

Explanation: LOS: Reading 52-a

II. refer to the weak and strong forms of the efficient market hypothesis respectively

III. refers to allocative efficiency. Internally efficient simply means transaction costs are minimized.

**Reference:** CFA® Program Curriculum, Volume 5, pp. 6-8.

---

2. (QID 278) In the primary market Treasury bonds are sold:

A. by private placement.

***B. by Federal Reserve auction.**

C. on a best efforts basis by a consortium of investment banks.

Explanation: LOS: Reading 52-b

Treasury bonds (and notes and bills) are all sold through Federal Reserve auctions.

**Reference:** CFA® Program Curriculum, Volume 5, pp. 8-9.

3. (QID 279) Value Line indexes are calculated as follows:

| Weighting of constituent stocks | Holding period returns |
|---|---|
| A. unweighted | arithmetic mean |
| B. unweighted | geometric mean |
| C. price-weighted | arithmetic mean |

---

4. (QID 280) In a continuous dealer market:

A. I. the market is open for 24 hours a day with market makers providing liquidity.

B. II. there are always dealers available when the market is open who are willing to make a market in a stock.

C. III. there is sufficient liquidity to assume that dealers who are submitting bid and ask prices will be able to deal.

3. (QID 279) Value Line indexes are calculated as follows:

| Weighting of constituent stocks | Holding period returns |
|---|---|
| A. unweighted | arithmetic mean |
| ***B. unweighted** | **geometric mean** |
| C. price-weighted | arithmetic mean |

Explanation: LOS: Reading 53-a

Value Line uses a geometric average of holding period returns to compute an unweighted index. Each stock therefore has an equal weight in the index and note that the geometric mean calculation gives it a downward bias compared to an arithmetic mean being used.

**Reference:** CFA® Program Curriculum, Volume 5, pp. 45-46.

---

4. (QID 280) In a continuous dealer market:

A. I. the market is open for 24 hours a day with market makers providing liquidity.

***B. II. there are always dealers available when the market is open who are willing to make a market in a stock.**

C. III. there is sufficient liquidity to assume that dealers who are submitting bid and ask prices will be able to deal.

Explanation: LOS: Reading 52-c

I. A continuous market only needs to be liquid during its opening hours, it is not necessary for trading to be open for 24 hours.

III. is a continuous auction market.

**Reference:** CFA® Program Curriculum, Volume 5, pp. 13-15.

5. (QID 281) Which of the following is least likely to make the computation of bond market indexes more complex than stock market indexes in the U.S.?

A. Difficulties in establishing prices for bonds.

B. The universe of bonds is constantly changing due to the volume of new issues and bonds reaching maturity.

C. Investors receive a higher percentage of their return from coupon income from bonds than they receive from dividends with equities.

---

6. (QID 282) The third market refers to:

A. I. a regional exchange.

B. II. direct trading between two institutions.

C. III. over-the-counter trading of shares which are listed on an exchange.

5. (QID 281) Which of the following is least likely to make the computation of bond market indexes more complex than stock market indexes in the U.S.?

A. Difficulties in establishing prices for bonds.

B. The universe of bonds is constantly changing due to the volume of new issues and bonds reaching maturity.

***C. Investors receive a higher percentage of their return from coupon income from bonds than they receive from dividends with equities.**

Explanation: LOS: Reading 53-b

Two of the choices points are true plus there is also the issue of the change in volatility of bond indexes as durations are constantly changing.

"Investors receive a higher percentage" is not a factor that would make the computation of the index more complex, either the index would include reinvestment of income or it would not.

**Reference:** CFA® Program Curriculum, Volume 5, pp. 52-53.

---

6. (QID 282) The third market refers to:

A. I. a regional exchange.

B. II. direct trading between two institutions.

***C. III. over-the-counter trading of shares which are listed on an exchange.**

Explanation: LOS: Reading 52-d

The third market refers to trading outside an exchange

so I. is not correct.

Direct trading without the use of a broker is the fourth market

so II. is not correct.

The third market is over-the-counter trading of shares which are listed on an exchange.

**Reference:** CFA® Program Curriculum, Volume 5, p. 23.

7. (QID 283) If the performance of the Merrill Lynch-Wilshire Capital Markets Index was substantially higher than the Merrill Lynch Investment-Grade Bond Index over the same period this is most likely to be explained by:

A. U.S. Treasury bonds performed better than U.S. corporate bonds.

B. U.S. mortgage bonds performed better than U.S. corporate bonds.

C. the U.S. stock market performed better than the U.S. bond market.

---

8. (QID 284) If an investor buys a stock that is trading at $150 on margin and the percent margin is 25% then the leverage factor is:

A. 0.25.

B. 4.00.

C. 6.00.

7. (QID 283) If the performance of the Merrill Lynch-Wilshire Capital Markets Index was substantially higher than the Merrill Lynch Investment-Grade Bond Index over the same period this is most likely to be explained by:

A. U.S. Treasury bonds performed better than U.S. corporate bonds.

B. U.S. mortgage bonds performed better than U.S. corporate bonds.

***C. the U.S. stock market performed better than the U.S. bond market.**

Explanation: LOS: Reading 53-b

The Merrill Lynch-Wilshire Capital Markets Index is a combination of U.S. fixed income instruments and U.S. equities, therefore the outperformance of this index against the Merrill Lynch bond index is likely to be because equity markets provided superior returns to bonds.

**Reference:** CFA® Program Curriculum, Volume 5, pp. 53-56.

---

8. (QID 284) If an investor buys a stock that is trading at $150 on margin and the percent margin is 25% then the leverage factor is:

A. 0.25.

***B. 4.00.**

C. 6.00.

Explanation: LOS: Reading 52-g

The leverage factor is 1/(percent margin) which is 1/ 0.25 = 4

**Reference:** CFA® Program Curriculum, Volume 5, pp. 26-29.

9. (QID 285) In the U.S. a person who quotes bid and ask prices for a stock is called a:

A. specialist.

B. floor broker.

C. registered trader.

10. (QID 286) The cost of information explains why:

A. markets are not completely efficient.

B. there tends to be an upward bias to prices.

C. arbitrageurs cannot exploit pricing anomalies.

9. (QID 285) In the U.S. a person who quotes bid and ask prices for a stock is called a:

***A. specialist.**

B. floor broker.

C. registered trader.

Explanation: LOS: Reading 52-e

A specialist makes markets in stocks. They also act as brokers and match buy and sell orders.

**Reference:** CFA® Program Curriculum, Volume 5, pp. 29-31.

---

10. (QID 286) The cost of information explains why:

***A. markets are not completely efficient.**

B. there tends to be an upward bias to prices.

C. arbitrageurs cannot exploit pricing anomalies.

Explanation: LOS: Reading 55-a

The cost of information is one of the reasons why markets cannot be completely efficient; there must be some reward for analyzing or sourcing new information to justify the cost.

**Reference:** CFA® Program Curriculum, Volume 5, pp. 97-98.

11. (QID 287) We should be skeptical of any claims by institutional fund managers to have found a pricing anomaly because:

A. there are biases in the way stock trading strategies are researched.

B. markets are highly efficient so anomalies will only persist for very short periods.

C. most anomalies are exploited by individual investors and not institutional fund managers.

---

12. (QID 288) An investor buys 1,000 shares priced at $100 on margin and the initial margin required is 40%. If the maintenance margin is 30% the investor will have to pay the first margin call if the share price falls below:

A. $70.00.

B. $85.71.

C. $90.00.

11. (QID 287) We should be skeptical of any claims by institutional fund managers to have found a pricing anomaly because:

***A. there are biases in the way stock trading strategies are researched.**

B. markets are highly efficient so anomalies will only persist for very short periods.

C. most anomalies are exploited by individual investors and not institutional fund managers.

Explanation: LOS: Reading 55-d

Research that 'discovers' trading anomalies is often subject to survivorship bias, selection bias or small sample bias.

**Reference:** CFA® Program Curriculum, Volume 5, pp. 100-104.

---

12. (QID 288) An investor buys 1,000 shares priced at $100 on margin and the initial margin required is 40%. If the maintenance margin is 30% the investor will have to pay the first margin call if the share price falls below:

A. $70.00.

***B. $85.71.**

C. $90.00.

Explanation: LOS: Reading 52-g

The initial margin requirement of 40% allows the investor to borrow 60%, or $60,000 of the $100,000 cost of the shares. If the price of the shares moves to P the value of the equity is 1,000P - $60,000. This must equal 30% of 1,000P. This gives:

1,000P - $60,000 = 300P or P = $85.71

**Reference:** CFA® Program Curriculum, Volume 5, pp. 26-29.

13. (QID 289) Specialists are expected to:

A. sell stock from their own inventory when the market for a stock is declining.

B. buy and sell against the market when a stock is moving clearly in one direction.

C. widen the bid-ask spread for a stock when there is excessive volatility in the stock price movement.

---

14. (QID 290) The Dow Jones Industrial Average:

A. is a price-weighted index and automatically adjusts for a stock split by leaving the security weighting unchanged.

B. is a value-weighted index and has a downward bias since when there is a stock split of a constituent security the security weighting in the index will be reduced.

C. is a price-weighted index and has a downward bias since when there is a stock split of a constituent security the security weighting in the index will be reduced.

13. (QID 289) Specialists are expected to:

A. sell stock from their own inventory when the market for a stock is declining.

***B. buy and sell against the market when a stock is moving clearly in one direction.**

C. widen the bid-ask spread for a stock when there is excessive volatility in the stock price movement.

Explanation: LOS: Reading 52-e

The obligation of a market maker is to ensure a fair and orderly market for shares by providing reasonable liquidity. This would involve narrowing the spread for an illiquid stock, buying stock for their own inventory if the stock price is declining and visa versa if the stock price is rising, i.e. buying and selling against the market when shares are moving in one direction. Although this may dampen stock price moves there is not the expectation that specialists will try to stop stock prices moving.

**Reference:** CFA® Program Curriculum, Volume 5, pp. 29-31.

---

14. (QID 290) The Dow Jones Industrial Average:

A. is a price-weighted index and automatically adjusts for a stock split by leaving the security weighting unchanged.

B. is a value-weighted index and has a downward bias since when there is a stock split of a constituent security the security weighting in the index will be reduced.

***C. is a price-weighted index and has a downward bias since when there is a stock split of a constituent security the security weighting in the index will be reduced.**

Explanation: LOS: Reading 53-a

The Dow Jones Industrial Average is the price-weighted average of the 30 constituent stocks. It is computed by taking the sum of the prices of the stocks and dividing by a divisor that adjusts to take account of stock splits, so the index value is not altered by a stock split. However when a company does a stock split leading to a fall in the price, the weighting of the stock in the index will thereafter be smaller. Since more successful companies have, on average, rising share prices which lead to them having more stock splits this leads to their weighting being repeatedly reduced creating a downward bias in the index.

**Reference:** CFA® Program Curriculum, Volume 5, pp. 42-43.

15. (QID 291) An underwriter of a bond issue, if it is a negotiated bid, is least likely to do which of the following?

A. Origination.

B. Distribute the bonds to investors.

C. Return the unsold portion of bonds to the issuer.

---

16. (QID 292) There are three shares, A, B and C in a price-weighted index and the following information is given:

| | Share Price | Number of shares Outstanding |
|---|---|---|
| X | $50 | 100,000 |
| Y | $100 | 40,000 |
| Z | $75 | 10,000 |

If the share price of A doubles and the share prices of B and C remain unchanged then the index will rise by:

A. 22.22%.

B. 33.33%.

C. 44.44%.

15. (QID 291) An underwriter of a bond issue, if it is a negotiated bid, is least likely to do which of the following?

A. Origination.

B. Distribute the bonds to investors.

***C. Return the unsold portion of bonds to the issuer.**

Explanation: LOS: Reading 52-b

In a negotiated bid, the underwriter will take on the risk of selling the bonds at a price equal to, or higher than, the price paid to the issuer. Any unsold bonds will remain on the underwriter's book.

**Reference:** CFA® Program Curriculum, Volume 5, p. 9.

---

16. (QID 292) There are three shares, A, B and C in a price-weighted index and the following information is given:

| | Share Price | Number of shares Outstanding |
|---|---|---|
| X | $50 | 100,000 |
| Y | $100 | 40,000 |
| Z | $75 | 10,000 |

If the share price of A doubles and the share prices of B and C remain unchanged then the index will rise by:

***A. 22.22%.**

B. 33.33%.

C. 44.44%.

Explanation: LOS: Reading 53-a

Assume that the initial index is the sum of the prices = $50 + $100 + $75 =$225

If X doubles the index = $100 + $100 + $75 =$275, an increase of 22.22%.

**Reference:** CFA® Program Curriculum, Volume 5, pp. 42-44.

17. (QID 293) The geometric mean of the holding period returns of the constituents of an index are used, rather than the arithmetic mean, to compute an index level. If an investor replicates the index by holding the shares in the same weighting as they are represented in the index:

A. he will see the value of the shares move exactly in line with the index.

B. he will see the value of the shares increase by less than the index in a rising market.

C. he will see the value of the shares increase by more than the index in a rising market.

18. (QID 294) In Japan, if the share price of a company with a small market capitalization, that is in both the Nikkei Dow Jones Index and the TOPIX index, rises sharply then:

A. there is insufficient information to determine which index will rise the most.

B. the TOPIX will rise by more than the Nikkei-Dow Jones Average index since the Nikkei is a price-weighted index.

C. the Nikkei-Dow Jones Average index will rise by more than the TOPIX index since the Nikkei is a price-weighted index.

17. (QID 293) The geometric mean of the holding period returns of the constituents of an index are used, rather than the arithmetic mean, to compute an index level. If an investor replicates the index by holding the shares in the same weighting as they are represented in the index:

A. he will see the value of the shares move exactly in line with the index.

B. he will see the value of the shares increase by less than the index in a rising market.

***C. he will see the value of the shares increase by more than the index in a rising market.**

Explanation: LOS: Reading 53-a

In all types of index the geometric mean will be less than the arithmetic mean (unless each share moves by an identical amount in each time period) in a rising market.

**Reference:** CFA® Program Curriculum, Volume 5, pp. 45-46.

---

18. (QID 294) In Japan, if the share price of a company with a small market capitalization, that is in both the Nikkei Dow Jones Index and the TOPIX index, rises sharply then:

***A. there is insufficient information to determine which index will rise the most.**

B. the TOPIX will rise by more than the Nikkei-Dow Jones Average index since the Nikkei is a price-weighted index.

C. the Nikkei-Dow Jones Average index will rise by more than the TOPIX index since the Nikkei is a price-weighted index.

Explanation: LOS: Reading 53-a

Unless we know the Yen price relative to the market capitalization of the company's stock we cannot calculate which index will rise the most. The Nikkei is a price-weighted index and the TOPIX is a market-weighted index.

**Reference:** CFA® Program Curriculum, Volume 5, pp. 42-44.

19. (QID 295) Which of the following statements regarding NASDAQ is least accurate?

A. Dealers are obligated to execute transactions at the prices shown on the NASDAQ system.

B. A broker can access the bid and ask quotes for a stock from various dealers on the NASDAQ system.

C. Dealers are free to make markets on as many or as few OTC stocks as they wish on the NASDAQ system.

---

20. (QID 296) Security-market indexes are least likely to be used for:

A. constructing index funds.

B. computing total risk of portfolios.

C. benchmarks, to measure the performance of portfolios.

19. (QID 295) Which of the following statements regarding NASDAQ is least accurate?

***A. Dealers are obligated to execute transactions at the prices shown on the NASDAQ system.**

B. A broker can access the bid and ask quotes for a stock from various dealers on the NASDAQ system.

C. Dealers are free to make markets on as many or as few OTC stocks as they wish on the NASDAQ system.

Explanation: LOS: Reading 52-d

A broker will call a dealer who is showing the most attractive prices on the screen and verify the price; at that point the trade could be executed.

**Reference:** CFA® Program Curriculum, Volume 5, pp. 20-22.

---

20. (QID 296) Security-market indexes are least likely to be used for:

A. constructing index funds.

***B. computing total risk of portfolios.**

C. benchmarks, to measure the performance of portfolios.

Explanation: LOS: Reading 53-a

Index performance is used to compute systematic or market risk of portfolios.

Reference CFA® Program Curriculum, Volume 5, pp. 40-41.

**Reference:** CFA® Program Curriculum, Volume 5, pp. 52-53.

21. (QID 297) Two indexes contain exactly the same stocks; one is a value-weighted index which increased by 12% whereas the other is an unweighted index which increased by 5% over the same period. This is explained by:

A. there were a large number of stock splits over the period.

B. there were a small number of stock splits over the period.

C. large capitalization stocks outperformed small capitalization stocks.

---

23. (QID 299) The initial margin requirement for a stock purchase is:

A. the market value of the stock less the amount borrowed.

B. the market value of the stock less the amount paid in cash.

C. the percentage of the transaction value that must be paid for in cash.

21. (QID 297) Two indexes contain exactly the same stocks; one is a value-weighted index which increased by 12% whereas the other is an unweighted index which increased by 5% over the same period. This is explained by:

A. there were a large number of stock splits over the period.

B. there were a small number of stock splits over the period.

***C. large capitalization stocks outperformed small capitalization stocks.**

Explanation: LOS: Reading 53-a

Stock splits will not affect either index since in the market-value-weighted index when there is a stock split the number of shares outstanding will increase but the share price will fall by a corresponding amount. An unweighted index will be computed on an equal amount of money invested in each stock regardless of price or market value.

In a value-weighted index companies with a larger market capitalization will have a higher weighting so "large capitalization stocks" is the correct choice.

**Reference:** CFA® Program Curriculum, Volume 5, pp. 44-46.

---

22. (QID 299) The initial margin requirement for a stock purchase is:

A. the market value of the stock less the amount borrowed.

B. the market value of the stock less the amount paid in cash.

***C. the percentage of the transaction value that must be paid for in cash.**

Explanation: LOS: Reading 52-g

The initial margin is simply the percentage or proportion of the transaction value that must be paid for in cash, rather than borrowed.

**Reference:** CFA® Program Curriculum, Volume 5, pp. 26-29.

23. (QID 298) There are two stocks ABC and XYZ included in an unweighted index and the following data is provided:

| Stock | Number of shares | Price at end Year 1 | Price at end Year 2 |
|---|---|---|---|
| ABC | 10,000 | $25.00 | $30.00 |
| XYZ | 50,000 | $35.00 | $36.75 |

If the index is computed using geometric averages, the increase in the index over 2007 is closest to:

A. 11.25%.

B. 12.25%.

C. 12.50%.

24. (QID 363) A value-weighted index is made up of two stocks, X and Y, and the following data is provided:

| | December 31st 2006 | | December 31st 2007 | |
|---|---|---|---|---|
| Stock | Price | Shares Outstanding | Price | Shares Outstanding |
| X | $25 | 10,000 | $15 | 20,000* |
| Y | $50 | 6,000 | $65 | 6,000 |

* after a 2 for 1 stock split

The base index is set at 100 on December 31st 2007. The index on December 31st 2008 is closest to:

A. 98.18.

B. 125.45.

C. 126.67.

23. (QID 298) There are two stocks ABC and XYZ included in an unweighted index and the following data is provided:

| Stock | Number of shares | Price at end Year 1 | Price at end Year 2 |
|---|---|---|---|
| ABC | 10,000 | $25.00 | $30.00 |
| XYZ | 50,000 | $35.00 | $36.75 |

If the index is computed using geometric averages, the increase in the index over 2007 is closest to:

A. 11.25%.

***B. 12.25%.**

C. 12.50%.

Explanation: LOS: Reading 53-a

An unweighted index is computed on the basis that an equal dollar amount is invested in each of stocks ABC and XYZ. ABC rose by 20% and XYZ by 5% so the index performance is given by .

$$(1.20 \times 1.05)^{1/2} - 1 = 0.1225 = 12.25\%.$$

**Reference:** CFA® Program Curriculum, Volume 5, pp. 44-46.

24. (QID 363) A value-weighted index is made up of two stocks, X and Y, and the following data is provided:

| | December 31st 2006 | | December 31st 2007 | |
|---|---|---|---|---|
| Stock | Price | Shares Outstanding | Price | Shares Outstanding |
| X | $25 | 10,000 | $15 | 20,000* |
| Y | $50 | 6,000 | $65 | 6,000 |

* after a 2 for 1 stock split

The base index is set at 100 on December 31st 2007. The index on December 31st 2008 is closest to:

A. 98.18.

***B. 125.45.**

C. 126.67.

Explanation: LOS: Reading 53-a

Total market value on DeC. 31st 2006 is ($25 x 10,000) + ($50 x 6,000) = $550,000

Total market value on DeC. 31st 2007 is ($15 x 20,000) + ($65 x 6,000) = $690,000

The index = ($690,000/$550,000) x100 = 125.45

**Reference:** CFA® Program Curriculum, Volume 5, pp. 44-45.

# Study Session 14: Equity Investments: Industry and Company Analysis

This study session focuses on industry and company analysis and describes the tools used in forming an opinion about investing in a particular stock or group of stocks.

This study session begins with the essential tools of equity valuation: the discounted cash flow technique and the relative valuation approach. These techniques provide the means to estimate reasonable price for a stock. The readings on industry analysis are an important element in the valuation process, providing the top–down context crucial to estimating a company's potential. Also addressed is estimating a company's earnings per share by forecasting sales and profit margins.

The last reading in this study session focuses on price multiples, one of the most familiar and widely used tools in estimating the value of a company, and introduces the application of four commonly used price multiples to valuation.

**Reading 56: An Introduction to Security Valuation: Part I**

**Reading 57: Industry Analysis**

**Reading 58: Company Analysis and Stock Valuation**

**Reading 59: Introduction to Price Multiples**

1. (QID 300) The required rate of return of an investor buying an asset is least likely to depend on the:

A. risk premium of the asset.

B. real risk-free rate of the economy.

C. growth rate of the asset's earnings.

---

2. (QID 301) An industry has a Herfindahl index of 0.05. Which of the following statements might explain this?

A. The industry is an oligopoly.

B. The industry has a large number of participants with no single firm holding a large market share.

C. The industry has very few participants, each with an approximately equal market share.

1. (QID 300) The required rate of return of an investor buying an asset is least likely to depend on the:

A. risk premium of the asset.

B. real risk-free rate of the economy.

***C. growth rate of the asset's earnings.**

Explanation: LOS: Reading 56-e

The required rate of return depends on three factors: the real risk-free rate, the expected inflation rate and a risk premium.

**Reference:** CFA® Program Curriculum, Volume 5, pp. 141-143.

---

2. (QID 301) An industry has a Herfindahl index of 0.05. Which of the following statements might explain this?

A. The industry is an oligopoly.

***B. The industry has a large number of participants with no single firm holding a large market share.**

C. The industry has very few participants, each with an approximately equal market share.

Explanation: LOS: Reading 58-e

A Herfindahl index of 0.05 indicates low concentration in the industry. For example if there were 20 firms with equal market shares the Herfindahl index would be 0.05.

**Reference:** CFA® Program Curriculum, Volume 5, pp. 196-199.

3. (QID 302) When economies move from being industrially based to service based this could be most appropriately described as:

A. value chain competition.

B. cyclical economic change.

C. structural economic change.

---

4. (QID 303) Which of the following is most likely to lead to estimated earnings per share for a stock being lower than in the previous period?

A. Tax rates are declining.

B. Industry sales are rising.

C. Unit labor costs are rising.

3. (QID 302) When economies move from being industrially based to service based this could be most appropriately described as:

A. value chain competition.

B. cyclical economic change.

***C. structural economic change.**

Explanation: LOS: Reading 57

A structural economic change is when an economy goes through a major change in the way it functions. A move from an industry-based to a service-based economy is an example of this. Business or economic cycles are shorter term ups and downs in economic activity.

**Reference:** CFA® Program Curriculum, Volume 5, pp. 155-157.

---

4. (QID 303) Which of the following is most likely to lead to estimated earnings per share for a stock being lower than in the previous period?

A. Tax rates are declining.

B. Industry sales are rising.

***C. Unit labor costs are rising.**

Explanation: LOS: Reading 58-b

Higher unit labor costs will depress operating margins. The other factors will tend to increase earnings per share.

**Reference:** CFA® Program Curriculum, Volume 5, pp. 162-166.

5. (QID 304) The major difference between portfolio managers who follow the top-down rather than the bottom-up approach to stock valuation is that they:

A. they focus on selecting stocks that will outperform the market regardless of the market outlook.

B. they focus on selecting stocks that will outperform the market regardless of the industry outlook.

C. they place emphasis on the market and industry outlook in determining stocks' performance.

---

6. (QID 305) Estimating the earnings per share for a firm's stock is least likely to involve analyzing which of the following?

A. The firm's earnings multiplier.

B. The firm's competitive strategy.

C. The firm's operating profit margins.

5. (QID 304) The major difference between portfolio managers who follow the top-down rather than the bottom-up approach to stock valuation is that they:

A. they focus on selecting stocks that will outperform the market regardless of the market outlook.

B. they focus on selecting stocks that will outperform the market regardless of the industry outlook.

***C. they place emphasis on the market and industry outlook in determining stocks' performance.**

Explanation: LOS: Reading 56-a

A top-down portfolio manager will look at market factors first, then industry factors and finally individual securities.

The other three refer to bottom-up portfolio managers.

Reference CFA® Program Curriculum, Volume 5, pp. 115-119.

---

6. (QID 305) Estimating the earnings per share for a firm's stock is least likely to involve analyzing which of the following?

***A. The firm's earnings multiplier.**

B. The firm's competitive strategy.

C. The firm's operating profit margins.

Explanation: LOS: Reading 58-b

The earnings multiplier (P/E) multiplied by the earnings per share estimate will give the expected stock price.

**Reference:** CFA® Program Curriculum, Volume 5, pp. 162-166.

7. (QID 306) A company's current stock price is \$3.20, the estimated earnings per share are \$0.24, the dividend payout ratio is 35%, and the estimated P/E ratio in one year's time is 15. The expected rate of return from the stock over the next year is closest to:

A. 12.5%.

B. 15.1%.

C. 25.3%.

---

8. (QID 307) If the real risk-free rate of return is 2% and the expected inflation rate is 5%, then the nominal risk-free rate is closest to:

A. 2.5%.

B. 2.9%.

C. 7.1%.

7. (QID 306) A company's current stock price is $3.20, the estimated earnings per share are $0.24, the dividend payout ratio is 35%, and the estimated P/E ratio in one year's time is 15. The expected rate of return from the stock over the next year is closest to:

A. 12.5%.

***B. 15.1%.**

C. 25.3%.

Explanation: LOS: Reading 58-b

The end year stock price is estimated to be $0.24 x 15 = $3.60

The dividend is $0.24 x 0.35 = $0.084

The return is ($3.60 – $3.20 +$0.084)/$3.20 = 15.1%

**Reference:** CFA® Program Curriculum, Volume 5, pp. 175-177.

---

8. (QID 307) If the real risk-free rate of return is 2% and the expected inflation rate is 5%, then the nominal risk-free rate is closest to:

A. 2.5%.

B. 2.9%.

***C. 7.1%.**

Explanation: LOS: Reading 56-e

Nominal RFR = (1 + real RFR)(1 + expected inflation) – 1 = 1.02 x 1.05 – 1 = 7.1%

**Reference:** CFA® Program Curriculum, Volume 5, pp. 141-142.

9. (QID 308) A company maintains a stable dividend payout ratio of 30% and the rate of return on existing equity is 15%. If new projects available to the company earn a return of only 12%, and the company does not raise any outside capital, then the earnings growth rate will be:

A. 4.5%.

B. 8.4%.

C. 10.5%.

---

10. (QID 309) If investors' required rate of return from a stock increases then the P/E of the stock will generally:

A. increase.

B. decrease.

C. either increase or decrease depending on whether investors' required rate of return from the overall market has changed.

9. (QID 308) A company maintains a stable dividend payout ratio of 30% and the rate of return on existing equity is 15%. If new projects available to the company earn a return of only 12%, and the company does not raise any outside capital, then the earnings growth rate will be:

A. 4.5%.

***B. 8.4%.**

C. 10.5%.

Explanation: LOS: Reading 56-f

Growth rate = retention rate x return on equity (for new investment)

= 0.7 x 12% = 8.4%

**Reference:** CFA® Program Curriculum, Volume 5, pp. 146-149.

---

10. (QID 309) If investors' required rate of return from a stock increases then the P/E of the stock will generally:

A. increase.

***B. decrease.**

C. either increase or decrease depending on whether investors' required rate of return from the overall market has changed.

Explanation: LOS: Reading 56-d

$P/E = (D_1/E_1)/(k - g)$

where:

k = required rate of return

$D_1/E_1$ = expected dividend payout ratio.

g = expected growth rate of dividends

If k increases the P/E will decline.

**Reference:** CFA® Program Curriculum, Volume 5, pp. 136-138.

11. (QID 310) A company has a dividend payout ratio of 40%, dividends are expected to grow by 5% per annum and the required rate of return is 12%. The price/earnings ratio is closest to:

A. 5.71.

B. 5.93.

C. 8.57.

---

12. (QID 311) The mature growth stage of an industry's life cycle is usually characterized in the following way:

A. I. sales are growing rapidly and profit growth is high.

B. II. sales are growing at above the rate of growth of the economy but profit margins are no longer rising since competitors are entering the industry.

C. III. sales are growing at the same rate as the economy and the industry is subject to heavy competition.

11. (QID 310) A company has a dividend payout ratio of 40%, dividends are expected to grow by 5% per annum and the required rate of return is 12%. The price/earnings ratio is closest to:

***A. 5.71.**

B. 5.93.

C. 8.57.

Explanation: LOS: Reading 56-d

$$P/E = P/E = (D_1/E_1)/(k - g)$$
$$= 0.4/(0.12 - 0.05) = 5.71$$

where:

$k$ = required rate of return

$D_1/E_1$ = expected dividend payout ratio.

$g$ = expected growth rate of dividends

**Reference:** CFA® Program Curriculum, Volume 5, pp. 136-138.

---

12. (QID 311) The mature growth stage of an industry's life cycle is usually characterized in the following way:

A. I. sales are growing rapidly and profit growth is high.

***B. II. sales are growing at above the rate of growth of the economy but profit margins are no longer rising since competitors are entering the industry.**

C. III. sales are growing at the same rate as the economy and the industry is subject to heavy competition.

Explanation: LOS: Reading 58-c

I. is rapid accelerating growth, III. is market maturity.

**Reference:** CFA® Program Curriculum, Volume 5, pp. 137-138.

13. (QID 312) Which of the following is least likely to be a major factor in determining the value added at each transformation stage in the value chain?

A. Economies of scale.

B. Economies of scope.

C. Vertical integration.

---

14. (QID 313) A preferred stock has a par value of $100, is trading at $90, and pays a 6% annual dividend. Assume that there is no risk that the company will default on dividend payments. If an investor's required rate of return is 6.5% the preferred stock looks:

A. attractive.

B. expensive.

C. fairly valued.

13. (QID 312) Which of the following is least likely to be a major factor in determining the value added at each transformation stage in the value chain?

A. Economies of scale.

B. Economies of scope.

***C. Vertical integration.**

Explanation: LOS: Reading 56-b

The value chain is the process by which raw material is transformed into a product or service. Each transformation in the chain adds value; the amount of value added depends on four main factors:

" Learning curve - cost per unit declines as a company gains experience.

" Economies of scale - average cost declines as output expands.

" Economies of scope - as a company moves into related products, experience and reputation with the original product may help demand.

" Network externalities - some products and services gain value as more and more customers use them.

" Vertical integration refers to when a manufacturer delivers the entire value chain.

**Reference:** CFA® Program Curriculum, Volume 5, pp. 136-137.

---

14. (QID 313) A preferred stock has a par value of $100, is trading at $90, and pays a 6% annual dividend. Assume that there is no risk that the company will default on dividend payments. If an investor's required rate of return is 6.5% the preferred stock looks:

***A. attractive.**

B. expensive.

C. fairly valued.

Explanation: LOS: Reading 56-c

The value of the preferred stock, since it pays dividends in perpetuity, is $6/0.065 = $92.30. Therefore, at a price of $90, the stock looks attractive.

**Reference:** CFA® Program Curriculum, Volume 5, pp. 1122-123.

15. (QID 314) If the price to book value of a company is higher than the market and industry average, this could be explained by:

A. the company has just purchased new machinery.

B. the company has significant off-balance-sheet liabilities.

C. it is a new company which has a small capital base but it is expected to grow rapidly.

---

16. (QID 315) Which of the following would be expected to lead to a high risk premium for a market?

A. High liquidity.

B. A volatile exchange rate.

C. Low levels of financial leverage.

15. (QID 314) If the price to book value of a company is higher than the market and industry average, this could be explained by:

A. the company has just purchased new machinery.

***B. the company has significant off-balance-sheet liabilities.**

C. it is a new company which has a small capital base but it is expected to grow rapidly.

Explanation: LOS: Reading 59-b

The purchase of new machinery would not immediately change the book value. Off-balance-sheet liabilities would reduce the price to book value that investors are willing to pay. If it is a new company with good growth prospects investors may be willing to pay a high multiple of the current book value of assets.

**Reference:** CFA® Program Curriculum, Volume 5, pp. 188-190.

---

16. (QID 315) Which of the following would be expected to lead to a high risk premium for a market?

A. High liquidity.

***B. A volatile exchange rate.**

C. Low levels of financial leverage.

Explanation: LOS: Reading 56-e

A volatile exchange rate would increase the exchange rate risk, one of the five components of risk that affects the risk premium.

**Reference:** CFA® Program Curriculum, Volume 5, pp. 141-146.

17. (QID 316) An investor forecasts that the economy is going to peak within the next year. His most likely strategy would be to purchase:

A. bonds.

B. commodities.

C. property.

---

18. (QID 317) It is assumed that a company's dividends will grow at a constant growth rate of 4%, and the current dividend is $2.50 per share. If an investor's required rate of return is 9% then using the dividend discount model, the value of the company is closest to:

A. $27.77.

B. $28.89.

C. $52.00.

17. (QID 316) An investor forecasts that the economy is going to peak within the next year. His most likely strategy would be to purchase:

***A. bonds.**

B. commodities.

C. property.

Explanation: LOS: Reading 56-a

At the end of an economic boom stocks, property and commodities will have performed well and will be peaking. Interest rates will be high reflecting strong demand for borrowing and therefore bonds offer the best potential performance. As demand for borrowing slows interest rates will fall providing attractive returns for bonds.

**Reference:** CFA® Program Curriculum, Volume 5, pp. 130-132.

---

18. (QID 317) It is assumed that a company's dividends will grow at a constant growth rate of 4%, and the current dividend is $2.50 per share. If an investor's required rate of return is 9% then using the dividend discount model, the value of the company is closest to:

A. $27.77.

B. $28.89.

***C. $52.00.**

Explanation: LOS: Reading 56-c

$$V = D_1/(k - g) = 2.50(1.04)/(0.09 - 0.04) = \$52.00$$

**Reference:** CFA® Program Curriculum, Volume 5, pp. 126-132.

19. (QID 318) In an industry the largest two firms have a market share of 20% each and six firms have a market share of 10% each. The five firm concentration ratio and Herfindahl index are:

| Concentration ratio | Herfindahl index |
|---|---|
| A. 62.5% | 0.11 |
| B. 70.0% | 0.14 |
| C. 70.0% | 0.11 |

---

20. (QID 423) The top down approach to security valuation is supported by:

A. stock pickers who believe that industry analysis is an important part of the decision making process.

B. academic studies which identify a link between stock price moves and movements in the aggregate stock market and the stock's industry.

C. investors who believe it is difficult to add value through asset allocation and the inefficiency in the pricing of stocks provides opportunities for investment managers.

19. (QID 318) In an industry the largest two firms have a market share of 20% each and six firms have a market share of 10% each. The five firm concentration ratio and Herfindahl index are:

| Concentration ratio | Herfindahl index |
|---|---|
| A. 62.5% | 0.11 |
| ***B. 70.0%** | **0.14** |
| C. 70.0% | 0.11 |

Explanation: LOS: Reading 58-a

$$H = M_1^2 + M_2^2 + \dots + M_i^2 = 2 \times (0.20)^2 + 6 \times (0.10)^2 = 0.14$$

**Reference:** CFA® Program Curriculum, Volume 5, pp. 160-162.

---

20. (QID 423) The top down approach to security valuation is supported by:

A. stock pickers who believe that industry analysis is an important part of the decision making process.

***B. academic studies which identify a link between stock price moves and movements in the aggregate stock market and the stock's industry.**

C. investors who believe it is difficult to add value through asset allocation and the inefficiency in the pricing of stocks provides opportunities for investment managers.

Explanation: LOS: Reading 56-a

Stock pickers often agree on the importance of industry analysis but essentially believe in a 'bottom up' rather than a top down process. Top down analaysts generally agree that asset allocation can add value so B is the best answer.

**Reference:** CFA® Program Curriculum, Volume 5, pp. 115-119.

21. (QID 320) ABC Commodities is sensitive to the economic cycle and an analyst decides that the six years ending 2008 reflect a business cycle for the company. He collects the following data: earnings per share (EPS), book value per share ( BVPS) and return on equity (ROE):.

| | 2003 | 2004 | 2005 | 2006 | 2007 | 2008 |
|---|---|---|---|---|---|---|
| Adjusted* EPS, $ | 1.30 | 2.65 | 5.50 | 4.30 | 3.25 | 1.00 |
| ROE* % | 0.04 | 0.13 | 0.22 | 0.18 | 0.12 | 0.03 |
| BVPS, $ | | | | | 32.00 | |

* Adjusted for non-recurring items

The current share price of ABC Commodities is $30.00

The P/E of ABC commodities based on the method of average ROE is closest to:

A. 7.81.

B. 9.37.

C. 10.00.

22. (QID 321) A firm with a high business risk is most likely to:

A. have cyclical stock.

B. have defensive stock.

C. be a cyclical company.

21. (QID 320) ABC Commodities is sensitive to the economic cycle and an analyst decides that the six years ending 2008 reflect a business cycle for the company. He collects the following data: earnings per share (EPS), book value per share ( BVPS) and return on equity (ROE):.

| | 2003 | 2004 | 2005 | 2006 | 2007 | 2008 |
|---|---|---|---|---|---|---|
| Adjusted* EPS, $ | 1.30 | 2.65 | 5.50 | 4.30 | 3.25 | 1.00 |
| ROE* % | 0.04 | 0.13 | 0.22 | 0.18 | 0.12 | 0.03 |
| BVPS, $ | | | | | | 32.00 |

* Adjusted for non-recurring items

The current share price of ABC Commodities is $30.00

The P/E of ABC commodities based on the method of average ROE is closest to:

***A. 7.81.**

B. 9.37.

C. 10.00.

Explanation: LOS: Reading 59-b

Use the average ROE over the period, and multiply by the current book value.

Average ROE = (0.04 + 0.13 + 0.22 + 0.18 + 0.12 + 0.03)/6 = 0.12

Normal EPS = 0.12 x 32.0 = 3.84

P/E = 30.00/3.84 = 7.81

**Reference:** CFA® Program Curriculum, Volume 5, pp. 184-188.

---

22. (QID 321) A firm with a high business risk is most likely to:

A. have cyclical stock.

B. have defensive stock.

***C. be a cyclical company.**

Explanation: LOS: Reading 58-a

High business risk (sales leverage and/or operating leverage) leads to a company having volatile earnings, it usually does well in times of economic expansion and badly in times of economic slowdown. This is the definition of a cyclical company.

**Reference:** CFA® Program Curriculum, Volume 5, pp. 160-162.

23. (QID 322) Which of the following is one of the reasons why price to book value is a useful valuation measure?

A. It can be used to value loss-making companies.

B. Book value has proved to be a good indicator of the market value of a company's assets.

C. Book value is not usually distorted by the accounting methods used.

24. (QID 420) Which of the following would be the most likely to explain why a firm's price to sales ratio is higher than its competitors?

A. The firm is highly geared relative to its competitors.

B. The firm has a high asset backing per share relative to its competitors.

C. The firm uses aggressive revenue recognition policies relative to its competitors.

23. (QID 322) Which of the following is one of the reasons why price to book value is a useful valuation measure?

***A. It can be used to value loss-making companies.**

B. Book value has proved to be a good indicator of the market value of a company's assets.

C. Book value is not usually distorted by the accounting methods used.

Explanation: LOS: Reading 59-a

Loss making companies cannot be valued using current P/E and will often also have negative cash flow so P/B, which is based on book value representing cumulative earnings and paid up capital, is a method that can usually be applied.

**Reference:** CFA® Program Curriculum, Volume 5, pp. 210-218.

---

24. (QID 420) Which of the following would be the most likely to explain why a firm's price to sales ratio is higher than its competitors?

A. The firm is highly geared relative to its competitors.

***B. The firm has a high asset backing per share relative to its competitors.**

C. The firm uses aggressive revenue recognition policies relative to its competitors.

Explanation: LOS: Reading 59-a

High gearing would tend to reduce the market capitalization of the firm relative to its sales, leading to a lower P/S ratio, is not correct.

Aggressive sales recognition would reduce the price investors are willing to pay for sales, so will lead to a lower P/S ratio, is not correct.

If the firm has high asset backing this would increase the value of the company and might lead to a higher P/S ratio, is the best answer.

**Reference:** CFA® Program Curriculum, Volume 6, pp. 196-199.

25. (QID 421) Historically using price to book value ratios to compare companies' valuations is most likely to have been useful in which of the following sectors?

A. Financial sector.

B. Technology sector.

C. Pharmaceutical sector.

---

26. (QID 422) Which of the following statements is most accurate regarding the earnings number used in the price to earnings measure?

A. Earnings are one of the most stable accounting numbers over time.

B. It is important to use an earnings number that includes both recurring and nonrecurring earnings.

C. Normalized earnings will be lower than current earnings for a company that is at the peak of its business cycle.

---

27. (QID 521) A company has a dividend retention ratio of 60%, dividends are expected to grow by 3% per annum and the investors' required rate of return is 8%. The theoretical price earnings ratio is:

A. 5.0.

B. 8.0.

C. 12.5.

25. (QID 421) Historically using price to book value ratios to compare companies' valuations is most likely to have been useful in which of the following sectors?

***A. Financial sector.**

B. Technology sector.

C. Pharmaceutical sector.

Explanation: LOS: Reading 59-a

In financial companies the assets tend to be more liquid (until the recent credit crunch) and therefore traditionally market values are closer to book values, which mean P/B ratios can be a useful valuation method. In the case of pharmaceutical and technology companies treatment of R&D can distort balance sheet numbers. Service companies are often dependent on the quality of staff which is not reflected in the balance sheet.

**Reference:** CFA® Program Curriculum, Volume 6, pp. 188-191.

---

26. (QID 422) Which of the following statements is most accurate regarding the earnings number used in the price to earnings measure?

A. Earnings are one of the most stable accounting numbers over time.

B. It is important to use an earnings number that includes both recurring and nonrecurring earnings.

***C. Normalized earnings will be lower than current earnings for a company that is at the peak of its business cycle.**

Explanation: LOS: Reading 59-a

Cumulative numbers such as book values tend to be the most stable.

Nonrecurring earnings should not be included since they do not reflect the underlying earnings of the company.

**Reference:** CFA® Program Curriculum, Volume 5, pp. 182-200.

27. (QID 521) A company has a dividend retention ratio of 60%, dividends are expected to grow by 3% per annum and the investors' required rate of return is 8%. The theoretical price earnings ratio is:

A. 5.0.

***B. 8.0.**

C. 12.5.

Explanation: LOS: Reading 56-d

P/E = D/[E(k - g)] = 0.4/(0.08 - 0.03) = 8.0

**Reference:** CFA® Program Curriculum, Volume 5, pp. 136-138.

# Study Session 15: Fixed Income: Basic Concepts

This study session presents the foundation for fixed income investments, one of the largest and fastest growing segments of global financial markets. It begins with an introduction to the basic features and characteristics of fixed income securities and the associated risks. The session then builds by describing the primary issuers, sectors, and types of bonds. Finally, the study session concludes with an introduction to yields and spreads and the effect of monetary policy on financial markets. These readings combined are the primary building blocks for mastering the analysis, valuation, and management of fixed income securities.

**Reading 60: Features of Debt Securities**

**Reading 61: Risks Associated with Investing in Bonds**

**Reading 62: Overview of Bond Sectors and Instruments**

**Reading 63: Understanding Yield Spreads**

1. (QID 323) A floating-rate note has a cap and a floor with the coupon formula:

coupon rate = 25% – 3 x (six-month LIBOR)

This floating-rate note is called:

A. a step-up note.

B. an inverse floater.

C. a deleveraged floater.

---

2. (QID 324) Information asymmetry between a central bank and the market is most likely to result in:

A. inaction by the central bank.

B. loss of credibility of the central bank.

C. central bank policies that are unexpected by the market participants.

1. (QID 323) A floating-rate note has a cap and a floor with the coupon formula:

coupon rate = 25% – 3 x (six-month LIBOR)

This floating-rate note is called:

A. a step-up note.

***B. an inverse floater.**

C. a deleveraged floater.

Explanation: LOS: Reading 60-b

An inverse floater has a coupon formula where the coupon rate rises if the reference rate falls and vice versA. There are often caps and floors on an inverse floater to prevent there being a negative coupon if LIBOR increases sharply or an excessively high coupon if LIBOR drops sharply.

**Reference:** CFA® Program Curriculum, Volume 5, pp. 218-221.

---

2. (QID 324) Information asymmetry between a central bank and the market is most likely to result in:

A. inaction by the central bank.

B. loss of credibility of the central bank.

***C. central bank policies that are unexpected by the market participants.**

Explanation: LOS: Reading 60-c

If the central bank has access to information which is not known by the market, the risk is its actions will not be correctly anticipated.

**Reference:** CFA® Program Curriculum, Volume 5, pp. 325-327.

3. (QID 325) Which of the following statements is least accurate regarding the term to maturity of a bond?

A. The term to maturity is always fixed.

B. The yield offered on a bond depends on the term to maturity.

C. It tells the investor the number of years before the principal is paid in full and the period over which interest payments can be expected.

---

4. (QID 326) A floating-rate note has the following coupon formula:

Six-month Treasury bill rate + 60 basis points with a cap of 7% and a floor of 6.5%

The 6-month Treasury bill rates are as follows:

| | 6-month Treasury bill rate |
|---|---|
| First reset date | 6.5% |
| Second reset date | 5.8% |
| Third reset date | 6.3% |
| Fourth reset date | 6.1% |

What would be the coupon rates at the first and the second reset dates, respectively?

A. 6.5% 6.5%

B. 7.0% 6.5%

C. 7.6% 7.1%

3. (QID 325) Which of the following statements is least accurate regarding the term to maturity of a bond?

***A. The term to maturity is always fixed.**

B. The yield offered on a bond depends on the term to maturity.

C. It tells the investor the number of years before the principal is paid in full and the period over which interest payments can be expected.

Explanation: LOS: Reading 60-a

There may be provisions in the indenture that allow the issuer or the bondholder to alter the term to maturity.

**Reference:** CFA® Program Curriculum, Volume 5, pp. 215-216.

---

4. (QID 326) A floating-rate note has the following coupon formula:

Six-month Treasury bill rate + 60 basis points with a cap of 7% and a floor of 6.5%

The 6-month Treasury bill rates are as follows:

| | 6-month Treasury bill rate |
|---|---|
| First reset date | 6.5% |
| Second reset date | 5.8% |
| Third reset date | 6.3% |
| Fourth reset date | 6.1% |

What would be the coupon rates at the first and the second reset dates, respectively?

A. 6.5% 6.5%

***B. 7.0% 6.5%**

C. 7.6% 7.1%

Explanation: LOS: Reading 60-b

The coupon rate at the first reset date is 6.5% + 0.6% = 7.1% which is higher than the cap rate. Therefore it takes on the cap rate, which is 7.0%.

The coupon rate at the second reset date is 5.8% + 0.6% = 6.4% which is lower than the floor rate. Therefore it takes on the floor rate, which is 6.5%.

**Reference:** CFA® Program Curriculum, Volume 5, pp. 218-222.

5. (QID 327) A bond is priced at 90. If yields decline by 25 basis points the price rises to 94.8 and if yields rise by 25 basis points the price falls to 84.9. The duration is closest to:

A. 9.9.

B. 22.0.

C. 44.0.

---

6. (QID 328) Which of the following tools is least likely to be used to manage the level of interest rates in an economy?

A. The discount rate.

B. Corporate tax rates.

C. Open market operations.

5. (QID 327) A bond is priced at 90. If yields decline by 25 basis points the price rises to 94.8 and if yields rise by 25 basis points the price falls to 84.9. The duration is closest to:

A. 9.9.

***B. 22.0.**

C. 44.0.

Explanation: LOS: Reading 61-f

The duration formula is

$$\frac{\text{price if yields decline} - \text{price of yield rise}}{2 \times (\text{initial price}) \times (\text{change in yield in decimal})}$$

$= (94.8 - 84.9)/(2 \times 90 \times 0.0025) = 22.0$

**Reference:** CFA® Program Curriculum, Volume 5, pp. 245-247.

---

6. (QID 328) Which of the following tools is least likely to be used to manage the level of interest rates in an economy?

A. The discount rate.

***B. Corporate tax rates.**

C. Open market operations.

Explanation: LOS: Reading 63-a

Adjusting corporate tax rates is a tool that is used as part of fiscal, not monetary, policy.

**Reference:** CFA® Program Curriculum, Volume 5, pp. 320-321.

7. (QID 329) Which of the following is least likely to be used as a type of external credit enhancement?

A. Letters of credit.

B. Corporate guarantee.

C. Sequential disbursement.

---

8. (QID 330) The role of credit rating agencies is to:

A. I. perform valuations of companies.

B. II. extend a credit guarantee to bond issues.

C. III. report on the likelihood of an issuer defaulting.

7. (QID 329) Which of the following is least likely to be used as a type of external credit enhancement?

A. Letters of credit.

B. Corporate guarantee.

***C. Sequential disbursement.**

Explanation: LOS: Reading 62-c

Sequential disbursement rules are techniques for internal credit enhancement that are commonly used in structured securities such as collateralized mortgage obligations (CMOs).

**Reference:** CFA® Program Curriculum, Volume 5, pp. 281-288.

---

8. (QID 330) The role of credit rating agencies is to:

A. I. perform valuations of companies.

B. II. extend a credit guarantee to bond issues.

***C. III. report on the likelihood of an issuer defaulting.**

Explanation: LOS: Reading 61-j

I. is the role of investment bankers or accounting firms,

II. is the role of a bank or a credit insurance company.

**Reference:** CFA® Program Curriculum, Volume 5, pp. 254-257.

9. (QID 331) Which of the following factors is least likely to affect the yield spread of a bond?

A. The type of issuer.

B. The coupon rate of the bond.

C. The expected liquidity of the issue.

10. (QID 332) Which of the following will be least important in explaining a bond price's volatility?

A. Its coupon.

B. Its par value.

C. The direction of any yield change.

9. (QID 331) Which of the following factors is least likely to affect the yield spread of a bond?

A. The type of issuer.

***B. The coupon rate of the bond.**

C. The expected liquidity of the issue.

Explanation: LOS: Reading 63-e

Coupon rates generally do not affect the yield spread as the price of the bond will adjust according to investors' required returns.

**Reference:** CFA® Program Curriculum, Volume 5, pp. 331-332.

---

10. (QID 332) Which of the following will be least important in explaining a bond price's volatility?

A. Its coupon.

***B. Its par value.**

C. The direction of any yield change.

Explanation: LOS: Reading 61-c

A bond's par value determines the pricing of a bond but its interest rate sensitivity mainly depends on its coupon, its term to maturity, market level of yields and the direction of the yield change.

**Reference:** CFA® Program Curriculum, Volume 5, pp. 242-243.

11. (QID 333) The most recently auctioned Treasury bonds are called:

A. flower bonds.

B. on-the-run issues.

C. benchmark bonds.

---

12. (QID 334) Which one of the following descriptions relates to yield curve risk? The risk that investors face when

A. a crossover yield is reached for a callable bond.

B. reinvestment rates are lower than the yield to maturity.

C. yields of bonds with different maturities do not move in parallel.

11. (QID 333) The most recently auctioned Treasury bonds are called:

A. flower bonds.

***B. on-the-run issues.**

C. benchmark bonds.

Explanation: LOS: Reading 62-b

The most recently auctioned Treasury bonds are called the on-the-run issues.

**Reference:** CFA® Program Curriculum, Volume 5, pp. 274-275.

---

12. (QID 334) Which one of the following descriptions relates to yield curve risk? The risk that investors face when

A. a crossover yield is reached for a callable bond.

B. reinvestment rates are lower than the yield to maturity.

***C. yields of bonds with different maturities do not move in parallel.**

Explanation: LOS: Reading 61-g

Yield curve risk exists when the bonds in the portfolio have different exposures to how the yield curve shifts. Yield curves usually do not shift in parallel.

**Reference:** CFA® Program Curriculum, Volume 5, pp. 247-251.

13. (QID 335) Which one is the least likely to be a characteristic of a revenue-type of municipal bond?

A. It is guaranteed by the federal government.

B. It is exempt from federal tax for certain investors.

C. The source of repayment is from revenue-generating projects.

---

14. (QID 336) Which of the following is least likely to be a characteristic of a Collateralized Mortgage Obligation (CMO?

A. The structure is a pass-through instead of a pay-through.

B. The credit quality of most tranches is equivalent to the collateral.

C. The CMOs are serviced with the cash flows from a pool of mortgages.

13. (QID 335) Which one is the least likely to be a characteristic of a revenue-type of municipal bond?

***A. It is guaranteed by the federal government.**

B. It is exempt from federal tax for certain investors.

C. The source of repayment is from revenue-generating projects.

Explanation: LOS: Reading 62-g

Municipal bonds are not guaranteed by the federal government.

**Reference:** CFA® Program Curriculum, Volume 5, pp. 288-291.

---

14. (QID 336) Which of the following is least likely to be a characteristic of a Collateralized Mortgage Obligation (CMO?

***A. The structure is a pass-through instead of a pay-through.**

B. The credit quality of most tranches is equivalent to the collateral.

C. The CMOs are serviced with the cash flows from a pool of mortgages.

Explanation: LOS: Reading 62-e

The main difference between a MBS and a CMO is that the former is a pass-through structure and the latter is a pay-through.

**Reference:** CFA® Program Curriculum, Volume 5, pp. 281-288.

15. (QID 337) Which of the following is least likely to be a characteristic of a pass-through Government National Mortgage Association (Ginnie Mae) mortgage-backed security?

A. The average life is the same as the maturity.

B. The outgoing cash flows follow the pattern of the incoming cash flows.

C. Each monthly payment to investors consists of interest and principal components.

---

16. (QID 338) Bankers acceptances are:

A. guarantees issued by a bank on a municipal bond.

B. nonnegotiable longer-term (over one year) certificates of deposit.

C. a money market instrument that is created by a non-financial firm and guaranteed by a bank.

15. (QID 337) Which of the following is least likely to be a characteristic of a pass-through Government National Mortgage Association (Ginnie Mae) mortgage-backed security?

***A. The average life is the same as the maturity.**

B. The outgoing cash flows follow the pattern of the incoming cash flows.

C. Each monthly payment to investors consists of interest and principal components.

Explanation: LOS: Reading 62-e

The monthly payments of a MBS consist of principal and interest components. They are not certain, primarily because prepayment events may modify the statistical characteristics of the pool. The maturity of the pool follows the longest maturity of a loan, but the average life is generally less than the maturity due in part to prepayment events. In pass-through securities, the outgoing pattern of cash flows reflects the incoming cash flows.

**Reference:** CFA® Program Curriculum, Volume 5, pp. 281-288.

---

16. (QID 338) Bankers acceptances are:

A. guarantees issued by a bank on a municipal bond.

B. nonnegotiable longer-term (over one year) certificates of deposit.

***C. a money market instrument that is created by a non-financial firm and guaranteed by a bank.**

Explanation: LOS: Reading 62-h

A bankers acceptance is when a bank accepts the ultimate responsibility to repay a loan to its holder, it is a vehicle which is commonly issued to facilitate commercial trade transactions.

**Reference:** CFA® Program Curriculum, Volume 5, pp. 302-304.

17. (QID 339) The motivation for a corporation to issue an asset-backed security is:

A. to dispose of unproductive assets.

B. to strengthen the affirmative covenants of all the issued debt securities.

C. to obtain funding which is lower in cost than the corporation's rating allows.

---

18. (QID 340) A downward-sloping yield curve may be caused by:

A. investors expect short-term interest rates to fall.

B. investors expect short-term interest rates to rise.

C. demand outstrips supply for short-term securities.

17. (QID 339) The motivation for a corporation to issue an asset-backed security is:

A. to dispose of unproductive assets.

B. to strengthen the affirmative covenants of all the issued debt securities.

***C. to obtain funding which is lower in cost than the corporation's rating allows.**

Explanation: LOS: Reading 62-i

The motivation is often that a corporation's credit rating is less than the rating that is given to the collateral being used in the asset-backed security. An example of this is when a company's customers have a higher average rating than the company itself so the receivables can be securitized to form an asset-backed security.

**Reference:** CFA® Program Curriculum, Volume 5, pp. 304-306.

---

18. (QID 340) A downward-sloping yield curve may be caused by:

***A. investors expect short-term interest rates to fall.**

B. investors expect short-term interest rates to rise.

C. demand outstrips supply for short-term securities.

Explanation: LOS: Reading 63-c

A downward-sloping yield curve may be caused by expectations that short-term rates are going to fall, or by demand outstripping supply for long-term securities, pushing down long-term rates, or by supply outstripping demand for short-term securities, pushing up short-term rates.

**Reference:** CFA® Program Curriculum, Volume 5, pp. 323-328.

19. (QID 341) If a country's economy is entering a recession then one would expect that the yield spread between government bonds and corporate bonds that are rated single A to:

A. be wider than normal, since the risk of the A-rated bonds defaulting is lower.

B. be wider than normal, since the risk of the A-rated bonds defaulting is higher.

C. be tighter than normal, since the risk of the A-rated bonds defaulting is higher.

---

20. (QID 342) An increase in yield volatility means that:

| Prices of callable bonds | Value of embedded call option |
|---|---|
| A. rise | increases |
| B. rise | decreases |
| C. fall | increases |

19. (QID 341) If a country's economy is entering a recession then one would expect that the yield spread between government bonds and corporate bonds that are rated single A to:

A. be wider than normal, since the risk of the A-rated bonds defaulting is lower.

***B. be wider than normal, since the risk of the A-rated bonds defaulting is higher.**

C. be tighter than normal, since the risk of the A-rated bonds defaulting is higher.

Explanation: LOS: Reading 63-f

If an economy is entering recession then the risk of default of the corporate bonds will increase and therefore the extra return required for holding these bonds should be higher than normal.

**Reference:** CFA® Program Curriculum, Volume 5, pp. 331-332.

---

20. (QID 342) An increase in yield volatility means that:

| Prices of Callable bonds | Value of embedded call option |
|---|---|
| A. rise | increases |
| B. rise | decreases |
| ***C. fall** | **increases** |

Explanation: LOS: Reading 61-d

Price of callable bond = Price of option-free bond – Price of embedded call option

The value of the embedded option goes up when yield volatility increases. So if the price of the embedded call option increases, then the price of callable bond will decrease if the price of the option-free bond remains the same.

**Reference:** CFA® Program Curriculum, Volume 5, p. 243.

21. (QID 343) Commercial paper:

A. pays interest on a semiannual basis.

B. is actively traded in the secondary market.

C. is issued by both financial and nonfinancial companies.

---

22. (QID 344) Which of the following types of bond will generally have the highest reinvestment risk?

A. Zero-coupon bonds.

B. High-coupon callable bonds.

C. Low-coupon Treasury bonds.

21. (QID 343) Commercial paper:

A. pays interest on a semiannual basis.

B. is actively traded in the secondary market.

***C. is issued by both financial and nonfinancial companies.**

Explanation: LOS: Reading 62-h

Commercial paper is a short-term unsecured promissory note, which is usually zero-coupon. It is issued by both financial companies (usually direct paper) and non-financial companies, and not normally traded in the secondary market.

**Reference:** CFA® Program Curriculum, Volume 5, p. 301.

---

22. (QID 344) Which of the following types of bond will generally have the highest reinvestment risk?

A. Zero-coupon bonds.

***B. High-coupon callable bonds.**

C. Low-coupon Treasury bonds.

Explanation: LOS: Reading 61-i

Reinvestment risk will be highest with callable bonds with a high coupon rate. When a callable bond is called, it generally means that interest rates are low. So the investor will have cash in hand which he or she will have to invest in a low interest rate environment.

**Reference:** CFA® Program Curriculum, Volume 5, pp. 252-253.

23. (QID 424) The implication of liquidity preference theory is that:

A. an on-the-run issue tends to have a lower yield than an off-the-run bond issue.

B. the yield curve tends to be downward sloping when investors expect the inflation rate to decline.

C. the yield curve tends to be upward sloping reflecting investors' preference for shorter-term maturities.

---

24. (QID 419) Which a firm issues bonds that are nonrefundable this means that:

A. the bonds can be called but the investor cannot be offered a replacement bond with a similar yield.

B. an investor cannot exercise an embedded put option whilst they are in a prespecified nonrefunding period.

C. the bonds cannot be redeemed using proceeds of another debt issue that has provided a lower cost source of funds.

---

25. (QID 523) Which of the following statements is least accurate?

A. The yields of on-the-run issues are generally lower than off-the-run issues.

B. The financing rates (repo rates) of on-the-run issues are generally lower than off-the-run issues.

C. The interest rate risks of on-the-run and off-the-run issues with the same maturity are identical.

23. (QID 424) The implication of liquidity preference theory is that:

A. an on-the-run issue tends to have a lower yield than an off-the-run bond issue.

B. the yield curve tends to be downward sloping when investors expect the inflation rate to decline.

***C. the yield curve tends to be upward sloping reflecting investors' preference for shorter-term maturities.**

Explanation: LOS: Reading 60-c

The liquidity preference theory asserts that investors require compensation for holding long-term bonds. Therefore the yields for long-term bonds should be progressively higher as their maturities lengthen. 'Liquidity' here refers to interest rate risk: the more the interest rate risk, the less the liquidity.

**Reference:** CFA® Program Curriculum, Volume 5, pp. 215-216.

---

24. (QID 419) Which a firm issues bonds that are nonrefundable this means that:

A. the bonds can be called but the investor cannot be offered a replacement bond with a similar yield.

B. an investor cannot exercise an embedded put option whilst they are in a prespecified nonrefunding period.

***C. the bonds cannot be redeemed using proceeds of another debt issue that has provided a lower cost source of funds.**

Explanation: LOS: Reading 60-e

When a callable bond is issued it may have restrictions on when it can be called, nonrefundable is such a restriction and means that the firm cannot issue a new bond on a lower yield to pay back the original bond holders.

**Reference:** CFA® Program Curriculum, Volume 5, pp. 223-227.

25. (QID 523) Which of the following statements is least accurate?

A. The yields of on-the-run issues are generally lower than off-the-run issues.

***B. The financing rates (repo rates) of on-the-run issues are generally lower than off-the-run issues.**

C. The interest rate risks of on-the-run and off-the-run issues with the same maturity are identical.

Explanation: LOS: Reading 62-b

Choice C is false because bonds with identical maturities may not have identical coupon rates, hence the durations may differ.

**Reference:** CFA® Program Curriculum, Volume 5, pp. 274-275.

# Study Session 16: Fixed Income: Analysis and Valuation

This study session illustrates the primary tools for valuation and analysis of fixed income securities and markets. It begins with a study of basic valuation theory and techniques for bonds and concludes with a more in-depth explanation of the primary tools for fixed income investment valuation, specifically, interest rate and yield valuation and interest rate risk measurement and analysis.

**Reading 64: Introduction to the Valuation of Debt Securities**

**Reading 65: Yield Measures, Spot Rates, and Forward Rates**

**Reading 66: Introduction to the Measurement of Interest Rate Risk**

1. (QID 345) A bond has a yield of 7.50% and the on-the-run Treasury yield is 6.55%. The yield spread and yield ratio are:

| Relative yield spread | Yield ratio |
|---|---|
| A. 14.50% | 0.873 |
| B. 14.50% | 1.145 |
| C. 12.67% | 0.873 |

---

2. (QID 346) The arbitrage-free value of a Treasury bond is:

A. the price of an on-the-run Treasury bond with the same maturity.

B. the value of a bond calculated as the present value of each cash flow discounted at the corresponding Treasury spot rate.

C. the value of a bond calculated as the present value of each cash flow discounted back at the average yield to maturity of Treasury bonds with the same maturity.

1. (QID 345) A bond has a yield of 7.50% and the on-the-run Treasury yield is 6.55%. The yield spread and yield ratio are:

| Relative yield spread | Yield ratio |
|---|---|
| A. 14.50% | 0.873 |
| ***B. 14.50%** | **1.145** |
| C. 12.67% | 0.873 |

Explanation: LOS: Reading 63-c

The market practice is to measure the spread and ratio against Treasuries.

Relative yield spread:

= (Yield on Bond A - Yield on Treasury)/Yield on Treasury

= (7.5% - 6.55%)/6.55% = 14.50%

Yield ratio:

= Yield on Bond A/Yield on Treasury

= 1.145

**Reference:** CFA® Program Curriculum, Volume 5, pp. 328-330.

---

2. (QID 346) The arbitrage-free value of a Treasury bond is:

A. the price of an on-the-run Treasury bond with the same maturity.

***B. the value of a bond calculated as the present value of each cash flow discounted at the corresponding Treasury spot rate.**

C. the value of a bond calculated as the present value of each cash flow discounted back at the average yield to maturity of Treasury bonds with the same maturity.

Explanation: LOS: Reading 64-f

The arbitrage-free value of a Treasury bond is the value of a bond calculated as the present value of each cash flow discounted at the corresponding Treasury spot rate rather than at the yield to maturity.

**Reference:** CFA® Program Curriculum, Volume 5, pp. 372-374.

3. (QID 347) The following data has been provided:

| Years to maturity | Spot rate |
|---|---|
| 0.5 | 8.75% |
| 1.0 | 6.25% |
| 1.5 | 5.00% |

The six-month forward rate one year from now is closest to:

A. 1.26%.

B. 2.52%.

C. 3.78%.

---

4. (QID 368) Which of the following is a characteristic of Macaulay duration? Macaulay duration

A. cannot be used for zero-coupon bonds.

B. can be used to compute modified duration.

C. can be used for bonds with embedded options.

3. (QID 347) The following data has been provided:

| Years to maturity | Spot rate |
|---|---|
| 0.5 | 8.75% |
| 1.0 | 6.25% |
| 1.5 | 5.00% |

The six-month forward rate one year from now is closest to:

A. 1.26%.

***B. 2.52%.**

C. 3.78%.

Explanation: LOS: Reading 65-h

$$_1f_2 = [(1+ 0.025)^3/(1 + 0.03125)^2] - 1$$

$$= 1.26\%$$

The forward rate is 1.26% x 2 = 2.52%

**Reference:** CFA® Program Curriculum, Volume 5, pp. 421-425.

---

4. (QID 368) Which of the following is a characteristic of Macaulay duration? Macaulay duration

A. cannot be used for zero-coupon bonds.

***B. can be used to compute modified duration.**

C. is the same as Modified duration when a bond pays annual coupons.

Explanation: LOS: Reading 69-e

Macaulay duration can be used to calculate modified duration, but has the same problems as modified duration; it cannot be used for bonds where the cash flows are altered by interest rate moves. Modified duration is less than Macaulay duration, for an annual-pay bond we need to divide Macaulay duration by (1 + yield) to get modified duration.

**Reference:** CFA® Program Curriculum, Volume 5, p. 497.

5. (QID 349) For a given large change in yields, if the price gain of a bond is less than the price loss then the cause can be explained by:

A. positive duration.

B. negative duration.

C. negative convexity.

---

6. (QID 350) A zero-coupon bond with two years remaining to maturity is currently trading at $82.65. If the par value is $100, the yield to maturity is closest to:

A. 8.7%.

B. 9.0%.

C. 9.8%.

5. (QID 349) For a given large change in yields, if the price gain of a bond is less than the price loss then the cause can be explained by:

A. positive duration.

B. negative duration.

***C. negative convexity.**

Explanation: LOS: Reading 66-c

Negative convexity will make the price gain smaller than the price fall.

**Reference:** CFA® Program Curriculum, Volume 5, pp. 452-456.

---

6. (QID 350) A zero-coupon bond with two years remaining to maturity is currently trading at $82.65. If the par value is $100, the yield to maturity is closest to:

A. 8.7%.

B. 9.0%.

***C. 9.8%.**

Explanation: LOS: Reading 64-e

Let x be the semiannual yield we are looking for, then:

$$82.65 = \frac{100}{(1+x)^4}$$

$$(1+x)^4 = 100/82.65 = 1.21$$

$x = 0.0488$ or 9.8% annual yield

**Reference:** CFA® Program Curriculum, Volume 5, pp. 366-367.

7. (QID 351) A bond without any embedded options has a remaining life of three years, carries an 8% coupon rate payable annually, and has a yield to maturity of 7%. If the one- and three-year spot rates are 8.0% and 7.0%, respectively, then the two-year spot rate is closest to:

A. 6.0%.

B. 6.5%.

C. 7.5%.

8. (QID 353) The yield-to-maturity calculation assumes that coupon payments can be reinvested at:

A. the coupon rate.

B. the current yield.

C. the yield to maturity.

7. (QID 351) A bond without any embedded options has a remaining life of three years, carries an 8% coupon rate payable annually, and has a yield to maturity of 7%. If the one- and three-year spot rates are 8.0% and 7.0%, respectively, then the two-year spot rate is closest to:

A. 6.0%.

***B. 6.5%.**

C. 7.5%.

Explanation: LOS: Reading 65-h

The following relationship must hold, where z is the two-year spot rate:

$$8/(1.07) + 8/(1.07)^2 + 108/(1.07)^3$$
$$= 8/(1.08) + 8/(1+ z)^2 + 108/(1.07)^3$$

$14.46 \quad = 7.41 + 8/(1+z)^2$

$(1 + z)^2 = 8/7.06$

$1 + z \quad = (1.1337)^{1/2}$

$z \quad = 6.45\%$

**Reference:** CFA® Program Curriculum, Volume 5, pp. 436-429.

---

8. (QID 353) The yield-to-maturity calculation assumes that coupon payments can be reinvested at:

A. the coupon rate.

B. the current yield.

***C. the yield to maturity.**

Explanation: LOS: Reading 65-b

The yield to maturity will only be realized if the following assumptions hold:

A1. The bond is held to maturity.

A2. The coupon payments can be reinvested at a yield equivalent to the yield to maturity.

**Reference:** CFA® Program Curriculum, Volume 5, pp. 392-393.

9. (QID 352) Modified duration is:

A. shorter than Macaulay duration for any given bond.

B. shorter or longer than the time to maturity of a bond.

C. a useful measure of duration for mortgage-backed securities.

---

10. (QID 359) The yield to worst for a callable bond is:

A. the yield assuming the bond is called at the lowest possible call price.

B. the yield assuming that the bond is called at the first possible call date.

C. the lowest of the yield to maturity and yields to call, calculated using all possible call dates.

9. (QID 352) Modified duration is:

***A. shorter than Macaulay duration for any given bond.**

B. shorter or longer than the time to maturity of a bond.

C. a useful measure of duration for mortgage-backed securities.

Explanation: LOS: Reading 66-e

Modified duration is based on Macaulay duration which is the weighted-average time until an investor receives payments from a bond, so it cannot be a negative number, and it is shorter than or equal to the time to maturity. It is not used for bonds such as mortgage-backed securities where there are uncertain cash flows.

The link between modified duration and Macaulay duration is given below:

$$\text{Modified duration} = \frac{\text{Macaulay duration}}{(1 + \text{yield}/k)}$$

We can see that modified duration is shorter than Macaulay duration since the yield is positive.

**Reference:** CFA® Program Curriculum, Volume 5, pp. 464-465.

---

10. (QID 359) The yield to worst for a callable bond is:

A. the yield assuming the bond is called at the lowest possible call price.

B. the yield assuming that the bond is called at the first possible call date.

***C. the lowest of the yield to maturity and yields to call, calculated using all possible call dates.**

Explanation: LOS: Reading 65-b

The yield to worst for a callable bond is the lowest yield that an investor could receive so it is the lowest of the yield to maturity and all possible yields to call.

**Reference:** CFA® Program Curriculum, Volume 5, p. 402.

11. (QID 355) If the bond-equivalent yield on a U.S. bond is 5%, the yield on an annual-pay basis is closest to:

A. 4.94%.

B. 5.06%.

C. 5.51%.

---

12. (QID 356) An investor purchases a ten-year bond at par of $100 on June 3 2006, which has an annual coupon of 10%. The reinvestment rate at the first coupon date is 9% and at the second coupon date is 8%. The investor expects 12.5% annualized total return for the three years ending on June 1 2009. To reach the investment goal, the bond should be sold on June 1, 2009 at a price closest to:

A. $110.

B. $127.

C. $138.

11. (QID 355) If the bond-equivalent yield on a U.S. bond is 5%, the yield on an annual-pay basis is closest to:

A. 4.94%.

***B. 5.06%.**

C. 5.51%.

Explanation: LOS: Reading 65-d

yield on annual-pay bond
$= (1 + \text{bond-equivalent yield}/2)^2 - 1$
$= 5.06\%$

**Reference:** CFA® Program Curriculum, Volume 5, p. 399.

---

12. (QID 356) An investor purchases a ten-year bond at par of $100 on June 3 2006, which has an annual coupon of 10%. The reinvestment rate at the first coupon date is 9% and at the second coupon date is 8%. The investor expects 12.5% annualized total return for the three years ending on June 1 2009. To reach the investment goal, the bond should be sold on June 1, 2009 at a price closest to:

***A. $110.**

B. $127.

C. $138.

Explanation: LOS: Reading 65-c

The future value of the investment on June 1 2008:

$$100(1.125)^3 = 10(1.09)(1.08) + 10(1.08) + 10 + P$$
$$P = 109.81$$

**Reference:** CFA® Program Curriculum, Volume 56, pp. 393-397.

13. (QID 357) To determine whether a bond is undervalued or overvalued, which of the following information is least likely to be required?

A. The convexity measure.

B. The current market price.

C. The appropriate spot rates.

---

14. (QID 358) The following data has been gathered:

| Maturity (years) | Spot rates |
|---|---|
| 1.0 | 7.6% |
| 1.5 | 7.8% |
| 2.0 | 8.2% |
| 2.5 | 8.4% |
| 3.0 | 9.0% |

The six-month forward rate two years from now is closest to:

A. 4.6%.

B. 8.4%.

C. 9.2%.

13. (QID 357) To determine whether a bond is undervalued or overvalued, which of the following information is least likely to be required?

***A. The convexity measure.**

B. The current market price.

C. The appropriate spot rates.

Explanation: LOS: Reading 64-c

Given a bond's cash flows, appropriate spot rates or yield to maturity, the 'theoretical' price or arbitrage-free value can be calculated. Comparing it to the current market price, we can determine if a bond is undervalued or overvalued.

**Reference:** CFA® Program Curriculum, Volume 5, pp. 372-374.

---

14. (QID 358) The following data has been gathered:

| Maturity (years) | Spot rates |
|---|---|
| 1.0 | 7.6% |
| 1.5 | 7.8% |
| 2.0 | 8.2% |
| 2.5 | 8.4% |
| 3.0 | 9.0% |

The six-month forward rate two years from now is closest to:

A. 4.6%.

B. 8.4%.

***C. 9.2%.**

Explanation: LOS: Reading 65-h

$_1f_4 = [(1+0.042)^5/(1+0.041)^4] - 1$

$= 4.6\%$

The forward rate is 4.6% x 2 = 9.2%

**Reference:** CFA® Program Curriculum, Volume 5, pp. 421-426.

15. (QID 367) Bootstrapping is used to calculate:

A. theoretical spot rates.

B. the value of an embedded option.

C. forward rates from a series of spot rates.

---

16. (QID 360) Which of the following statements regarding reinvestment risk is least accurate?

A. The higher the coupon rate the higher the reinvestment risk.

B. Long-dated zero coupon bonds have significant reinvestment risk.

C. A bond selling at a premium will have a higher reinvestment risk than a bond selling at a discount.

15. (QID 367) Bootstrapping is used to calculate:

***A. theoretical spot rates.**

B. the value of an embedded option.

C. forward rates from a series of spot rates.

Explanation: LOS: Reading 65-e

Bootstrapping is used to calculate theoretical default-free spot rates from on-the-run Treasury bonds.

**Reference:** CFA® Program Curriculum, Volume 5, pp. 408-413.

---

16. (QID 360) Which of the following statements regarding reinvestment risk is least accurate?

A. The higher the coupon rate the higher the reinvestment risk.

***B. Long-dated zero coupon bonds have significant reinvestment risk.**

C. A bond selling at a premium will have a higher reinvestment risk than a bond selling at a discount.

Explanation: LOS: Reading 65-c

The higher the coupon rate the more difficult to obtain a comparable high reinvestment yield.

A bond selling at a premium means that the reinvestment income will have to compensate for the capital loss due to the premium.

A zero coupon bond will have no coupons to reinvest, so no reinvestment risk.

**Reference:** CFA® Program Curriculum, Volume 5, pp. 397-400.

17. (QID 361) A bond with five years remaining term to maturity and a 10% coupon payable annually is trading at $95. The current yield is closest to:

A. 9.5%.

B. 10.0%.

C. 10.5%.

---

18. (QID 362) The following data is collected:

| Years to maturity | Spot rate |
|---|---|
| 0.5 | 5.75% |
| 1.0 | 6.25% |
| 1.5 | 7.00% |
| 2.0 | 7.25% |

Based on the above data, the six-month implied forward rate one and a half years from now is closest to:

A. 4.00%.

B. 6.25%.

C. 8.00%.

17. (QID 361) A bond with five years remaining term to maturity and a 10% coupon payable annually is trading at $95. The current yield is closest to:

A. 9.5%.

B. 10.0%.

***C. 10.5%.**

Explanation: LOS: Reading 65-b

The current yield is then 10/95 = 10.52%

**Reference:** CFA® Program Curriculum, Volume 5, p. 391.

---

18. (QID 362) The following data is collected:

| Years to maturity | Spot rate |
|---|---|
| 0.5 | 5.75% |
| 1.0 | 6.25% |
| 1.5 | 7.00% |
| 2.0 | 7.25% |

Based on the above data, the six-month implied forward rate one and a half years from now is closest to:

A. 4.00%.

B. 6.25%.

***C. 8.00%.**

Explanation: LOS: Reading 65-h

$${}_2r_1 = (1.07)^3/(1.0625)^2 - 1$$
$$= 8.52\%$$

The forward rate is 4.0% x 2 = 8.0%

**Reference:** CFA® Program Curriculum, Volume 5, pp. 421-426.

19. (QID 363) An option-free bond has a remaining life of three years and carries an 8
coupon rate payable annually and has a yield to maturity of 9%. If the one- and two-year spot
rates are 6.0% and 6.5%, respectively, then the three-year spot rate is closest to:

A. 7.0%.

B. 8.1%.

C. 9.2%.

---

20. (QID 364) An investor who requires a return of 10% will value an 8-year zero-coupon bond with a redemption value of $10,000 at a price closest to:

A. $2,000.

B. $4,580.

C. $9,000.

19. (QID 363) An option-free bond has a remaining life of three years and carries an 8% annual coupon rate payable annually and has a yield to maturity of 9%. If the one- and two-year spot rates are 6.0% and 6.5%, respectively, then the three-year spot rate is closest to:

A. 7.0%.

B. 8.1%.

***C. 9.2%.**

Explanation: LOS: Reading 65-h

The following relationship must hold, where the three-year spot rate is z:

$$8/(1.09)+8/(1.09)^2+108/(1.09)^3$$
$$=8/(1.06)+8/(1.065)^2+108/(1+z)^3$$

$$97.47 = 14.60+108/(1+z)^3$$

$$(1+z)^3 = 108/82.87$$

$$1+z = (1.3032)^{1/3}$$

$$z = 9.23\%$$

**Reference:** CFA® Program Curriculum, Volume 5, pp. 426-429.

---

20. (QID 364) An investor who requires a return of 10% will value an 8-year zero-coupon bond with a redemption value of $10,000 at a price closest to:

A. $2,000.

***B. $4,580.**

C. $9,000.

Explanation: LOS: Reading 64-e

Using a semiannual discount rate to arrive at bond-equivalent yield pricing:

$$\textbf{Price} = \mathbf{10{,}000/(1.05)^{16} = \$4{,}580}$$

**Reference:** CFA® Program Curriculum, Volume 5, pp. 366-367.

21. (QID 365) Which of the following statements is least accurate when referring to the characteristics of effective duration?

A. Effective duration can be a negative value.

B. Effective duration can only be calculated for bonds where the cash flows are certain.

C. Effective duration is useful for estimating price changes of bonds with embedded options.

---

22. (QID 366) For a given basis point change in interest rates, the percentage price increase of a bond is more than the price decrease. This indicates that the bond has:

A. low duration.

B. high duration.

C. positive convexity.

21. (QID 365) Which of the following statements is least accurate when referring to the characteristics of effective duration?

A. Effective duration can be a negative value.

***B. Effective duration can only be calculated for bonds where the cash flows are certain.**

C. Effective duration is useful for estimating price changes of bonds with embedded options.

Explanation: LOS: Reading 66-e

Effective duration is calculated by empirical observation and a pricing model taking into account changes in cash flows due to yield changes. It can take on a negative value and be greater than maturity, particularly for unconventional securities such as MBS derivatives such as IOs and POs.

Effective duration is the most common tool for estimating price changes of bonds with embedded options or uncertain cash flows.

**Reference:** CFA® Program Curriculum, Volume 5, p. 464.

---

22. (QID 366) For a given basis point change in interest rates, the percentage price increase of a bond is more than the price decrease. This indicates that the bond has:

A. low duration.

B. high duration.

***C. positive convexity.**

Explanation: LOS: Reading 66-c

Positive convexity occurs when the percentage price increase of a bond is more than the price decrease for a given yield change.

**Reference:** CFA® Program Curriculum, Volume 5, pp. 448-456.

23. (QID 348) A 6% coupon bond pays interest semiannually, has duration of 10, sells for $800, and is priced at a yield to maturity (YTM) of 8%. If the YTM increases to 9%, the expected decrease in price is:

A. $10.

B. $72.

C. $80.

---

24. (QID 447) A short-term forward rate curve is plotted on the same chart as the Treasury yield curve. If the yield curve is upward sloping then we can conclude that the forward rate curve will be

A. above the yield curve.

B. below the yield curve.

C. flatter than the yield curve.

---

25. (QID 354) A bond with a coupon of 11.5% and 10 years remaining maturity has an effective duration of 6.2 and convexity of 5.5. The bond is quoted at $125¾. If the yield to maturity rises by 125 basis points the bond price will be closest to:

A. $97.50.

B. $115.89.

C. $116.12.

23. (QID 348) A 6% coupon bond pays interest semiannually, has duration of 10, sells for $800, and is priced at a yield to maturity (YTM) of 8%. If the YTM increases to 9%, the expected decrease in price is:

A. $10.

B. $72.

***C. $80.**

Explanation: LOS: Reading 66-d

Percentage change in price

= -D x ? y x 100 = -10 x 0.01 x 100 = -10

The predicted decrease in price

= 10% x $800 = $80

**Reference:** CFA® Program Curriculum, Volume 5, pp. 456-457.

---

24. (QID 447) A short-term forward rate curve is plotted on the same chart as the Treasury yield curve. If the yield curve is upward sloping then we can conclude that the forward rate curve will be

***A. above the yield curve.**

B. below the yield curve.

C. flatter than the yield curve.

Explanation: LOS: Reading 65-h

When the yield curve is upward sloping investors are expecting yields to rise so the forward rates will be above the spot rates. We cannot conclude whether the forward rate curve will be steeper or flatter without more information about the yield curve shape.

**Reference:** CFA® Program Curriculum, Volume 5, pp. 421-425.

25. (QID 354) A bond with a coupon of 11.5% and 10 years remaining maturity has an effective duration of 6.2 and convexity of 5.5. The bond is quoted at \$125¾. If the yield to maturity rises by 125 basis points the bond price will be closest to:

A. \$97.50.

B. \$115.89.

***C. \$116.12.**

Explanation: LOS: Reading 66-g

| | | |
|---|---|---|
| Duration effect | = | -D x ?y x 100 |
| | = | - 6.2 x (0.0125) x 100 |
| | = | -7.75 |
| Convexity effect | = | Convexity x ?$y^2$ x 100 |
| | = | 5.5 x $(0.0125)^2$ x 100 |
| | = | 0.0859 |
| ?P | = | \$125.75 x (-7.75 + 0.089)% |
| | = | \$9.634 |

The new price is:

\$125.75 – \$9.634 = \$116.12

**Reference:** CFA® Program Curriculum, Volume 5, pp. 469-470.

# Study Session 17: Derivatives:

Derivatives—financial instruments that offer a return based on the return of some underlying asset—have become increasingly important and fundamental in effectively managing financial risk and creating synthetic exposures to asset classes. As in other security markets, arbitrage and market efficiency play a critical role in establishing prices and maintaining parity.

This study session builds the conceptual framework for understanding derivative investments (forwards, futures, options, and swaps), derivative markets, and the use of options in risk management.

**Reading 67: Derivative Markets and Instruments**

**Reading 68: Forward Markets and Contracts**

**Reading 69: Futures Markets and Contracts**

**Reading 70: Option Markets and Contracts**

**Reading 71: Swap Markets and Contracts**

**Reading 72: Risk Management Applications of Option Strategies**

1. (QID 369) If a party to a swap agreement wishes to terminate the agreement prior to the expiry of the swap, it might consider:

A. I. entering into an offsetting swap agreement.

B. II. selling the swap at its market value through the swaps exchange.

C. III. offsetting a long position with a short position in the futures market.

---

2. (QID 370) A put option on a stock has an exercise price of $25.00, the stock is trading at $22.00 and the price of the put option is $3.50. The option is:

A. $3.00 in-the-money.

B. $0.50 out-of-the-money.

C. $6.50 out-of-the-money.

1. (QID 369) If a party to a swap agreement wishes to terminate the agreement prior to the expiry of the swap, it might consider:

***A. I. entering into an offsetting swap agreement.**

B. II. selling the swap at its market value through the swaps exchange.

C. III. offsetting a long position with a short position in the futures market.

Explanation: LOS: Reading 70-a

II. is not correct since swaps are dealt over-the-counter.

III. is not correct: long and short are terms applied to futures positions.

**Reference:** CFA® Program Curriculum, Volume 6, pp. 125-126.

---

2. (QID 370) A put option on a stock has an exercise price of $25.00, the stock is trading at $22.00 and the price of the put option is $3.50. The option is:

***A. $3.00 in-the-money.**

B. $0.50 out-of-the-money.

C. $6.50 out-of-the-money.

Explanation: LOS: Reading 70-a

The put option is in-the-money since the exercise price is above the stock price, and the difference between the two prices is $3.

**Reference:** CFA® Program Curriculum, Volume 6, pp. 79-82.

3. (QID 371) The clearing house of a futures exchange:

A. acts as counterparty to each transaction on the exchange.

B. acts as market maker in futures contracts traded on the exchange.

C. stabilizes futures prices by buying futures when the market is weak and selling futures when the market is strong.

---

4. (QID 372) When an institution does a swap transaction the counterparty to the transaction is the:

A. exchange.

B. clearing house.

C. party who is the end user of the transaction.

3. (QID 371) The clearing house of a futures exchange:

***A. acts as counterparty to each transaction on the exchange.**

B. acts as market maker in futures contracts traded on the exchange.

C. stabilizes futures prices by buying futures when the market is weak and selling futures when the market is strong.

Explanation: LOS: Reading 69-c

The clearing house does not intentionally take positions in futures or act as market maker. Once a trade is done it acts as counterparty to both parties and they both settle with the clearing house.

**Reference:** CFA® Program Curriculum, Volume 6, pp. 51-54.

---

4. (QID 372) When an institution does a swap transaction the counterparty to the transaction is the:

A. exchange.

B. clearing house.

***C. party who is the end user of the transaction.**

Explanation: LOS: Reading 67-b

Swaps differ from exchange-traded futures and options where the counterparty risk is the risk that the exchange or clearing house defaults (not likely to happen). The parties to a swap take on the risk of counterparty default.

**Reference:** CFA® Program Curriculum, Volume 6, pp. 9-10.

5. (QID 373) Which of the following statements is most accurate with respect to forward and futures contracts?

A. A forward contract refers to a futures contract traded outside the U.S.

B. A forward contract is another term for, and is identical to, a futures contract.

C. A futures contract is a type of forward contract but futures contracts have highly standardized contract terms.

---

6. (QID 374) The lower bound for an American call option compared to a European call option with the same underlying, exercise date and time to maturity is:

A. always equal to the lower bound for the European call.

B. equal to or less than the lower bound for the European call.

C. equal to or more than the lower bound for the European call.

5. (QID 373) Which of the following statements is most accurate with respect to forward and futures contracts?

A. A forward contract refers to a futures contract traded outside the U.S.

B. A forward contract is another term for, and is identical to, a futures contract.

***C. A futures contract is a type of forward contract but futures contracts have highly standardized contract terms.**

Explanation: LOS: Reading 69-a

A forward contract is the general term applied to an agreement that leads to an exchange of assets at a later time. A futures contract has specific contract terms and is traded on a recognized exchange with the contract guaranteed by a clearing house.

**Reference:** CFA® Program Curriculum, Volume 6, pp. 47-48.

---

6. (QID 374) The lower bound for an American call option compared to a European call option with the same underlying, exercise date and time to maturity is:

***A. always equal to the lower bound for the European call.**

B. equal to or less than the lower bound for the European call.

C. equal to or more than the lower bound for the European call.

Explanation: LOS: Reading 70-h

The lower bound for a European call is either zero or the underlying price minus the present value of the exercise price, whichever is greater. Since an American call option is worth the same or more than a European call the lower bound is the same.

**Reference:** CFA® Program Curriculum, Volume 6, pp. 98-103.

7. (QID 375) The value of a call option on a stock at expiration is:

A. the greater of (i) zero and (ii) the stock price minus the exercise price.

B. the greater of (i) zero and (ii) the exercise price minus the stock price.

C. the smaller of (i) zero and (ii) the stock price minus the exercise price.

---

8. (QID 376) If an investor wants to protect his stock portfolio against losses he could:

A. sell calls on the stock market index.

B. buy puts on the stock market index.

C. sell puts on the stock market index.

7. (QID 375) The value of a call option on a stock at expiration is:

***A. the greater of (i) zero and (ii) the stock price minus the exercise price.**

B. the greater of (i) zero and (ii) the exercise price minus the stock price.

C. the smaller of (i) zero and (ii) the stock price minus the exercise price.

Explanation: LOS: Reading 70-e

At expiration the holder of the call option can either exercise the option or let it lapse. If the stock price has ended higher than the exercise price then the investor will exercise the option since he can sell the stock in the market at a higher price. If the stock price has fallen below the exercise price he will let the option lapse worthless.

**Reference:** CFA® Program Curriculum, Volume 6, pp. 94-98.

---

8. (QID 376) If an investor wants to protect his stock portfolio against losses he could:

A. sell calls on the stock market index.

***B. buy puts on the stock market index.**

C. sell puts on the stock market index.

Explanation: LOS: Reading 72-b

If he buys put options and the market falls he will make a profit on the put options. This will offset his loss on the stock portfolio.

**Reference:** CFA® Program Curriculum, Volume 6, pp. 160-163.

9. (QID 377) In the case that a stock price falls below the exercise price of a call option at the expiration of the option, then:

A. the profit made by the writer of the option is larger than the loss made by the buyer.

B. the loss made by the writer of the option is larger than the profit made by the buyer.

C. the profit made by the writer of the option is the same as the loss made by the buyer.

10. (QID 378) If a trader has opened a position by buying a call option, he can close the position by:

A. selling a put.

B. buying a put.

C. selling a call.

9. (QID 377) In the case that a stock price falls below the exercise price of a call option at the expiration of the option, then:

A. the profit made by the writer of the option is larger than the loss made by the buyer.

B. the loss made by the writer of the option is larger than the profit made by the buyer.

***C. the profit made by the writer of the option is the same as the loss made by the buyer.**

Explanation: LOS: Reading 72-a

Options are a zero-sum gain, the profit (loss) made by the writer of the option will equal the loss (profit) made by the buyer.

**Reference:** CFA® Program Curriculum, Volume 6, pp. 147-151.

---

10. (QID 378) If a trader has opened a position by buying a call option, he can close the position by:

A. selling a put.

B. buying a put.

***C. selling a call.**

Explanation: LOS: Reading 70-a

The 'opposite' of buying a call is simply selling the same call option.

**Reference:** CFA® Program Curriculum, Volume 6, pp. 78-80.

11. (QID 379) Which of the following combination of factors will tend to lead to the highest price of a put option:

A. a low strike price and a short time to expiry.

B. a high strike price and a short time to expiry.

C. a high strike price and a long time to expiry.

---

12. (QID 380) Which of the following statements is most accurate concerning two options that have the same terms except that one is an American option and one is a European option?

A. The European option can be exercised at any point before expiry and is worth at least as much as the American option.

B. The American option can be exercised at any point before expiry and is worth at least as much as the European option.

C. The American option can be exercised at any point before expiry and is worth less than, or the same as, the European option.

11. (QID 379) Which of the following combination of factors will tend to lead to the highest price of a put option:

A. a low strike price and a short time to expiry.

B. a high strike price and a short time to expiry.

***C. a high strike price and a long time to expiry.**

Explanation: LOS: Reading 70-i

The profit on a put option will be determined by the difference between the stock price and the strike price: the higher the strike price the higher the potential profit. A longer time to expiry gives the holder a longer period in which to sell the shares at the exercise price so it will be worth more.

**Reference:** CFA® Program Curriculum, Volume 6, pp. 93-98.

---

12. (QID 380) Which of the following statements is most accurate concerning two options that have the same terms except that one is an American option and one is a European option?

A. The European option can be exercised at any point before expiry and is worth at least as much as the American option.

***B. The American option can be exercised at any point before expiry and is worth at least as much as the European option.**

C. The American option can be exercised at any point before expiry and is worth less than, or the same as, the European option.

Explanation: LOS: Reading 70-a

Since an American option can be exercised at any time up to expiry, whereas a European option can only be exercised at expiry, an American option gives the holder more flexibility and therefore must be worth more (or the same).

**Reference:** CFA® Program Curriculum, Volume 6, p. 79.

13. (QID 381) There is a European put option expiring in 60 days, the exercise price is 110 and the underlying is trading at 100. The risk-free rate is 6%, the lower bound on the option value is closest to:

A. 3.77.

B. 8.95.

C. 10.00.

---

14. (QID 382) An investor holds an asset with a current price of 120; a put option is purchased with an exercise price of 105. If the breakeven point for the hedged position is an asset price of 135 at expiration, then the value of the put option at the time of purchase must have been:

A. 15.

B. 20.

C. 30.

13. (QID 381) There is a European put option expiring in 60 days, the exercise price is 110 and the underlying is trading at 100. The risk-free rate is 6%, the lower bound on the option value is closest to:

A. 3.77.

***B. 8.95.**

C. 10.00.

Explanation: LOS: Reading 70-h

The lower bound is given by:

$$p_0 ? \text{Max}[0, X/(1 + r)^T - S_0] = \text{Max}[0, 110/(1.06)^{0.1644} - 100] = 8.95$$

**Reference:** CFA® Program Curriculum, Volume 6, pp. 98-103.

---

14. (QID 382) An investor holds an asset with a current price of 120; a put option is purchased with an exercise price of 105. If the breakeven point for the hedged position is an asset price of 135 at expiration, then the value of the put option at the time of purchase must have been:

***A. 15.**

B. 20.

C. 30.

Explanation: LOS: Reading 72-b

Breakeven is when:

Cost of put option

= change in value of asset + value of put option

= (135 -120) + 0 = 15

**Reference:** CFA® Program Curriculum, Volume 6, pp. 152-156.

15. (QID 383) The swap markets:

A. are highly regulated.

B. developed in the last five years.

C. offer an effective way of hedging.

---

16. (QID 384) An investor deposits an initial margin of $40,000 for a futures trade and the following day makes a $15,000 loss on the trade. If the maintenance requirement is $30,000 then he must deposit a variation margin of:

A. $0.

B. $5,000.

C. $15,000.

15. (QID 383) The swap markets:

A. are highly regulated.

B. developed in the last five years.

***C. offer an effective way of hedging.**

Explanation: LOS: Reading 71-a

The swap markets are mainly used by institutions, are virtually unregulated, and have been active for a long period. They can be used for hedging, e.g. interest rate swaps are used to hedge interest rate risk.

**Reference:** CFA® Program Curriculum, Volume 6, pp. 124-126.

---

16. (QID 384) An investor deposits an initial margin of $40,000 for a futures trade and the following day makes a $15,000 loss on the trade. If the maintenance requirement is $30,000 then he must deposit a variation margin of:

A. $0.

B. $5,000.

***C. $15,000.**

Explanation: LOS: Reading 69-b

The variation margin must be paid if the investor's margin balance falls below the maintenance requirement and must bring the margin balance back to the initial level. In this case the balance has fallen to $25,000 so he must make up the difference of $15,000 in variation margin.

**Reference:** CFA® Program Curriculum, Volume 6, pp. 53-58.

17. (QID 385) A series of cash settled forward contracts is:

A. a swap.

B. a futures option.

C. a futures contract.

---

18. (QID 386) An investor holds 1,000 shares of ABC Corp. and the current stock price is $45. He buys 1,000 put options with an exercise price of $46 at a premium of $6 each. If the stock price falls to $35 at the expiration date then the value of his insured portfolio is:

A. $40,000.

B. $46,000.

C. $51,000.

17. (QID 385) A series of cash settled forward contracts is:

***A. a swap.**

B. a futures option.

C. a futures contract.

Explanation: LOS: Reading 67-b

A swap is an agreement between two parties to exchange a series of cash flows in the future. It is dealt OTC so is effectively a series of cash settled forward contracts.

**Reference:** CFA® Program Curriculum, Volume 6, pp. 9-10.

---

18. (QID 386) An investor holds 1,000 shares of ABC Corp. and the current stock price is $45. He buys 1,000 put options with an exercise price of $46 at a premium of $6 each. If the stock price falls to $35 at the expiration date then the value of his insured portfolio is:

***A. $40,000.**

B. $46,000.

C. $51,000.

Explanation: LOS: Reading 72-b

The value of the portfolio will be $35,000 - $6,000 (option premium) + $11,000 (profit on exercising option) = $40,000 i.e. the minimum value is the exercise price less the premium.

**Reference:** CFA® Program Curriculum, Volume 6, pp. 156-160.

19. (QID 387) The least appropriate way to close a futures position is by:

A. offset.

B. exercise.

C. delivery.

---

20. (QID 388) Daily settlement in the futures market refers to:

A. I. closing prices which are reported daily by the exchange.

B. II. when a trader enters into a futures contract he has one day to deposit the initial margin.

C. III. gains and losses are added or deducted from the margin position held with a broker on a daily basis.

19. (QID 387) The least appropriate way to close a futures position is by:

A. offset.

***B. exercise.**

C. delivery.

Explanation: LOS: Reading 69-d

Exercise is a term used for options.

**Reference:** CFA® Program Curriculum, Volume 6, pp. 58-60.

---

20. (QID 388) Daily settlement in the futures market refers to:

A. I. closing prices which are reported daily by the exchange.

B. II. when a trader enters into a futures contract he has one day to deposit the initial margin.

***C. III. gains and losses are added or deducted from the margin position held with a broker on a daily basis.**

Explanation: LOS: Reading 69-c

II. is not correct since the initial margin must be deposited before the trade is done.

**Reference:** CFA® Program Curriculum, Volume 6, pp. 53-54.

21. (QID 389) An investor purchases a call option on a stock, with an exercise price of $8.00, at a premium of $0.70 and writes a call option on the same stock, with an exercise price of $9.00, at a premium of $0.10. Both options have the same expiration date. Which of the following statements is most accurate regarding the profit/loss the investor makes?

A. I. The investor has the risk of making an unlimited loss.

B. II. The investor has the potential to make unlimited gains.

C. III. If the stock price rises sharply the investor will make a profit.

---

22. (QID 390) A trader writes a put option on a stock which has a current price of $50, the option price is $5 and the exercise price is $52. At expiration the stock closes at $54. The intrinsic value of the option at expiration is:

A. $0.

B. $2.

C. $4.

21. (QID 389) An investor purchases a call option on a stock, with an exercise price of $8.00, at a premium of $0.70 and writes a call option on the same stock, with an exercise price of $9.00, at a premium of $0.10. Both options have the same expiration date. Which of the following statements is most accurate regarding the profit/loss the investor makes?

A. I. The investor has the risk of making an unlimited loss.

B. II. The investor has the potential to make unlimited gains.

***C. III. If the stock price rises sharply the investor will make a profit.**

Explanation: LOS: Reading 72-a

I. and II. are not correct since if the stock price falls sharply neither option will be exercised so the loss is the difference in premium of $0.60. If the stock price rises, then the loss on the short call will be more than made up by the profit on the long call, but the maximum gain will $1.00 - $0.70 + $0.10 = $0.40.

III. If the stock price rises then the investor will make a profit since the profit on the long call will be more than the loss on the short call (due to the lower exercise price) and the gain will $1.00 - $0.70 + $0.10 = $0.40.

**Reference:** CFA® Program Curriculum, Volume 6, pp. 149-156.

---

22. (QID 390) A trader writes a put option on a stock which has a current price of $50, the option price is $5 and the exercise price is $52. At expiration the stock closes at $54. The intrinsic value of the option at expiration is:

***A. $0.**

B. $2.

C. $4.

Explanation: LOS: Reading 70-a

The intrinsic value of a put option is the greater of zero or the (exercise price – strike price). The exercise price is less than the strike price so the intrinsic value is zero.

**Reference:** CFA® Program Curriculum, Volume 6, pp. 94-98.

23. (QID 391) A portfolio insurance strategy for a diversified stock portfolio can be implemented by:

A. buying a put option on the stock index representing the underlying stock portfolio.

B. writing a put option on the stock index representing the underlying stock portfolio.

C. buying a call option on the stock index representing the underlying stock portfolio.

---

24. (QID 475) An investor writes a put option at a premium of $6 on a stock with an exercise price of $62. If the stock price is $70 at expiration the investor will make a profit of:

A. $2.

B. $6.

C. $8.

---

25. (QID 476) A portfolio insurance strategy for a diversified stock portfolio can be implemented by:

A. buying a put option on the stock index representing the underlying stock portfolio.

B. writing a put option on the stock index representing the underlying stock portfolio.

C. writing a covered call option on the stock index representing the underlying stock portfolio.

23. (QID 391) A portfolio insurance strategy for a diversified stock portfolio can be implemented by:

***A. buying a put option on the stock index representing the underlying stock portfolio.**

B. writing a put option on the stock index representing the underlying stock portfolio.

C. buying a call option on the stock index representing the underlying stock portfolio.

Explanation: LOS: Reading 70-b

In the situation that the stock market index falls, the losses on the underlying portfolio will be offset by the profits on the put option.

**Reference:** CFA® Program Curriculum, Volume 6, pp. 106-111.

---

24. (QID 475) An investor writes a put option at a premium of $6 on a stock with an exercise price of $62. If the stock price is $70 at expiration the investor will make a profit of:

A. $2.

***B. $6.**

C. $8.

Explanation: LOS: Reading 72-a

The put option will lapse worthless since the exercise price is lower than the market price, so the investor makes a profit of the premium that he collected.

**Reference:** CFA® Program Curriculum, Volume 6, pp. 152-156.

25. (QID 476) A portfolio insurance strategy for a diversified stock portfolio can be implemented by:

***A. buying a put option on the stock index representing the underlying stock portfolio.**

B. writing a put option on the stock index representing the underlying stock portfolio.

C. writing a covered call option on the stock index representing the underlying stock portfolio.

Explanation: LOS: Reading 72-b

In the situation that the stock market index falls, the losses on the underlying portfolio will be offset by the profits on the put option.

**Reference:** CFA® Program Curriculum, Volume 6, pp. 160-163.

# Study Session 18: Alternative Investments:

Due to diversification benefits and higher expectations of investment returns, investors are increasingly turning to alternative investments. This study session describes the common types of alternative investments, methods for their valuation, unique risks and opportunities associated with them, and the relation between alternative investments and traditional investments.

Although finding a single definition of an "alternative" investment is difficult, certain features (e.g., limited liquidity, infrequent valuations, and unique legal structures) are typically associated with alternative investments. This study session discusses these features and how to evaluate their impact on expected returns and investment decisions in more detail. The reading provides an overview of the major categories of alternative investments, including real estate, private equity, venture capital, hedge funds, closely held companies, distressed securities, and commodities.

Each one of these categories has several unique characteristics, and the readings discuss valuation methods for illiquid assets (such as direct real estate or closely held companies), performance measures for private equity and venture capital investments, differences between various hedge fund strategies, and implementation vehicles for investments in alternative assets.

**Reading 73: Alternative Investments**

**Reading 74: Investing in Commodities**

1. (QID 392) Which of the following statements best describes real estate markets? Real estate markets are:

A. inefficient since prices are dependent on many different factors.

B. efficient since most real estate is heavily promoted prior to sale.

C. inefficient since there is no central market place and information is not circulated quickly between investors.

---

2. (QID 393) Early-stage venture capital investments are least likely to be:

A. illiquid.

B. invested in companies that will require further financing.

C. invested in companies that are looking to expand their commercial production.

1. (QID 392) Which of the following statements best describes real estate markets? Real estate markets are:

A. inefficient since prices are dependent on many different factors.

B. efficient since most real estate is heavily promoted prior to sale.

***C. inefficient since there is no central market place and information is not circulated quickly between investors.**

Explanation: LOS: Reading 73-d

Real estate markets are regarded as informationally inefficient, which provides opportunities for investors who can identify mispriced properties.

**Reference:** CFA® Program Curriculum, Volume 6, pp. 186-188.

---

2. (QID 393) Early-stage venture capital investments are least likely to be:

A. illiquid.

B. invested in companies that will require further financing.

***C. invested in companies that are looking to expand their commercial production.**

Explanation: LOS: Reading 73-g

Early–stage financing is used to help companies move into operations and occurs before commercial production has started.

**Reference:** CFA® Program Curriculum, Volume 6, pp. 198-200.

3. (QID 394) The market cap rate that is used to value a property:

A. is the appreciation in market value over the previous one-year period.

B. is the operating expense incurred in owning and managing the property.

C. reflects the rate of return required by investors in a comparable property.

---

4. (QID 395) Exchange Traded Funds (ETFs) have 'in kind' redemption. This means that:

A. an ETF can redeem shares in its underlying portfolio by giving two days' notice.

B. an investor will receive the cash equivalent to the net asset value of the shares they hold when they redeem them.

C. an authorized participant can redeem shares and receive a portfolio of shares that was used to track the index.

3. (QID 394) The market cap rate that is used to value a property:

A. is the appreciation in market value over the previous one-year period.

B. is the operating expense incurred in owning and managing the property.

***C. reflects the rate of return required by investors in a comparable property.**

Explanation: LOS: Reading 73-f

The market cap rate is the rate that is used to discount the net operating cash flows from the property to arrive at the present value.

**Reference:** CFA® Program Curriculum, Volume 6, pp. 191-193.

---

4. (QID 395) Exchange Traded Funds (ETFs) have 'in kind' redemption. This means that:

A. an ETF can redeem shares in its underlying portfolio by giving two days' notice.

B. an investor will receive the cash equivalent to the net asset value of the shares they hold when they redeem them.

***C. an authorized participant can redeem shares and receive a portfolio of shares that was used to track the index.**

Explanation: LOS: Reading 73-b

When an authorized participant or market maker redeems shares he receives a basket of the underlying securities rather than cash.

**Reference:** CFA® Program Curriculum, Volume 6, pp. 178-182.

5. (QID 396) The advantages of investing in a fund of hedge funds rather directly into a single strategy hedge fund include:

A. lower fees.

B. superior returns.

C. diversification reducing the volatility of returns.

6. (QID 397) Hedge funds usually:

A. hedge out all market and currency risks.

B. use leverage to increase the returns from arbitrage strategies.

C. take short positions to enhance returns when prices are rising.

5. (QID 396) The advantages of investing in a fund of hedge funds rather directly into a single strategy hedge fund include:

A. lower fees.

B. superior returns.

***C. diversification reducing the volatility of returns.**

Explanation: LOS: Reading 73-j

A fund of hedge funds will invest across a number of different hedge funds which often follow different strategies so the volatility of the fund of funds' returns is reduced below the volatility of the individual hedge funds' returns.

**Reference:** CFA® Program Curriculum, Volume 6, pp. 210-213.

---

6. (QID 397) Hedge funds usually:

A. hedge out all market and currency risks.

***B. use leverage to increase the returns from arbitrage strategies.**

C. take short positions to enhance returns when prices are rising.

Explanation: LOS: Reading 73-k

Hedge funds have the flexibility to borrow to increase their returns. This is a strategy often used by arbitrage funds. They take short positions to enhance returns when prices are falling, many strategies do not hedge out all market and currency exposure (despite their name) and they frequently use OTC derivatives.

**Reference:** CFA® Program Curriculum, Volume 6, pp. 205-213.

7. (QID 398) In the U.S. most equity real estate investment trusts (REITs):

A. are open-end investment companies.

B. are only available to institutional investors.

C. have shares which are traded on a stock market.

8. (QID 399) The Sharpe ratio for hedge fund indexes is:

A. often understated due to survivorship bias.

B. generally higher than those for equity and bond indexes.

C. a suitable measure of risk-adjusted return since returns are not always symmetrically distributed.

7. (QID 398) In the U.S. most equity real estate investment trusts (REITs):

A. are open-end investment companies.

B. are only available to institutional investors.

***C. have shares which are traded on a stock market.**

Explanation: LOS: Reading 73-e

A REIT is a closed-end investment company that is usually listed on a stock market making it available to retail and institutional investors.

**Reference:** CFA® Program Curriculum, Volume 6, p. 188.

---

8. (QID 399) The Sharpe ratio for hedge fund indexes is:

A. often understated due to survivorship bias.

***B. generally higher than those for equity and bond indexes.**

C. a suitable measure of risk-adjusted return since returns are not always symmetrically distributed.

Explanation: LOS: Reading 73-l

Survivorship bias means that returns are overstated and risk understated, and hence Sharpe ratios are overstated.

If a hedge fund invests in options or other derivatives, standard deviation, and hence the Sharpe ratio, may underestimate the risk of big losses.

The standard deviation of hedge funds returns is lower than those of equities.

**Reference:** CFA® Program Curriculum, Volume 6, pp. 214-218.

9. (QID 400) A property was purchased one year ago for $175,000. If the annual net operating income is $24,000 and the market capitalization rate is 12% then, using the income approach, the value of the property is:

A. $196,000.

B. $200,000.

C. $220,000.

---

10. (QID 401) The discounted after-tax cash flow approach to real estate valuation is often considered more relevant than the market value approach for all of the following reasons except:

A. it is not influenced by the tax status of the investor.

B. it looks at the individual return requirements of the investor.

C. it takes into account the leverage used to purchase real estate.

9. (QID 400) A property was purchased one year ago for $175,000. If the annual net operating income is $24,000 and the market capitalization rate is 12% then, using the income approach, the value of the property is:

A. $196,000.

***B. $200,000.**

C. $220,000.

Explanation: LOS: Reading 73-f

Market value = net operating income/market capitalization rate

= $24,000/0.12 = $200,000

**Reference:** CFA® Program Curriculum, Volume 6, pp. 191-193.

---

10. (QID 401) The discounted after-tax cash flow approach to real estate valuation is often considered more relevant than the market value approach for all of the following reasons except:

***A. it is not influenced by the tax status of the investor.**

B. it looks at the individual return requirements of the investor.

C. it takes into account the leverage used to purchase real estate.

Explanation: LOS: Reading 73-f

The discounted cash flow approach takes into account the cash flows after tax for the investor.

**Reference:** CFA® Program Curriculum, Volume 6, pp. 193-196.

11. (QID 402) The least appropriate reason why after-tax cash flows rather than net operating income are used in the discounted cash flow approach to real estate valuation is:

A. investors usually pay federal taxes.

B. property taxes are payable in many locations.

C. different investors have different costs of borrowing.

---

12. (QID 403) Real estate appraisal refers to:

A. the process of establishing the current market value of a property.

B. checking the quality of construction of a property.

C. examining the legal documentation concerning a property.

11. (QID 402) The least appropriate reason why after-tax cash flows rather than net operating income are used in the discounted cash flow approach to real estate valuation is:

A. investors usually pay federal taxes.

***B. property taxes are payable in many locations.**

C. different investors have different costs of borrowing.

Explanation: LOS: Reading 73-f

Property taxes would be deducted in the calculations of both net operating income and after-tax cash flows.

**Reference:** CFA® Program Curriculum, Volume 6, pp. 193-196.

---

12. (QID 403) Real estate appraisal refers to:

***A. the process of establishing the current market value of a property.**

B. checking the quality of construction of a property.

C. examining the legal documentation concerning a property.

Explanation: LOS: Reading 73-e

Real estate appraisal establishes the value of a property which might include investigating the location, checking the quality of construction and legal documentation.

**Reference:** CFA® Program Curriculum, Volume 6, pp. 186-187.

13. (QID 404) An investor calculates that the net operating income from a property will be $40,000 for each of the next two years. Depreciation expense will be $8,000 per year and her marginal tax rate is 40%. She will pay for the property with cash rather than using a mortgage. At the end of two years she believes that she will be able to sell the property for $200,000 net of tax. If the investor's required rate of return is 15%, the value of the property to the investor is closest to:

A. $182,443.

B. $195,448.

C. $216,257.

14. (QID 405) An investment company is least likely to:

A. offer investment advisory services to investors.

B. appoint an investment manager to manage its assets.

C. have its assets invested in securities that are referred to as a fund.

13. (QID 404) An investor calculates that the net operating income from a property will be $40,000 for each of the next two years. Depreciation expense will be $8,000 per year and her marginal tax rate is 40%. She will pay for the property with cash rather than using a mortgage. At the end of two years she believes that she will be able to sell the property for $200,000 net of tax. If the investor's required rate of return is 15%, the value of the property to the investor is closest to:

A. $182,443.

***B. $195,448.**

C. $216,257.

Explanation: LOS: Reading 73-f

The net income each year is

($40,000 - $8,000)0.60 = $19,200

so the after-tax cash flow is

$19,200 + $8,000 = $27,200 in the first year.

In the second year we need to add the expected sale proceeds of $200,000 .

The cash flows discount back to give a present value of:

$$\frac{\$27{,}200}{1.15} + \frac{\$227{,}200}{1.15^2} = \$23{,}652 + \$171{,}796 = \$195{,}448$$

**Reference:** CFA® Program Curriculum, Volume 6, pp. 193-196.

---

14. (QID 405) An investment company is least likely to:

***A. offer investment advisory services to investors.**

B. appoint an investment manager to manage its assets.

C. have its assets invested in securities that are referred to as a fund.

Explanation: LOS: Reading 73-a

An investment company is the name for a company that receives cash from a number of investors, uses this money to invest in securities and is often managed by a professional fund manager. It is not the same as an investment management or advisory company.

**Reference:** CFA® Program Curriculum, Volume 6, pp. 175-176.

15. (QID 406) At the beginning of the year a hedge fund has assets of $500 million and the fee structure is a fixed fee of 1% of the portfolio value at the beginning of the year plus a 20% incentive fee. The incentive fee is applied to the annual gross return in excess of the previous high watermark or maximum value since inception. The maximum value was two years ago when the value was $520 million. If the gross return over the next year is 10% the fee earned by the manager is:

A. $10 million.

B. $11 million.

C. $15 million.

---

16. (QID 407) Which of the following is the fee that is least likely to be charged by an investment company?

A. Redemption fee.

B. Deferred sales load.

C. A premium to the net asset value.

15. (QID 406) At the beginning of the year a hedge fund has assets of $500 million and the fee structure is a fixed fee of 1% of the portfolio value at the beginning of the year plus a 20% incentive fee. The incentive fee is applied to the annual gross return in excess of the previous high watermark or maximum value since inception. The maximum value was two years ago when the value was $520 million. If the gross return over the next year is 10% the fee earned by the manager is:

A. $10 million.

***B. $11 million.**

C. $15 million.

Explanation: LOS: Reading 73-i

Fixed fee = 1% x $500 million = $5 million

The new value of the fund is $550 million, which is $30 million above the high watermark so the incentive fee is 20% x $30 million = $6 million

Total fee = $5 million + $6 million = $11 million

**Reference:** CFA® Program Curriculum, Volume 6, pp. 206-207.

---

16. (QID 407) Which of the following is the fee that is least likely to be charged by an investment company?

A. Redemption fee.

B. Deferred sales load.

***C. A premium to the net asset value.**

Explanation: LOS: Reading 73-a

The premium to net asset value refers to a closed-end fund which is trading in the market at a premium above its net asset value; this premium goes to the seller of the mutual fund.

**Reference:** CFA® Program Curriculum, Volume 6, pp. 176-178.

17. (QID 408) Which of the following is a characteristic of the real estate market?

A. Frequent transactions.

B. There is no central market place.

C. Supply and demand are in balance.

---

18. (QID 409) Start-up financing from a venture capital company is for:

A. I. market research of a new product idea.

B. II. starting commercial production and sales.

C. III. product development and initial marketing of a product before it is sold commercially.

17. (QID 408) Which of the following is a characteristic of the real estate market?

A. Frequent transactions.

***B. There is no central market place.**

C. Supply and demand are in balance.

Explanation: LOS: Reading 73-d

Property markets often have infrequent transactions and there is no central market place.

It takes time for supply to adjust to changes in demand so they usually are not in balance.

**Reference:** CFA® Program Curriculum, Volume 6, pp. 186-187.

---

18. (QID 409) Start-up financing from a venture capital company is for:

A. I. market research of a new product idea.

B. II. starting commercial production and sales.

***C. III. product development and initial marketing of a product before it is sold commercially.**

Explanation: LOS: Reading 73-g

I. refers to seed financing.

II. is first-stage financing.

**Reference:** CFA® Program Curriculum, Volume 6, pp. 198-200.

19. (QID 410) Shares in a closed-end investment company usually trade at:

    A. the net asset value of the shares.

    B. the net asset value less the liabilities of the fund.

    C. a discount or premium to the net asset value of the shares.

---

20. (QID 411) A hedge fund charges a 0.5% base management fee plus 20% of any gross return above the risk-free rate. The gross return on the fund is 30% and the risk–free rate is 5%. The net return for an investor is closest to:

    A. 24.5%.

    B. 19.5%.

    C. 23.5%.

19. (QID 410) Shares in a closed-end investment company usually trade at:

A. the net asset value of the shares.

B. the net asset value less the liabilities of the fund.

***C. a discount or premium to the net asset value of the shares.**

Explanation: LOS: Reading 73-a

Historically closed-end funds have generally traded at a discount. The price is set by supply and demand for the shares. Open-end funds trade at NAV, plus or minus sales and redemption charges.

**Reference:** CFA® Program Curriculum, Volume 6, p. 175-176.

---

20. (QID 411) A hedge fund charges a 0.5% base management fee plus 20% of any gross return above the risk-free rate. The gross return on the fund is 30% and the risk–free rate is 5%. The net return for an investor is closest to:

***A. 24.5%.**

B. 19.5%.

C. 23.5%.

Explanation: LOS: Reading 76-i

The fee = 0.5% + 20%(30% - 5%) = 5.5%

Net return = 30% - 5.5% = 24.5%

**Reference:** CFA® Program Curriculum, Volume 6, pp. 210-211.

21. (QID 412) Which of the following factors is the least likely to affect net operating income for a property?

A. Rental income.

B. Mortgage interest costs.

C. Property management costs.

---

22. (QID 413) If a fund is to invest in illiquid assets there will be advantages in establishing it as a closed-end fund since:

A. investors cannot draw money out of the fund if they wish to sell their shares.

B. the managers can charge a higher front-end load.

C. the annual investment management fees will be higher.

21. (QID 412) Which of the following factors is the least likely to affect net operating income for a property?

A. Rental income.

***B. Mortgage interest costs.**

C. Property management costs.

Explanation: LOS: Reading 76-f

Net operating income is before tax and interest costs.

**Reference:** CFA® Program Curriculum, Volume 6, pp. 193-194.

---

22. (QID 413) If a fund is to invest in illiquid assets there will be advantages in establishing it as a closed-end fund since:

***A. investors cannot draw money out of the fund if they wish to sell their shares.**

B. the managers can charge a higher front-end load.

C. the annual investment management fees will be higher.

Explanation: LOS: Reading 76-a

If the fund is structured as an open-end fund and at some point is faced with heavy redemptions the managers could have difficulty selling the assets to pay for the redemptions so a closed-end structure is often preferred.

**Reference:** CFA® Program Curriculum, Volume 6, pp. 177-179.

23. (QID 414) A property which is considered a lower risk investment than another property investment, assuming they both generate the same net operating income, will be likely to have a:

| Market capitalization rate | Valuation |
|---|---|
| A. lower | lower |
| B. lower | higher |
| C. higher | lower |

---

24. (QID 425) The roll yield for a long-only investor in a commodity:

A. is positive when producers are dominating the futures market.

B. is negative when the commodity futures market is in backwardation.

C. will be higher when the commodity futures market is in contango rather than backwardation.

---

25. (QID 502) An investor is looking at investing $1 million in a project, where the expected payout is $10 million at the end of five years. The investor's cost of equity for the project is 10%. However there is a significant risk of failure and the probability of failure in any year is given in the table below. The probability is based on the condition that the project has survived the previous year.

| Year | 1 | 2 | 3 | 4 | 5 |
|---|---|---|---|---|---|
| Probability of failure | 0.40 | 0.35 | 0.25 | 0.20 | 0.20 |

The expected net present value (NPV) of the project is closest to

A. $159,400.

B. $346,400.

C. $870,000.

23. (QID 414) A property which is considered a lower risk investment than another property investment, assuming they both generate the same net operating income, will be likely to have a:

| Market Capitalization rate | Valuation |
|---|---|
| A. lower | lower |
| ***B. lower** | **higher** |
| C. higher | lower |

Explanation: LOS: Reading 76-f

The market capitalization rate reflects the investors' required rate of return from the property, a low risk project will tend to have a low capitalization rate and therefore, for equal net operating income, a higher value.

**Reference:** CFA® Program Curriculum, Volume 6, pp. 193-194.

---

24. (QID 425) The roll yield for a long-only investor in a commodity:

***A. is positive when producers are dominating the futures market.**

B. is negative when the commodity futures market is in backwardation.

C. will be higher when the commodity futures market is in contango rather than backwardation.

Explanation: LOS: Reading 69-C

When producers dominate a market and are hedging production the futures market will be in backwardation, with the futures price below the spot, producing a positive roll yield.

**Reference:** CFA® Program Curriculum, Volume 6, pp. 53-54.

25. (QID 502) An investor is looking at investing $1 million in a project, where the expected payout is $10 million at the end of five years. The investor's cost of equity for the project is 10%. However there is a significant risk of failure and the probability of failure in any year is given in the table below. The probability is based on the condition that the project has survived the previous year.

| Year | 1 | 2 | 3 | 4 | 5 |
|---|---|---|---|---|---|
| Probability of failure | 0.40 | 0.35 | 0.25 | 0.20 | 0.20 |

The expected net present value (NPV) of the project is closest to

***A. $159,400.**

B. $346,400.

C. $870,000.

Explanation: LOS: Reading 73-h

The probability that the project survives throughout the five years is given by the product of the individual probabilities it survives each year, which is:

(1 – 0.40) (1 – 0.35) (1 – 0.25) (1 – 0.20) (1 – 0.20) = 18.7%

If the project survives the present value is:

$10 million/(1.10)5 - $1 million = $5.2 million

If the project fails the present value is:

– $1 million.

The expected NPV:

0.187($5.2 million) + 0.813(– $1 million) = $159,400

**Reference:** CFA® Program Curriculum, Volume 6, pp. 202-204.

# Download Instructions

The Financial Certification Center (TFCC) version 4.0 Chartered Financial Analyst (CFA) Level 1 Exam

**System Requirements:** Windows 95 & 98, Windows NT, Windows 2000/XP, and Windows Server 2003 with a minimum of 40 MB hard disk space and 64 MB RAM

**The Center For Financial Certification, InC.** will help you accomplish your CFA Certifications. This state of art software program is designed to cut your study time in half, and get you to a passing knowledge level in the easiest and shortest amount of time possible. The program will adapt to you personally, and then lay out a prioritized study plan that will visually show you your progress on a day to day basis. When the software has recognized that you are at a passing level in each objective category, you're ready to sit for the exam. It's really that easy!

**Installation Instructions:** To obtain the FE practice exam simply visit the engine download link.

TotalRecall CFA Level I Practice Exam and Engine Download *

1. Click on the link or copy it to your browser http://snipurl.com/2009CFAL1WB400 to download the software.

When the computer prompts you to open or save, choose "save this file to disk."

Select the location for the download file CFA2009CFA400.zip

**License Key**

**1. FE-JV 2009_ConceptCheckQuestions 400 = 312912131882**

**2. Financial Terminology Evaluation = 322478807587**

**Visit:**

http://www.financialexams.com/member_signup.php

http://www.financialcertification.com/forum/registration_rules.asp

or contact sales@totalrecallpress.com for Download and Installation Instructions:

Please use InsidersChoice Workbook as the Subject.

**Starting FinancialExams** To start the program the next time (if it doesn't start automatically), select FinancialExams from the Program's menu. Assistance with running and using FE is available under the Help menu.



**Good Luck with your certification!**
**Your Book Registration Number EW2009-900L1A**

Lightning Source UK Ltd.
Milton Keynes UK
30 October 2009

145609UK00001B/119/P

9 781590 959374